LEARNING THROUGH
SERVING

LEARNING THROUGH
SERVING

A Student Guidebook for Service-Learning and Civic Engagement across Academic Disciplines and Cultural Communities

SECOND EDITION

Christine M. Cress,
Peter J. Collier,
Vicki L. Reitenauer,
and Associates

STERLING, VIRGINIA

Published by Stylus Publishing, LLC
22883 Quicksilver Drive
Sterling, Virginia 20166-2102

Book design and composition by Susan Mark
Coghill Composition Company
Richmond, Virginia

Library of Congress Cataloging-in-Publication Data

Cress, Christine M. (Christine Marie), 1962–
    Learning through serving : a student guidebook for service-learning and civic engagement
across the disciplines and cultural communities / Christine M. Cress, Peter J. Collier, Vicki L.
Reitenauer and Associates. — Second edition.
        pages   cm
    Includes bibliographical references and index.
    ISBN 978-1-57922-989-4 (cloth : alk. paper) — ISBN 978-1-57922-990-0 (pbk. : alk. paper)
— ISBN 978-1-57922-991-7 (library networkable e-edition) — ISBN (invalid) 978-1-57922-992-4
(consumer e-edition)   1. Service learning—United States—Handbooks, manuals, etc.
2. Community and college—United States—Handbooks, manuals, etc.   3. Experiential
learning—United States—Handbooks, manuals, etc.   I. Title.
    LC220.5.C72 2013
    378.1'030973—dc23
                                        2012051423
        13-digit ISBN: 978-1-57922-989-4 (cloth)
        13-digit ISBN: 978-1-57922-990-0 (paper)
        13-digit ISBN: 978-1-57922-991-7 (library networkable e-edition)
        13-digit ISBN: 978-1-57922-992-4 (consumer e-edition)

Printed in the United States of America

All first editions printed on acid-free paper that meets the
American National Standards Institute Z39-48 Standard.

Bulk Purchases

Quantity discounts are available
for use in workshops and for staff
development.
Call 1-800-232-0223

First Edition, 2013

10   9   8   7   6   5   4   3   2   1

For our parents and families who taught us the importance of being contributing individual, team, and community members.

Contents

PART ONE

UNDERSTANDING THE *LEARNING-THROUGH-SERVING* PROPOSITION

PART TWO
LEARNING THE LANDSCAPE, LEARNING THE LANGUAGE

PART THREE
FACILITATING LEARNING AND MEANING-MAKING INSIDE AND OUTSIDE THE CLASSROOM

PART FOUR
ASSESSING THE ENGAGEMENT EFFORT

Figures

Exercises

Acknowledgments

The authors want to thank the following for permission to use their copyrighted material:

"Reflection and the Service Learning Cycle" diagram in chapter 6 (from Toole & Toole, 1991; revised 1993 and 2001) with permission of James C. Toole, Compass Institute.

Pearson Education, Inc., for the use of figure 6.2 (page 98), from David A. Kolb. *Experiential Learning: Experience as the Source of Learning and Development,* © 1984. Adapted with the permission of Pearson Education, Inc., Upper Saddle River, New Jersey

Alfred A. Knopf, a division of Random House, Inc., for permission to reprint the poem "The Low Road" from *The Moon Is Always Female* by Marge Piercy, © 1980 by Marge Piercy.

Preface

The first edition of *Learning through Serving* was published in 2005 and became a widely adopted classroom text by colleges across the United States committed to civic engagement and community-based learning. The book has also been translated into Arabic and is used by faculty and college students in countries around the world, including Australia, Saudi Arabia, India, Japan, Ireland, China, and Iraq. The content and activities have also provided substance for faculty professional development seminars on curricular integration, assessment of learning, and engaged scholarship focused on community impact.

During the last decade our global economic and environmental interdependence has become even more apparent through our digital connections and relationships. In keeping with these international developments, colleges have embraced the idea that our common future outcomes depend upon graduating students who can fully use their academic knowledge and skills for the greater good. Therefore, intentionally connecting community service with learning has become a featured teaching and learning strategy in many primary, secondary, and postsecondary educational institutions.

Indeed, research indicates that civic engagement is a robust educational tool for enhancing student retention, learning, and graduation gains. Thoughtful and purposefully designed civic engagement activities yield greater learning and increased graduation rates in K–12 schools, community colleges, and four-year institutions. In fact, some educators have argued that service-learning is one way to ensure that no student is left behind (see Cress, 2012).

But times and teaching have continued to evolve. Service-learning courses are frequently supported by electronic formats and even offered fully online. Advancing change and leveraging community assets are now achieved by service-learning students through multiple social media networks. While direct community service may be conducted, such as tutoring at-risk middle school students, interpersonal support may be achieved online in conjunction with in-person assistance. Moreover, indirect service projects have increased in frequency. Service-learning students may redesign a website or strategize a new marketing plan for a non-profit social service organization.

In addition, each year thousands of students participate in intensive service-learning experiences during alternative spring breaks and as a part of short-term international service-learning. And some higher education institutions, like Portland State University, now offer master's degree specializations and graduate certificates in service-learning and community-based learning for those pursuing a career in the civic engagement field as a teacher, researcher, or administrator (see http://pdx.edu/elp/service-learning).

With this second edition, the central tenets of the *Learning through Serving* student guidebook have not changed. It is designed to help students understand and reflect on their community service experiences as individuals and as citizens of communities in need of their compassionate expertise. It is designed to assist faculty in facilitating student development of compassionate expertise through the context of service in applying disciplinary knowledge to community issues and challenges. In sum, the book is about how to make academic sense of civic service in preparing for students' roles as future citizen leaders.

Therefore, to ensure that the content and activities are relevant to contemporary service-learning experiences the original authors and editors have reunited to write revised and expanded chapters to share their collective expertise. Specifically, each chapter now more fully addresses issues of social justice, privilege/power, diversity, intercultural communication, and technology. In addition, there are more examples from different academic disciplines, additional academic content for understanding service-learning issues (e.g., attribution theory), and information on issues related to students with disabilities and to international students. We have also added four new chapters on mentoring, leadership, becoming a change agent, and short-term global and immersive service-learning experiences.

We have also created an instructor manual that discusses the key areas for aligning a course with *Learning through Serving*. The manual is free to download at http://tinyurl.com/LearningthroughServing2E. The manual is also included in the e-book edition of this text.

As editors, we are deeply indebted to our associates for their willingness to engage in another collaborative effort to provide a scholarly framework for effective service-learning. We are also greatly appreciative of the leadership Portland State University has demonstrated over the past 20 years in making civic engagement a priority of its academic mission. With respect to John von Knorring of Stylus, his early vision for publishing intellectually sound textbooks has significantly contributed to the legitimacy of this pedagogical approach as a fulcrum for student learning and community improvement. And last but not least, we each wish to thank our families for their support of our pursuits in trying to make a difference.

Reference

Cress, C. M. (2012). Civic engagement and student success: Leveraging multiple degrees of achievement. *Diversity and Democracy, 15*(3).

Introduction

Why a Book about Learning through Serving?

CHRISTINE M. CRESS

Learning through Serving: A Student Guidebook for Service-Learning and Civic Engagement across Academic Disciplines and Cultural Communities is a textbook for students who, like yourself, are involved in service-learning experiences as part of the college or university program. We wrote this book because we care about your serving and learning experience. Whether you are performing service work in the community as a member of a course or engaging in service on your own, we offer exercises and activities to help you have a more effective, interesting, and meaningful experience.

The purpose of this book is to guide you through the essential elements of *learning* and *serving*. In other words, we focus on how you can best provide meaningful service to a community agency or organization while simultaneously gaining new skills, knowledge, and understanding as an integrated aspect of your academic program.

As you may know, service-learning courses are complex teaching and learning environments that are designed to enhance learning through the process of connecting academic course content with service opportunities in the community. This approach will require you and your instructor to participate in new roles and in different ways of learning than a traditional lecture course. What you are about to experience is an entirely new context for learning—one based in active practice in the community—that will challenge you to connect that learning back to classroom instruction, course readings, and discussion. We have developed this workbook to assist you in planning, processing, and evaluating your learning-through-serving experience.

The text first guides you over the initial hurdles faced in service-learning courses by addressing questions of meaning and values as you face the potential irony of "required volunteerism" and grapple with the essence of what it means to be a learner, a citizen, and a community member. For the most part, we assume that you are reading the text and completing the activities as part of a service-learning course. If you are not, however, you can still easily adapt any of the exercises to be completed on your own. You might also use these exercises to reflect upon your service experience even if your instructor does not assign all the activities to be completed as part of your class.

We have intentionally planned the book to be read over an academic term or semester. You will probably read about one chapter per week. Most important, though, is that you pace your reading of the text and completion of the exercises with the progression of your community-based experience for maximum benefit and insight.

The various inventories and reflective activities in this book are designed to help you understand your relationship to your classmates (viewing the classroom as a community), to the community organization (or wherever you are providing the service), and to the larger society. Further, the book prepares you to enter multicultural communities by addressing diversity issues that you may encounter in community-based work. We offer information, resources, and activities to explore issues of race, class, gender, ability, orientation, and other lived differences and likenesses that you may encounter in your classroom and extended community.

The text also provides academic scholarship and inquiry questions to help you glean lessons regarding the nature and process of societal change. We encourage you to think about how your academic program or major can be used as a framework for understanding and addressing complex community challenges. Moreover, we help you look for leverage points that you can use in considering the dynamics of power, collaboration, change, and transformation in communities. Finally, the text offers further reflective strategies for assessment so that you can make meaning of the service you have performed (the processes and the outcomes) and envision future roles you will play in your community (as a citizen, a volunteer, and an employee).

Thus, this book is designed as a practical guide to help you survive and thrive in service-learning experiences, whether that service to the community lasts a few weeks or a few months. The book can also be read as a companion text to your course readings in that it offers creative resources and ideas for bridging the gap between learning and serving across a variety of academic fields and a multitude of community-based experiences.

As you will see, each section's chapters include theoretical information in order to provide a contextual understanding of contemporary community issues. The bulk of each chapter, however, incorporates methods for self-reflection and assessment, offers questions for your individual thought and group discussion, suggests techniques for effectively interacting with the community, and details brief case-study examples of service-learning projects at other institutions.

To assist you, key symbols have been added to the exercises to highlight their relative importance in explaining chapter concepts. If applicable, check with your instructor in advance to see which exercises he or she may require you to complete on your own and which ones you might complete as part of a group.

Exercises with a star cluster (★★) are of utmost importance to complete (working either on your own or as part of a group); those with a lightbulb (💡) represent optional exercises (strategies for gaining deeper insights into the issues); and those with a question mark (❓) identify exercises that provide further resources and information in your quest for understanding community problem solving and change. Please note that, be-

cause of the range of community-based experiences, we will use the terms *service-learning* and *community-based learning* relatively interchangeably, although we will explore the differences between these terms in chapter 1.

For clarity and ease of understanding, the book is divided into four parts: (1) Understanding the *Learning-through-Serving* Proposition; (2) Learning the Landscape, Learning the Language; (3) Facilitating Learning and Meaning-Making Inside and Outside the Classroom; and (4) Assessing the Engagement Effort.

Part One: Understanding the *Learning-through-Serving* Proposition

The goal of part one is to prepare you for the experience of learning through serving. Some students begin their service-learning courses already understanding the foundations for this type of classroom-community experience through their own personal histories of volunteering and engaged citizenship. For others, the experience may be unfamiliar, untested territory. Chapters 1 through 3 will provide you with the steps for connecting yourself to the community and offer suggestions for how you might begin to experience yourself as a collaborator in learning through serving.

Chapter 1   What are Service-Learning *and* Civic Engagement?
In chapter 1, we look at the nature of "service" and "learning" as they are enacted in service-learning courses and connect this description to a larger conversation about democracy, citizenship, and civic responsibility. You will be introduced to reflection as a key practical element that distinguishes service from volunteerism. We also discuss the role of colleges in facilitating the development of your civic capacity, and the types of knowledge, skills, and motivation that will allow you to become a fully contributing member of your community.

Chapter 2   Building and Maintaining Community Partnerships
In chapter 2, we delve more deeply into the potentially transformative power of your partnership with a community organization. We discuss the key elements for successful partnerships by offering a case study example of entering, engaging with, and exiting a service-learning experience. You will also have an opportunity to develop an Action Learning Plan for Serving (ALPS)

as a strategy for making the most of your serving and learning.

Chapter 3   Becoming Community: Moving from I *to* We

In chapter 3, we discuss "community" as experienced in a service-learning course: the class as learning community, extended community as wall-less classroom, and the intersection of these learning landscapes. We discover that good intentions and communication are not always enough to ensure a fruitful serving experience, as multiple parties may have differences in values and goals. We also introduce you to a new leadership model as a framework for how to make the best use of collaboration in creating community change.

Part Two: Learning the Landscape, Learning the Language

As you participate in your learning-through-serving experience, you will come to understand yourself and others in new ways. In this section of the book (chapters 4 and 5), we provide you with information and exercises for interacting with diverse groups of individuals in order to maximize your effectiveness and empathy as a learner and server.

Chapter 4   Groups Are Fun, Groups Are Not Fun: Teamwork for the Common Good

Whether or not you are part of a formal team to perform your service, teamwork and collaboration in a group setting is a standard process in many, if not most, service-learning experiences. Chapter 4 specifically addresses the development of your knowledge and skills for creating effective group collaboration to further both course learning and service objectives.

Chapter 5   Creating Cultural Connections: Navigating Difference, Investigating Power, Unpacking Privilege

Chapter 5 builds on the experiential learning inherent in navigating differences in group practice to look more closely at multiculturalism. No doubt you hope to work respectfully, ethically, and effectively on behalf of classmates and community constituents, but to realize these goals you must look at underlying issues (power, privilege, discrimination, stereotypes, intercultural communication, cultural competence, and others) that affect the life of a community. In this chapter we examine how to incorporate multiple

voices to offer a chorus of viewpoints on community and discuss the politics of difference and the implications for community engagement.

Part Three: Facilitating Learning and Meaning-Making Inside and Outside the Classroom

The goal of part three (chapters 6–10) is to highlight multiple venues for understanding the community service experience—when things are going well and when things are not going well. Specifically, how can you use reflection to construct meaning and knowledge from your experience? How can you use these new insights to facilitate growth and development in others through mentoring and leadership? What can be done if the community interaction is a disappointment or is failing? How can the context and content of the course (and your academic major) provide learning about serving and offer ideas for future career directions?

Chapter 6   Reflection in Action: The Learning–Doing Relationship

Without numerous opportunities to reflect on your actions, you are at risk for leaving the service-learning class without having articulated the ways that your learning was amplified through engagement with your community partner and what that engagement meant to you. In chapter 6, we suggest strategies for structuring the on-going practice of reflection throughout the service-learning experience. We examine deeply what might be contributing to or hindering your learning and serving. Moreover, we help you understand how your learning style may be supported through multiple modes of reflection.

Chapter 7   Mentoring: Relationship Building for Empowerment

Peer-to-peer mentoring relationships can lead to empowerment and capacity building for mentees. We introduce the dual-function model of mentoring and illustrate how peer mentoring can provide both psychosocial support and role modeling that can contribute to mentee success. As part of a discussion of the relative benefits of in-person and online/e-mentoring, we discuss the concept of "credibility" and explain why it is important for effective mentor-mentee relationships. Finally, we share a tool for mentors—the New Johari Window—to increase credibility with mentees by helping mentees recognize that they possess unrealized problem-solving abilities.

Chapter 8   *Leadership and Service-Learning: Leveraging Change*

Leadership in the twenty-first century is complex because we tend to operate in varying intercultural contexts. Thus, we explore how a leadership approach that is effective in one service-learning site, like a community garden, may not be viewed as appropriate in another site, such as an elementary school; and an approach that works when working with inner-city residents may prove ineffective when working with migrant workers. We explain Lipman-Bulman's multiple leadership styles model and introduce the leadership toolkit as helpful strategies to move from idea to action. Finally, through a series of vignettes, we illustrate how success in different service contexts requires diverse leadership approaches and make the case that participation in service-learning classes provides students with opportunities to develop unique leadership skills.

Chapter 9   *Failure with the Best of Intentions: When Things Go Wrong*

Despite the best-laid plans of faculty and students, a host of things can go wrong when working with the community. Students can become bitterly embroiled with one another when working in groups; the community partner may not provide sufficient information or support for the learning experience; and financial and logistical requirements may not be met within expected timeframes. This chapter will help you anticipate and circumvent possible "failures," strategically problem-solve and confront issues, and persevere in the process irrespective of the odds for "success."

Chapter 10   *Expanding Horizons: New Views of Course Concepts*

Identifying and understanding the relationship between course content and service-learning experiences is often the most challenging aspect of community-based learning. This chapter provides you with critical leverage points for connecting theoretical concepts with concrete strategies for learning and change. The goal is to give you insights into how the content of various academic fields can better inform service and

practice in the community. In addition, you will read case studies and be presented with actual scenarios from service experiences to help you see how academic knowledge can be used to address community challenges and needs.

Part Four: Assessing the Engagement Effort

The goal of part four of the text (chapters 11–14) is to assist you with evaluating the outcomes of your community-based engagement. Did your efforts in the community actually make a difference to that community and its stakeholders? As for yourself, what skills, knowledge, and values did you gain in the process of connecting with community? How might you utilize this learning in future efforts to make positive change in your community?

Chapter 11   *Beyond a Grade: Are We Making a Difference?: The Benefits and Challenges of Evaluating the Impact of Learning and Serving*

There are a number of aspects to consider at the end of a service-learning experience. Specifically, determining whether or not your service made meaningful differences to you, your classmates, your instructor, and the community partner. Were community stakeholders positively impacted by your work? What did you learn that is directly connected to your academic major? Was positive change realized? This chapter will offer you a variety of assessment rubrics and tools to assist you in evaluating the multiple impacts of your service and this college-community relationship.

Chapter 12   *Global and Immersive Service-Learning: What You Need to Know as You Go*

Students whose service-learning experiences involve traveling to another country (global service-learning) or to another part of their home country for weeks or months (immersive service-learning) face unique opportunities and challenges with being far away from campus, friends, and family. This chapter will guide you in how to prepare, process, and evaluate this special kind of service-learning experience. Certainly, the information and strategies are applicable to any civic engagement experience so we encourage you to read the chapter for new understanding and insight. In particular, we cover issues associated with logistics, project preparation, and intercultural sensitivity. We emphasize the importance of engaged reflection as an intellectual and emotional tool for learning in deeper ways how concepts from your academic major can be applied to real-life community situations at home and abroad.

Chapter 13   Start Anywhere, Follow It Everywhere: Agents of Change

In this chapter we learn about how the community around Joubert Park in Johannesburg, South Africa, came together to transform a place of drug abuse and gang violence to a sustainable garden of celebration and art. The story encourages us to start from a heartset of abundance even in the midst of deficits. We begin by looking inward at our own strengths and passions, and proceeding outward in building alliances with like-minded individuals. Hopefully, your own experiences in service-learning will also teach you that we each have the power to act, and we can choose to act in our world in ways that not only link to our own interests, but which create positive change in the collective sphere.

Chapter 14   Looking Back, Looking Forward: Where Do You Go from Here?

The final chapter asks you to reflect in a holistic manner on your learning process. You will reexamine who you were when you began the service, who you have become, and how you leave this experience poised to act again in the future for serving the common good.

We hope that the multitude of ideas, strategies, and schemes in this text will prove to be a valuable resource to you, your classmates, your instructor, and your community partner in making academic and personal sense of learning and serving. If you are interested in learning more about the academic field of civic engagement, we encourage you to visit the Portland State University website in the Graduate School of Education (http://pdx.edu/elp/service-learning), which has a certificate and master's degree programs in service-learning and community-based learning.

Finally, we are sincerely indebted to our scholar-colleagues at Portland State University for sharing their expertise and wisdom, and to our students and community partners who are truly the best teachers. You have our deepest respect and gratitude.

PART ONE

Understanding the *Learning-through-Serving* Proposition

The goal of part one is to prepare you for the experience of learning through serving. Some students begin their service-learning courses already understanding the foundations for this type of classroom-community experience through their own personal histories of volunteering and engaged citizenship. For others of you, the experience may be unfamiliar, untested territory. Chapters 1 through 3 will provide you with the steps for connecting yourself to the community and offer suggestions for how you might begin to experience yourself as a collaborator in learning through serving.

KEY SYMBOLS

 Exercises of utmost importance to complete (working either on your own or in a group)

 Optional exercises (strategies for gaining deeper insights into the issues)

 Exercises that provide further resources and information in your quest for understanding community problem solving and change

CHAPTER 1

What are *Service-Learning* and *Civic Engagement?*

CHRISTINE M. CRESS

What are *Service-Learning* and *Civic Engagement?*

ACROSS THE UNITED STATES and around the world, students and their instructors are leaving the classroom and engaging with their communities in order to make learning come alive and to experience real-life connections between their education and everyday issues in their cities, towns, or states. If you are reading this book, you are probably one of these students. In some cases, you might even travel to a different part of the country or to another country to "serve and learn." Depending on the curriculum or program, the length of your experience can vary from a couple of hours to a few weeks or months, and occasionally to an entire year. (If you are traveling across the country or inter-nationally to your service-learning site, make sure to read chapter 12, "Global and Immersive Service-Learning: What You Need to Know as You Go.")

In fact, this may not be your first volunteer, service, or service-learning experience. Today, many high schools require community service hours for gradua-tion and many colleges require proof of previous civic engagement or community service as a part of the ad-mission application.

These experiences are often referred to by multi-ple names: *service-learning*, *community service*, or *community-based learning*. Throughout this text we use these terms relatively interchangeably, but we also explore some important distinctions. The activities differ from volunteering or internships because you will intentionally use your intellectual capacities and

---

- *Volunteerism*: Students engage in activities where the emphasis is on service for the sake of the beneficiary or recipient (client, partner).
- *Internship*: Students engage in activities to enhance their own vocational or career development.
- *Practicum*: Students work in a discipline-based venue in place of an in-class course experience.
- *Community Service*: Students engage in activities to meet actual community needs as an integrated as-pect of the curriculum.
- *Community-Based Learning*: Students engage in actively addressing mutually defined community needs (as a collaboration between community partners, faculty, and students) as a vehicle for achieving academic goals and course objectives.
- *Service-Learning*: Students engage in community service activities with intentional academic and learning goals and opportunities for reflection that connect to their academic disciplines.

skills to address community problems. While you will have an opportunity to put your knowledge and skills into direct practice, you will also learn how to reflect on those experiences in making your community a better place in which to live and work.

For example, volunteering to tutor at-risk middle-school students is certainly valuable to the community. Similarly, working as an intern writing news copy for a locally owned and operated radio station is great job experience. *Service-learning*, however, is different. In service-learning you will work with your classmates and instructor to use your academic discipline and course content in understanding the underlying social, political, and economic issues that contribute to community difficulties. In essence, you will learn how to become an educated community member and problem solver through serving the community and reflecting on the meaning of that service.

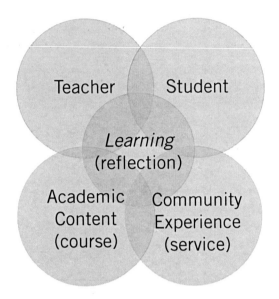

Figure 1.1. The Learning-through-Serving Model

How Is Service-Learning Different from Other Courses?

For clarity, we will most often use the term *service-learning* to characterize your community-based learning experience. Each faculty member may structure the experience slightly differently depending on the goals and objectives of the course and the needs of the community partner. What is most important for you to know is that service-learning is truly a different way of learning—thus the hyphen between "service" and "learning." These two facets are interdependent and dynamic and vary from other forms of traditional learning in that the focus is placed upon connecting course content with actual experience (see figure 1.1).

Instead of passively hearing a lecture, students involved in service-learning are active participants in creating knowledge. The role of teacher and learner are more fluid and less rigid. While the instructor guides the course, students share control for determining class outcomes. At first, this new kind of **pedagogy** (that is, teaching methods) can seem quite strange to students. As you and your classmates get more practice working with each other in groups and connecting with your community, though, you may find it far more interesting than "regular" classes.

In many traditional learning environments, the instructor delivers the content of the course through lectures, assignments, and tests. In some cases, students may also complete a practicum or other hands-on experience to further their learning. In contrast, learning through reflecting on experience is at the center of service-learning courses, and faculty guide students as they integrate intellectual knowledge with community interactions through the process of **reflection**.

One of the aspects of service-learning that may also make the experience enjoyable for you is that the experiential component connects to a wide range of learning styles. You may find that when you enter your service site, the needs of the community are quite different from what you expected. Say, for instance, that your service-learning involves teaching résumé writing to women staying at a "safe house" for survivors of domestic violence. In working with the women, you may discover that they also need professional clothing for job interviews. While they may still need your help in preparing résumés, their confidence in an interview may be undermined unless they feel appropriately dressed. As a service-learner, you might find yourself asking, "Now what do I do?"

You have probably succeeded thus far in your education because you have a certain level of ability to listen to lectures, take tests, do research, and write papers. However, for some students (including, perhaps, yourself) this does not come naturally. Instead, your skills may best emerge when interviewing community members or providing counseling assistance. Alternatively, you may excel at organizing tasks and developing project timelines, or you may be visually creative. In the previous example, you may be the best person to provide résumé assistance for the women, or it might make more sense for a classmate to assist with résumé writing while you call local agencies to inquire about clothing donations. Ideally, all students will find the opportunity to build from and contribute their strengths to the service-learning projects using different skill sets.

Along the way, your instructor and the course readings will further develop your range and repertoire of skills, knowledge, and insights, because service-learning courses invariably challenge students to consider where "truth" and wisdom reside. Moving more deeply into the previous scenario, for example, you might begin to wonder why domestic violence exists in your community. What role might the media play in portraying healthy and unhealthy domestic relationships? Do economic factors such as unemployment make any difference? What about substance abuse issues?

Stop for a moment and think about how you would answer the following questions as you ponder your own education and the relationship you see between in-classroom learning and the outside world:

- What is the relative value of solutions drawn from scholarly literature compared to ideas presented by students, faculty, and community partners?
- How can we move beyond stereotypes, preconceived ideas, misinformation, and biases to understand real people and real issues?

- How can we be solution centered?
- How can we examine external norms and societal structures?
- Which community values should we reinforce, which are open to question, and how should a community decide this?
- How can we develop and act from an ethical base while engaging as citizens in our communities?

As a student in a community-based learning course, you will be asked to be highly reflective about your learning experiences. Often, you will keep a journal or write reflective papers that emphasize various aspects of your learning. You may also be asked to post service-learning blogs or respond to online discussion questions. The goal is to help you cognitively and affectively process your thoughts and feelings about your experience, while using academic content to derive broader insights.

Here's an example of one way to reflect on your experience. In a senior-level course that provided after-school activities for at-risk students in an urban environment, the learners were asked to examine their experiences from a variety of viewpoints in their reflective journals:

- Describe what you *did* today.
- What did you *see* or observe at the site?
- How did you *feel* about the experience?
- What *connections* do you find between the *experience* and *course readings*?
- What new *ideas* or *insights* did you gain?
- What *skills* can you use and strengthen?

Exercise 1.1: Comparing Classrooms

Think back to traditional classrooms in which you have been a student/learner. What responsibilities did you have in this kind of class, and what responsibilities did the instructor have? How do you imagine your role as a student will be different in this community-based experience? What kinds of responsibilities do you imagine that you will have in this class? How about your instructor? The others in your classroom learning community? The community outside your classroom?

Make a list of the activities you did in a traditional classroom and compare those with any of your nontraditional learning experiences. What factors in each environment best facilitated your learning? What factors made it more challenging for you to learn?

- What will you *apply* from this experience in *future* work with the community?

Reflecting on our experiences lends new significance to what we are learning. It also allows us to compare initial goals and objectives with eventual outcomes—to assess what we have accomplished. We will cover more about reflection and assessment of our community-based learning experiences in later chapters. For now, let's turn our thoughts to why colleges and universities offer service-learning courses.

Why Is Service-Learning Required at Some Colleges?

Colleges and universities are increasingly including in their educational mission the preparation of graduates as future *citizens*. What, really, does this mean? Are colleges merely hoping that you will vote and pay your taxes as contributing members of society? What about job training and preparing you for the workforce? Aren't you, in fact, spending a lot of time and money on school? If so, why should you be required to perform volunteer service in the community? Isn't obligatory volunteerism like being an indentured servant? In other words, *Are you being forced to work for free*?

Perhaps the greatest single resistance voiced in service-learning classes is the argument that service is volunteerism and, by definition, cannot be required. However, in service-learning classes, the good that you will do in your community necessarily includes the learning you will gain as a result of your efforts. The whole point of service-learning is for you to grow in skills and knowledge precisely because you are bringing your capabilities to real-world problems. While you do this, your community benefits as well.

Colleges and universities do not want or intend to be social-service providers. A myriad of governmental offices, nonprofit agencies, and religiously affiliated organizations serve community needs. Instead, institutions of higher education want to be good neighbors in connecting with their communities. Colleges are most concerned about preparing citizens for the future, graduates who are well prepared to enter the job market and contribute to society. Institutions that require service-learning courses believe that such courses offer a fundamental way to develop and graduate involved citizens.

What Is a *Citizen* and Why Must I Learn to Be One?

Being a citizen in the United States implies that you were either born here or naturalized as one (meaning you passed the citizenship exam and took the citizenship oath). Generally, U.S. citizens do not tend to reflect on what **citizenship** means. In the wake of significant national or global events, such as the attacks on September 11, 2001, or the war against terrorism, citizenship may be associated with American patriotism. Those in the armed services may frequently consider what it means to be a citizen since they are charged with defending and protecting our country and its democratic values.

Certainly, citizens of the United States hold a variety of views about what precisely that means. If you are an international student or if you immigrated to this country, your ideas about citizenship may be different from those of many Americans. As you engage in your service-learning course, you will have many opportunities to explore what it means to be a citizen, an active participant in the life of American communities. What are the duties, as well as the rights, for participation in this democracy?

A college student originally from Bosnia wrote the following during her service-learning course:

> *I came to the United States five years ago as a refugee because of the war. Before, in my country, I hoped for freedom. To be free to make my own decisions and free to go wherever I wanted without any limitations. Back then, I didn't link it with democracy. Now, in the United States, I think about terms like freedom, democracy, and citizenship as interdependent. They can't exist without each other. If we live in a democratic society we have certain freedoms. But we must also be a good and responsible citizen to protect those freedoms for everyone.*

More than five decades ago, President John F. Kennedy said, "Ask not what your country can do for you—ask what you can do for your country." This statement most succinctly and aptly describes the fundamental concept behind service-learning and community service. As citizens, it is our obligation to contribute to the improvement of our nation. More-

---

⁎⁎ Exercise 1.2: What Is Citizenship?

If you are working on your own, list these words at the top of a large sheet of paper: *Citizenship, Democracy, Freedom, Community, Service, Volunteerism.* Below each of these keywords, brainstorm additional words and phrases that come to mind. You might add, across the top of the sheet, words that pertain directly to your community-based project as you currently understand it: *Homeless, Refugee, Elderly, Literacy.*

After you've completed your brainstorming, look at the lists of words you've created. Spend at least 10 minutes responding to these questions in writing: What patterns do you see among the lists? What connections? What disconnections? Are the words you chose "positive" or "negative" in meaning, or both, and how does that impact the insights you draw from the lists? What meaning do these lists have for you personally? What might be some implications of this word association for your work with your community partner?

If you are working with others, tape big sheets of newsprint or chart paper around the room, placing large pens or markers next to each sheet. In silence, walk around the room, adding words and phrases to the headers on each sheet.

After everyone has finished, take turns reading what you all have written, and then discuss the previous questions as a group.

---

over, many would argue that as citizens of the wealthiest nation in the world, it is our responsibility to be good *global citizens.*

We are all aware of the multiple issues that face our communities: homelessness, poverty, drug addiction, violence, pollution, racism, sexism, homophobia, lack of health care, poorly performing schools, urban blight—and the list goes on. Other difficulties face us as well: corporate fraud, dishonest politicians, and biased judicial systems. In light of such concerns, it is natural to feel overwhelmed, hopeless, and helpless. After all, what could you possibly do to change any of it? And while we might care about the issues (and maybe even donate a few dollars each year to charitable organizations), the guilty conscience that is prodding us to get involved may be overtaken by our own apathy. In the end, we feel bad but often go on with our day. We just do not know how to respond to President Kennedy's challenge. The problems seem too big.

Yet most of us have done "good" in our communities at one time or another. We might have served Thanksgiving dinner at a shelter; answered calls at a crisis center; helped to raise money for new playground equipment in a park; taught religious education to kids in churches, synagogues, or mosques; registered voters or gathered signatures for ballot measures; donated blood; picked up litter on the beach; or tutored someone to learn to read. All of these efforts are a part of what makes our communities stronger.

Still, the question remains: Why must I be "required" to participate in service-learning? If I want to make a positive difference in my neighborhood, why shouldn't I be left alone to decide for myself when and where I want to volunteer? Why should I be "forced" to serve in the community as a part of my education? Isn't this denying me freedom of choice? And isn't this even more problematic if I have to work at an organization or with others with whom I have differing political, religious, or ethical views?

The Role of Education in a Democracy

Some have described American *democracy* as a great experiment. Others have suggested that it is a work of art in progress. But unlike a laboratory experiment or a painting on the wall, democracy is the function of human interaction. Democracy is the attempt to balance differences in individual values, beliefs, and experiences with collective ideals of justice, equity, and security. Being a citizen in a democracy means that you possess both the rights of *freedom* and a *responsibility* to uphold democratic ideals such as fairness. In a way, it is a kind of double consciousness. We are accountable for ourselves *and* for the welfare of others.

We stand in a turmoil of contradictions without having the faintest idea how to handle them: Law/Freedom; Rich/Poor; Right/Left; Love/Hate—the list seems endless. Paradox lives and moves in this realm; it is the balancing of opposites in such a way that they do not cancel each other but shoot sparks of light across their points of polarity. It looks at our desperate either/ors and tells us that they are really both/ands—that life is larger than any of our concepts and can, if we let it, embrace our contradictions. (Morrison, 1983)

Institutions of education in U.S. democracy have attempted to bridge these complementary but competing forces—*individualism* and *society*, freedom and responsibility. Colleges and universities encourage us to live up to the "American dream" by working hard and increasing our intellectual capacities. The hope is that we will make use of our new insights to get good jobs and be good neighbors.

This is not a simple proposition. Our society, and our world for that matter, is plagued by incredibly complex problems. Pollution will not be stopped through curbside recycling alone, hunger will not be reduced by building larger food banks, and women will not be made safer merely by adding more streetlights.

Educational leaders have come to realize that the critical issues facing our nation can be solved only through the creation of educated citizens. Indeed, John Dewey (1916), in *Democracy and Education*, argued that students must be engaged not just in thought, but in action, and that this mode of education is crucial to the formation of responsible citizens. Two key elements—knowledge and skill—are the catalysts for developing civically engaged students and graduates.

Being civic-minded is more than just what you know. It is what you do with what you know. Institutions of higher education risk producing graduates who *know* without *doing*—and are increasingly incorporating service-learning to address this concern. Equally detrimental to our communities are those who *do* without knowing. What our country needs is more than either abstract visions or "blind" actions. We need mindful individuals who *choose* to "do good" for their country. In essence, community-based educa-

tional experiences increase our capacity for how to apply our knowledge and skills to civic issues. This is known as enhancing our **civic capacity.**

I knew that helping an underprivileged kid learn to read would be challenging and fun. But I never realized that as a class we could have an impact on the whole community. Because of the after-school program we started, parental involvement has increased and juvenile crime the last six months has decreased. I hope this trend continues.

Developing Civic Capacity: Charity versus Solidarity

Developing civic capacity—meaning knowing how to apply our knowledge and skills to community challenges—is also dependent upon our attitudes for performing service in the first place. Certainly, if service is required in the course then perhaps our only motivation for doing the service activities is to pass the class. Additionally, we may feel that serving others is simply part of our "duty," either because of religious values or because of our national obligations as citizens. However, when service is conducted from this mindset (or heartset) it is likely to be performed as "charity" work. With charity work, volunteers conceive of themselves as being above the person or group they are assisting. Charity workers believe that their volunteer work makes them "good people" and they see their assistance as one-sided (e.g., what I am doing for them). Charity workers don't see what benefits they get in exchange, such as learning from the people they are helping (Heldman, 2011).

In contrast, "solidarity" work shifts the focus from the volunteer to the community in identifying strengths, assets, and resources that can lift and sustain individuals and groups over the long term. With service as solidarity work, the volunteers see themselves as equal to the people they are serving, see a part of themselves in the person they are working with, and recognize that they are working together for the betterment of everyone (McClure, 2006).

Therefore, enhancing our civic capacity does not just mean cognitive enlightenment, it means viewing situations, people, and places from new perspectives. As we reach out our hand, we also imagine being in others' shoes—how they think and feel. The empathy we develop in service as solidarity is critical to the appropriate application of our academic and disciplinary content. We broaden our true understanding of community challenges thereby increasing our capacity for problem solving.

How Is Civic Capacity Developed in Service-Learning Courses?

The development of civic capacity occurs when we explore the connection between academic knowledge and experience-derived insight into the breadth and depth of societal and political issues. Having a surface understanding of deforestation, for instance, is not enough to address all the associated environmental and economic questions. Knowing that our schools need additional resources is not enough to ensure that children learn mathematics. We can no longer afford to take a singular or microscopic view of our world. Instead, through your service-learning course readings, discussion, research, lecture, and community experiences, you might come to understand how the purchase of your new running shoes or morning coffee makes you an interdependent part of the global community, whether you examine it through the disciplinary lens of history, biology, psychology, architecture, computer science, English, po-

litical science, or urban studies. If we do not see how our individual lives are a part of the whole, we will lack the ability to identify leverage points for creative change. In other words, being an engaged citizen involves more than "thinking globally and acting locally"; it means deliberately applying our academic knowledge and skills to positively transform ourselves, others, and organizations.

Meeting homeless families personally allowed me to get to know the faces behind the statistics. It also helped me to see how social issues and political issues are connected. While I was taking my service-learning course we were electing a mayor in my hometown. One of the candidates wanted to institute a policy to charge parents with a misdemeanor if they failed to get their kids to school. Many of the homeless families I met struggled to enroll their children in schools when they were moving around so much. Never before did I understand how much my vote in local elections matters. How could I vote for something that would hurt these people?

Understanding problems and recognizing opportunities for improvement is a great starting point. From there, your service-learning course will help you

---

💡 Exercise 1.3: Making a Difference

If you are working on your own, divide a sheet of paper into four columns. At the top of each column write one of the following words: *Location*, *Action*, *Skill*, and *Knowledge*.

Next, make a list of the places you have helped out in the community and put them under the *Location* column. This does not have to be formal volunteerism. Maybe you planted trees in a park as part of your Girl Scout troop or maybe you walked in a fundraiser for juvenile diabetes. Everything counts.

Beside each *Location*, briefly describe what you did. What was the *Action*?

As you consider what you did, note the *Skills* (the concrete abilities) and *Knowledge* (the base of information) you used to accomplish the *Action*.

Read what you have written. What do you notice about the ways you have worked to make a difference in your community? What does this say to you about your own civic capacity? What might that mean for you as a service-learner in this new experience? What knowledge and skills, in particular, would you like to expand in this new experience?

develop the capacity to apply your skills. You will have frequent occasions to test your talents and abilities on real community issues. How, for example, do you best organize volunteers for a legislative rally to support public schools? How might you identify and provide health care services to people without insurance? How do you promote tolerance in a racially segregated community? How do you teach a refugee to surf the Internet?

Each day, our workforce and neighborhoods become more diverse. We need the knowledge and skills of mathematicians, anthropologists, chemists, writers, engineers, musicians, sociologists, and every other discipline, in order to learn to work and live together. Just as importantly, we must practice patience and tolerance in understanding each other. In the end, *empathy* will be the glue that effectively binds our knowledge and skills into a source for community growth.

What Else Will I Gain from a Service-Learning Course?

Many studies indicate that students who participate in community-based learning realize greater educational and learning gains than their peers (Cress, 2012). Their academic and social self-concept is higher, they tend to be more moral and ethical in their decision making, their tolerance and empathy for others is improved, their understanding of societal and community issues is broadened, their cognitive and problem-solving skills are more advanced, and their interest in influencing positive social and political change is increased.

After participating in service-learning courses, students stated the following:

The empowerment given to students created a sense of responsibility and commitment.

Reflective journals helped to organize my thoughts and experiences.

Students also commented on their communication and critical-thinking skills:

The experience benefited me in improving my communication skills and leadership abilities. It also helped me to further my conflict resolution skills. Most importantly, it gave me the opportunity to have an experience in a real environment.

I learned how to talk effectively with others and how to resolve professional differences without anger.

Students further noted how the course brought new insights and understanding to their own stereotypes, biases, and prejudices while expanding their appreciation for diverse others.

The most important aspect I learned in this experience was dealing with a sector of the community I might never have worked with otherwise, gaining insight into the juvenile justice system and the needs of the Southeast Asian immigrant community.

I learned to understand myself and to overcome a lot of biases I had toward the poor.

Service-learning courses should not be viewed as an educational utopia. Personality conflicts can arise, students may lack the ability to deal with others who are different from themselves, community partners may not follow through on their commitments, and group members may not meet their responsibilities. In addition, many community service projects are in neighborhoods or parts of the community unfamiliar to students. It's quite likely that you may experience a variety of emotions and reactions while performing your service, including fear, guilt, or outrage. Because service-learning experiences are grounded in relationships—the relationship of student to community, to other students, to the instructor, and to the self—the thoughts and feelings you have about your service experience may be quite intense at times. We address these issues of understanding, managing, and processing your feelings and reactions in later chapters in this book.

Also, there may be aspects about you, your life, or your classmates that make the service-learning fit especially challenging; not because of anything bad or wrong but simply because of the diverse uniqueness of each of us. For example, a group of computer science students resisted working with low-income third graders because they felt that their technological expertise was too advanced for the youngsters. It turned out that most of the kids already knew how to make PowerPoint presentations and they asked the college students intriguing questions about how to create gaming software.

Similarly, some male students in a sociology course approached the instructor questioning the appropriateness of their service at a domestic violence shelter for women and their children. Would their presence make the women uncomfortable or bring up difficult memories and feelings? The instructor appreciated their sensitivity and double checked with the community partner. In fact, the women welcomed positive male role models for their children and they all collaborated together to design and paint zoo animals on the walls of the children's playroom.

Obviously, the lesson here is that service-learning is a distinctive opportunity to combine our cognitive competence and compassion for short-term gains and long-term solutions. The fundamental principle underlying service-learning and community-based learning courses is that you as a student have knowledge and skills that can improve society. You just need a chance to practice them. Working with community partners compels us to assess and reevaluate our abstract ideas about societal and political problems. As a result, we will see that the community is more than just a place with "needs." Through working with the community, we will learn of the knowledge, skills, and expertise of our community partners. We will also learn from the individuals we are there to "serve." Ultimately, community-based experiences are a reciprocal learning process between the educational community (students, faculty, administration) and the community partners (organizations and individuals).

What We All Gain

Colleges and universities would be educationally remiss if they did not teach students how to connect themselves to their communities. A central premise of the U.S. Constitution is that, in order to form a more per-

fect union (of communities), we must work actively to establish justice and ensure liberty. Service-learning courses are an important tool for learning how to take a thoughtfully informed and rational approach to living and working in community that is tempered by active empathy, respect, and care.

Before I came to the United States from Chengdu, China, I thought that everyone here would be treated equally. Supposedly, everyone is born equal but that is not the case. Some people are treated badly because of their race, age, sexual orientation, physical situation, and gender. I did not expect this discrimination. We must learn about social problems, use the knowledge to solve social issues, help others, and strengthen social responsibility.

While individuals may choose to volunteer for a variety of reasons, and learning from that experience naturally takes place, service-learning allows for deeper individual and collaborative reflection on how to create positive societal transformation. We have the capacity, individually and collectively, to transform our communities to include those who have been disenfranchised due to race, ethnicity, gender, age, class, sexual orientation, socioeconomic background, disability, religion, or political view. As such, service-learning courses teach us how to address the issues of today and tomorrow.

In the beginning, you may find it a struggle to define the concept of civic responsibility and civic engagement in articulating the connections between your service-learning and broader community involvement. At times, even faculty are uncertain about how to differentiate between service, "doing good," and the enrichment of their own civic capacities through encounters with community organizations, community issues, and community members. By being patient and practicing reflection throughout the process, you *will* "learn through serving." As Benjamin Barber (1992) states:

[t]he fundamental task of education in a democracy is the apprenticeship of liberty—learning to be free. . . . [T]he literacy required to live in a civil society, the competence to participate in democratic communities, the ability

to act deliberately in a pluralistic world, the empathy that permits us to hear and thus accommodate others, all involve skills that must be acquired. (p. 4)

The following chapters are designed to help you become a civically engaged individual and community member as you participate in and make meaning of your service-learning experience.

Key Concepts

citizen	democracy	reflection
citizenship	empathy	responsibility
civic capacity	freedom	service-learning
community-based	global citizen	society
learning	individualism	volunteerism
community service	pedagogy	

Key Issues

- How is community-based learning different from traditional forms of learning?
- Why do colleges require community service and service-learning?
- What is the role of freedom and responsibility in a democracy?
- What knowledge and skills are involved in developing civic capacity?
- What does the community gain as a result of student engagement?

ADDITIONAL EXERCISE

Exercise 1.4: Reflection Questions

- What should be the role of education in preparing students to become citizens?
- What does an effective citizen do? Can you identify some behaviors and actions associated with being a "good" citizen?
- What is a global citizen?
- What, in your view, are the pros and cons of requiring community-based learning courses?
- What specific knowledge or skills have you learned in your courses that you can apply to this community site?
- How might you be able to use your academic major and its associated knowledge base to address community issues?
- Is the "American Dream" possible? If so, how and for whom?
- What connection do you see between societal issues and individual responsibility?
- How do issues of discrimination and prejudice inhibit societal change?
- What community issues concern you the most?

CHAPTER 2

Building and Maintaining Community Partnerships

VICKI L. REITENAUER, AMY SPRING, KEVIN KECSKES,
SEANNA M. KERRIGAN, CHRISTINE M. CRESS, AND
PETER J. COLLIER

ON A BEAUTIFUL TUESDAY morning in early July, several student grantwriters and their instructor from a service-learning course gathered during their class time at a huge warehouse in an industrial section of their city. The space they were about to tour—the former administrative and manufacturing headquarters of a local sportswear company—had been donated to their community partner, whose vision was to create an inclusive space for both emerging and established artists to come together outside of the competitive world of commercial galleries and conservative museums. This prospective artistic community center, which was to include spaces for exhibitions and performances and a resource center for working artists, now sat in front of them, behind a massive (and locked) front door. Those assembled waited 5, 10, 15 minutes. A few more students showed up. They all waited a bit longer. Now the community partner was *really* late. So were about half of the students from the class.

Though perhaps seemingly minor, the apparent breakdown in communication described previously is no trivial matter in a community partnership, but it is quite a common one. In this chapter, we explore the process of creating successful partnerships (those that serve not only the community, but also the students who are working on behalf of community change) and the outcomes that result from such partnerships. We will return to the previous scenario and examine others to investigate how these students might actively approach this opportunity to build their own knowledge and skills through effective collaboration with the world outside their college campus.

Orienting the Self toward Serving and Learning

Before we talk about the hallmarks of a successful partnership, let's think about "service" itself. In chapter 1, you learned why colleges and universities are increasingly focused on engaging with their communities. This commitment allows the expertise of those who make up the higher education community (students, faculty, and staff) to impact the surrounding community positively, in order to address societal and political challenges and to create positive change both for individuals and within systems.

That's not the only reason colleges and universities partner with the community, however. In addition to the social change possible from these partnerships, students may receive extraordinary benefits not accessed through traditional lecture-style courses. Because community-based learning environments energize, enhance, and make real the course curricula, students typically report significant growth in their abilities to communicate with diverse audiences in multiple ways, enhancement of leadership and project management skills, and development of their capacities for understanding themselves in relation to others who are both similar to and different from themselves. Participating in a service-learning course may also help students clarify career goals and provide a network of contacts (and even, in some cases, job opportunities). Like students before you, you may also experience a significant shift in your identification as an informed and involved participant in your communities and your world.

These outcomes don't result by accident. Thoughtful preparation for community-based learning on the part of all involved dramatically increases the chances of successful results. We all have individual gifts and skills to offer our classmates, the instructor, and the community. By participating in this experience, we implicitly agree to put these capacities to use to create a rich, meaningful, and vibrant experience in an environment of mutual respect and commitment.

As noted in chapter 1, you can also expect to build academic discipline skills, deepen your knowledge of the issues facing your communities, and develop greater capacities for self-awareness. In fact, it is precisely through the reciprocal action of all of the parties involved in community-based learning that everyone benefits from the endeavor. That is to say, the community is able to achieve its outcomes and objectives through your focused actions, and you expand your knowledge

and skills through putting theory into practice. This is the meaning of "partnership": All parties gain in the relationship, and they gain precisely because the others are gaining, too.

In chapter 3, you will complete an activity to help you identify specific objectives for your service-learning experience, and you will develop a plan for achieving these objectives within the context of your particular community site. For now, we are going to explore how best to initiate and create a community partnership for your service-learning experience, and we'll start by exploring "service."

Community Partnerships

Community partners are members of the community in businesses, government agencies, and social service organizations that agree to work with students individually or collectively in order to meet community needs. Partnerships are designed to create a service to the community while addressing educational opportunities for students. No two community partnerships are exactly alike. Each partnership occurs in a different

---

✯✯ Exercise 2.1: Exploring "Service"

Look up the words *community*, *service*, *partner*, and *reciprocity* in the dictionary and write down the definitions. How are these words and their definitions related to each other and to this course?

Now, as you write responses to the following questions, try to locate yourself within these terms and their meanings. Please be as concrete as possible, using examples, as you consider the following:

- How have you experienced a sense of community in other settings?
- When have you been of service to others? In what ways?
- When have you been served by others? In what ways?
- What did you give to others when you were providing service? What did you gain from your service experience?
- What images about those being served do you carry?
- Have you experienced situations in which benefit has resulted from a collaborative effort?
- What have been some of the critical elements of those partnerships that contributed to the success? What do you think and feel about them as a result of having been involved in them?
- What communication skills, critical thinking abilities, or other new skills did you develop as a result?
- How do you think your experience might prepare you for this current community-based learning opportunity?

community context, with multiple constituents who bring diverse sets of needs and assets to the table. In community-based learning courses, who *you* are—and how you and your classmates interact with one another—meets the particular nature of your community partner to create your unique partnership. Because the very character of collaboration is dynamic and relationship based, it is not possible to offer a single set of standardized steps that will ensure the success of your shared work.

It *is* possible, however, to look at the key elements of successful partnerships as a way to guide your current service-learning opportunity. The next few sections of this chapter are meant to provide you with a set of preparatory tools to help you work effectively in your unique community environment. For those students who are able to choose their community setting from among several possibilities, we will start by describing different kinds of community-based learning environments.

Community-Based Learning Environments

Your service-learning course is an opportunity for you to connect academic knowledge with community challenges. Broadly speaking, community-based learning environments can be characterized as two basic types: **direct-service** and **project-based** (or *indirect-service*). In a *direct-service* learning experience, students work directly with the persons served by the partnering community organization. For example, students might spend several hours a week tutoring non-native-language speakers who recently arrived in the United States, or they may interview elderly persons living in a nursing home in order to compile oral histories of their life experiences.

In a *project-based* learning experience, students are more likely to focus on an end product and develop the necessary processes to lead them to the achievement of that goal. Writing grant proposals to win funding for a community partner's programs and developing a public relations campaign for an organization are two examples of project-based experiences.

The nature of the work you will take on—and the methods you will use to accomplish your tasks—will help to frame the ways you will most effectively interact with your community partner. If you are part of a class that will be working one-on-one with homeless and low-income individuals (direct service) to provide resources for housing, for example, you should certainly expect to receive training from the organization involved to understand the policies and protocols to which you will be subject. You may need to fill out a series of forms (including, perhaps, a background check and confidentiality agreements). It is the responsibility of your instructor and community partner to prepare you for the work you will be engaged in, and it is your responsibility to take advantage of the preparation afforded by them.

If you are working in a project-based partnership, you still need to be oriented to your partnering organization, its mission, the methods it uses to fulfill its mission, the persons it serves, and the particular tasks you will be undertaking. In some cases, your faculty may be able to provide a comprehensive introduction to your community organization, but usually some time spent with **contact persons** from the organization will be vital, as well.

In some instances—such as a group of students creating a photo essay about a changing neighborhood to supplement their coursework on understanding community cultures—community-based learning happens without a formal community partner present.

⚇ Often, the decision about whether you will engage in a direct-service or in a project-based learning experience is made long before you step foot in the classroom. Instructors may determine this in advance and select the community partner. In other cases, one of the first tasks of your service-learning course might be to work collaboratively to decide the type of community service and the community partner. If you are embarking on a community-based learning adventure on your own and can make this choice yourself, turn to **Exercise 2.8: Which Type of Community-Based Learning Is Right for Me?** located on page 32. You may also want to contact your college's service-learning or community service office to inquire about potential community partners and to get a list of service-learning course offerings.

Even without an identifiable community organization to whom you are accountable, it is still important that you, your classmates, and your instructor understand the goals of the project and that you identify the roles and responsibilities each person has in a successful community experience. After all, while you are not providing direct service to a specific set of clients in the previous example, you are still serving the community in terms of the accuracy and honesty with which you represent it.

Am I Ready for This Challenge? Is My Community Partner Ready for Me?

Students engaged in the community are faced with unique responsibilities as workers and learners. As a service-learner, you will be a representative of your college or university, requiring you to think about how your individual actions will portray your institution. As an ambassador to the community, you should consider and stay attentive to the ways in which your behavior may influence how a community partner approaches working with students in the future.

Community partners also have a lot at stake. Frequently working on "shoestring budgets" subject to the changing perceptions of social need, many organizations rely on input and expertise from students and faculty to help them fulfill their missions. Not only are the contributions of students and faculty a cost-effective means of furthering the work of community organizations, but they also bring a diversity of perspectives into those organizations, creating entities with greater capacities to serve their constituents.

The organization Community-Campus Partnerships for Health (CCPH) has outlined a number of principles of good practice for effective partnerships, principles that delineate responsibilities shared by colleges and universities (and the students who represent them in community-based learning projects) and communities. In the view of CCPH, partners in effective community-based learning situations exhibit the following traits:

- Agreed-upon goals and values on how to progress toward accomplishing those goals
- Mutual trust, respect, authenticity, and commitment
- Intentional working out of identified strengths, addressing areas that need improvement
- A balance of power and a sharing of resources
- Open and accessible communication
- Collaborative processes established through the interaction of all
- Feedback for improvement
- Sharing credit for accomplishments
- Commitment to spending the time it takes to develop these elements

As a student you have both **responsibilities** and **rights** that attend your participation in a service-learning experience. Let's consider each of these areas and how they impact the community partnership and your own learning.

As a student you have *responsibilities*, including legal ones, to ensure that all persons associated with your partnership may achieve maximum benefit without experiencing undue risk or potential harm. Your instructor and community partner, for example, will have very clear ideas about the parameters within which you may operate. For example, most (if not all) partnerships will not permit students to transport clients of a community organization in their cars or to visit with clients in a private home. You are responsible for understanding the role you are fulfilling with regard to your community partnership and the expectations for your performance in that role. Also, as a community-based learner, you need to make good ethical and legal decisions that are consistent with and further the shared vision of the service-learning effort.

You are also responsible for negotiating time and time management issues. The majority of community partners we have worked with, when asked about the greatest challenges they have encountered, identify students' failure to manage their time well (and the resulting difficulty this causes) in their partnerships.

For an exercise that helps you to consider visually your weekly time commitments to assist you in creating space for community commitment, turn to **Exercise 2.9: As Time Goes By . . .** on page 33.

> ⚘ To review your responsibilities as a community-based learner, turn to **Exercise 2.10: Pre-Service Checklist of Student Responsibilities** on page 34.

Moreover, it is your responsibility to *learn* in this nontraditional learning environment (which you may remember seeing in schematic form in chapter 1), through engaging with the community, dialoguing with others, and reflecting on how your work connects to the content of your course, larger societal and political issues, and your own sense of yourself.

Now let's examine your *rights* in the community setting. Your community partner is responsible for creating an environment in which it is possible for you to learn through serving, an environment in which you may use what you know for the benefit of yourself and others. This environment must be free from the kinds of threats that prevent learning through serving from taking place, particularly sexual and other forms of harassment based in discrimina-

tion. If possible, review the pertinent sections of your community partner's personnel manual that articulate the rights of staff, volunteers, and clients of the agency. These rights apply to you, as well, when you are working on behalf of the community partner.

So far, we have looked at your rights and responsibilities as a community-based learner and your connection to a community partner's responsibilities to create an environment that supports your work as a learner. Further, we must address the rights of the community partner, what a collaborating organization may expect to count on from the students with whom it is working. The following activity (exercise 2.2)—which may be completed in writing, discussed with others, or both—is intended to further your understanding of the reasonable expectations of a community partner.

> ⚘ **Exercise 2.11: Pre-Service Checklist of Student Rights** on page 35 is intended to reaffirm those rights and identify any areas that need to be addressed before and/or during your work with your community partner.

> ### ☼ Exercise 2.2: What Can a Community Partner Expect?
>
> Imagine that you are the program director for an organization that serves the refugee community in your city by providing workforce readiness programs and tutoring in English. You are preparing to welcome a group of students from a local college involved in a service-learning course that combines both direct and indirect service: tutoring small groups of refugees in English language skills and revising the outdated tutoring manual that your organization uses as a guide for volunteer tutors.
>
> Because your organization has worked with student interns, you have a fairly good sense of your responsibilities to the students. You've prepared job descriptions for the students, scheduled training sessions, and identified a process for them to get feedback and to assess their efforts.
>
> In the past, though, some of these relationships have not worked so well for your organization. For example, students often arrived late for their sessions, and occasionally they did not show up at all. As a result, some tutoring sessions had to be doubled up or canceled. To prevent this from happening again, your supervisor has asked you to create a list of the organization's rights in relation to this service-learning class to share with the students before their first tutoring session.
>
> **Your task is to create that list.** What, fundamentally, can your organization expect to get from the students who are preparing to engage with you?

This section was designed to draw parameters around your upcoming experience and make transparent the fundamental rights and responsibilities inherent in the community-based learning endeavor. In the next section, we'll take a closer look at how you might flesh out these basic rights and responsibilities in the context of your particular community partnership.

What's This Place? What's *My* Place?

Before we discuss specific ways that you can formally learn more about your community organization and how your particular academic framework and skills might be of support, let's start with an exercise to identify what you hope to accomplish, what your concerns are, what you need to be successful, and what you expect from others.

Your service experience will be greatly enhanced if you can have a discussion with your community partner representatives about *their* hopes, fears, needs, and expectations and compare them to your own. If you are able to do so, plan a specific time within the next week to have a one-on-one or group discussion with your community partner representatives about goals for this partnership to increase the likelihood of success for all involved.

Assets, Interests, and Needs

Effective community engagement requires us to understand the mission and goals of the organization with which we are preparing to work. In addition, we must consider the assets, interests, and needs of all of the stakeholders in a service-learning course: students, faculty, and community partners and the persons served by that organization. Without this understanding we may be insensitive to the challenges and capacities of individuals within the organization; we may provide services that are actually of little use to the organization; or we may fail to comprehend the impact we have had on the organization, the community it represents, and the larger world.

Assets are tangible or intangible resources, qualities, and/or material items that each party brings to the table. *Interests* are what's at stake for each party, what each party hopes to achieve through the act of working collaboratively together. And *needs* are, essentially, gaps in assets, places where the resources of one of the partners can make a meaningful difference to another. All of the players in the service-learning endeavor bring assets, interests, and needs to their work with each other.

Further, while our community partner and those it serves have needs that we might hope to address, they are not just "needy." In fact, it is essential to a true collaboration that students understand that those they serve bring their own capacities, as well as their self-identified needs, to the table—just as students bring *their* needs as learners, along with their capacities and skills.

This is also true of faculty. It can often be challenging, at first, for students and community partners to even consider that a faculty member has needs. As students, we tend to think of faculty as those who have tons of expertise and virtually no needs to bring to the

---

✶ Exercise 2.3: Hopes, Fears, Needs, and Expectations

Divide a sheet of paper into four columns: *Hopes, Fears, Needs,* and *Expectations.* Fill in whatever comes to mind under each category as it relates to the service-learning experience you are beginning. Then answer the following questions by completing a 7- to 10-minute "freewrite":

• What steps can you next take to begin realizing your hopes?
• What are the sources of your fears? What can you do to minimize these fears?
• What do you need and how will you get it to accomplish your hopes?
• What are the sources of your expectations? Are these your own or someone else's?
• Using this information as a guide, list three action steps you can take in the next week to create the service-learning experience you desire.

table. Of course it's true that your instructor *does* have a lot of knowledge to offer you and your classmates, as well as many skills and capacities as a facilitator in a service-learning environment. But your faculty person is also hoping to get something of value from this experience. Perhaps it's a deep desire for meaningful and engaging community-based placements and partners where their students might test and apply the theories they are learning in class to the real-world challenges faced in the community. Perhaps your instructor is keenly interested in seeing positive change happen in your community and is excited to watch students interact to bring that change into being. Perhaps your instructor includes their partnerships in the community in their research agendas, seeking not only to create new knowledge but to also offer something of value to the community.

For service-learning classes to be most effective, all stakeholders need to be transparent about the assets they bring to the table and the outcomes they hope to gain from participation. This works best when all members of the partnership recognize that everyone involved has something—in fact, *many* things—to bring to the table. This levels the playing field and facilitates the development of a different type of educational dynamic; one where, ideally, everyone involved

not only *is* a teacher and a learner but also understands and reflects on how this is true.

Our initial impressions of an organization and their clients may be based in reality or influenced by our biases and lack of information. We risk an unproductive service-learning experience unless we clarify our own perceptions with the community partner and with others involved in the community experience. The next exercise is intended to bring into alignment our notions with the reality of the community partner. Take a look at figure 2.1 and then complete exercises 2.4 and 2.5 to explore your community partnership this term.

By now you have thought about what you bring to the partnership and what you hope to get out of it. You have considered your rights and responsibilities and the rights and responsibilities of your community partner. You have begun to develop your partnership by learning more about the community organization. In effect, things are off to positive start.

Because any collaboration is rooted in human relationship, there is the possibility—and, realistically, the *probability*—that something will arise to challenge you, your classmates, your instructor, and the community partner. In the next section, we will explore what to do when there are breakdowns in even the best-laid plans.

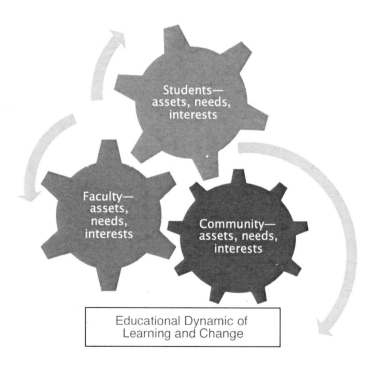

Figure 2.1.   Assets, Needs, Interests: Educational Dynamic

✥ Exercise 2.4: Mapping Assets, Interests, and Needs

Using figure 2.1 as a starting place, sketch a map of your partnership—students, faculty, and community partner. Identify each stakeholder's assets, interests, and needs. Some of these factors may be quite clear to you even in the early stages of your partnership. In other cases, you might have as many questions as answers about what each stakeholder is bringing to the table.

Indeed, your questions are just as valuable as your answers since they indicate gaps in understanding. Ultimately, how these questions are answered in working with your faculty and community partner may affect the outcomes that are realized in this educational dynamic.

After you've outlined your map, use the following questions to further reflect on what you need to know and what actions might be possible:

- What were the simplest and easiest elements to fill in on your map? What were the most difficult? What was most surprising to you in completing your map?
- What connections do you see between and among the assets, interests, and needs of each stakeholder group? How do you imagine the elements that each stakeholder brings to the table will interact with the elements that the other stakeholders bring?
- Where are the gaps in your understanding about assets, interests, and needs as they relate to this partnership and service-learning opportunity? How might you actively and intentionally work to fill in those gaps?

✥ Exercise 2.5: Organizational Action Research

Now that you've considered the assets, interests, and needs of each stakeholder in your service-learning course, let's deepen your familiarity with your community partner. This activity is designed for you to learn about the mission, history, staffing, structure, and budget of the community organization with which you are working through interviewing different persons associated with the organization. You are not limited to gathering information from the primary contact person at the organization. Instead, try to get a broad and comprehensive view of the organization by talking to as many people associated with the organization as possible. In addition to answering the following questions, gather one piece of organizational literature that best describes the organization's mission and services.

- Name of organization
- Brief history of the founding of the organization
- Mission statement
- Summary of vision: What would this organization like to accomplish/become? What is it trying to make happen?
- Describe the population the organization serves.
- Outline the public policy areas the organization might influence.
- What geographic area does the organization serve?
- How many paid staff are employed by the organization? What are their roles?
- What roles do volunteers play in the organization?

Adapted from R. Battistoni (2002), *Civic Engagement across the Curriculum: A Resource Book for Service-Learning Faculty in All Disciplines*.

What Now?—Navigating Breakdowns

Remember our half-formed group of students waiting outside their community partner's door at the beginning of this chapter? Rejoining their story, we find one of the students using his cell phone to call the executive director of the organization, who had visited the students' class the week before and confirmed that today's visit was on the organization's calendar. Reaching her, the student learned that she was in her car on her way to the organization's office site but was turning around to come meet the students at this exhibition space. There had apparently been a misunderstanding, she said; she thought that the artistic director had offered to facilitate today's visit, but now she wondered whether he thought *she* was scheduled to do it. She apologized for the miscommunication and asked the students to please wait.

The rest of the students from class arrived just as the executive director pulled in with more apologies and a key to the locked door. The students toured the cavernous space filled with art from a huge cross section of regional artists, taking notes for their grant proposals and asking questions of the executive director. Some stayed past the end of class, interested in interviewing the artists who were arriving to install even more art for the exhibition opening that weekend.

When the students were asked to reflect during their next class session on their visit to the gallery, many spoke about the negative impact the executive director's lateness had made on them. Several wondered aloud whether their grantwriting project was important to the community partner, let alone a priority; others maintained that the incident had soured them on the relationship and the project for good. Another student remarked that it was indicative of the flakiness of artists in general to blow off an important meeting. Many expressed that their time was valuable and that they resented having to wait.

Then one student offered an alternate view. He said that, from his perspective, the community partner's internal miscommunication signaled that they were working really hard with very little funding to pull off an enormous task—creating an inclusive exhibit of dozens of artists—and that proved to him how important his grantwriting would be to the organization. The small staff was so overtaxed with the basic work of the organization, he imagined, that they had failed to remember a meeting that would potentially benefit them. He said

he was impressed that the executive director acted so quickly to correct the mistake the organization had made, redirecting her entire day to accommodate their visit despite her understanding that someone else was responsible for it. Finally, he suggested that just as we were judging the community partner's lateness, so might the community partner judge the lateness of half of the students in the class—assuming that those who were late didn't care about and hadn't prioritized the visit, or were just "too flaky" to show up on time.

What these students were illustrating in a very practical way was the difference between ***intent*** and ***impact*** in communication. When interacting with others, all of us hold certain *intentions* for what we hope to communicate, and we use the various tools of communication (word choice, tone of voice, body language, behavior, and so on) to get that message across. Try as we might, we sometimes fail to have the *impact* on others that we intend; we also sometimes create impacts that inadvertently send a message that is directly opposed to our intentions. When the other students in the class heard that their lateness could be interpreted as flakiness or willful disregard of the community partner, they protested this perception: One argued that the bus had been late, several others that their bike rides had taken longer than they had imagined, and another that she had gotten lost on the way to the site. All of these quite legitimate reasons for lateness—like our contact person's—illustrated the fine line we walk as communicators between intent and impact.

Because service-learning courses are collaborations between persons (and groups of persons) with a variety of needs and resources, inevitably breakdowns in the process will occur. Students, faculty, and community partners may choose to view these glitches as fatal to the collaborative process and, as a result, shirk their commitment to the shared endeavor. On the other hand, students, faculty, and community partners may choose to understand that such mistakes are opportunities for learning and growth, as these are often exactly the things that expose areas ripe for improvement (for example, the need for greater communication between staff people within an organization, or the importance of getting accurate directions before driving to a new place for the first time).

You may have noticed that the word "choose" is used in the preceding paragraph to describe how students, faculty, and community partners assess the success of their efforts at partnership. At a basic level, the only things within the control of any single person involved in community-based learning are his or her own behavior and responses. The community partner, the instructor, and the on-time students did not control whether the other students were late or not, just as the instructor and students did not control the community partner's choices. However, all of these persons controlled how they reacted to the choices of the others and whether or not they used those outcomes to further their own learning.

Exercise 2.6: Exploring Breakdowns offers several situations of breakdown between community partners and students. Investigate your reactions to these situations either in writing, in discussion with others, or both.

As you may have noted, the perceptions and perspectives of any one person in a situation are impacted by many factors, some of which that person may have in common with others, and some of which will differ from person to person. Further, many of these differences in experience result from the multiple ways that persons do and do not experience privilege and access to power in the world. In chapter 5, we explore in depth what it means to investigate power, understand privilege, and navigate difference. As you begin to work with your community partner, however, you might start to think about how who you are and what you have experienced impact the way you see the world, including the current world of this partnership. Don't stop there, either: Get curious about the multiple realities you will encounter as a community-based learner. Think about how a genuine exchange, which is the promise of true collaboration, can leave all persons fuller, more whole, and better able to relate effectively to others than before they entered the partnership.

Developing an Action Learning Plan for Serving (ALPS)

Perhaps the best strategy for circumventing potential problems is the development of an Action Learning Plan for Serving (ALPS). Creating an ALPS can help you achieve your mountainous hopes because you have anticipated in advance the needs, resources, timelines, and obtainable objectives for the service-learning experience. The ALPS also includes the rights and responsibilities of all parties and offers an initial framework for assessing and evaluating your actions. Moreover, it allows you to track your progress during the experience to see if adjustments need to be made midstream. Exercise 2.7 (p. 31) introduces you to the ALPS, which you'll refer back to throughout your service-learning experience. Complete it with your class or on your own before continuing.

Conclusion

Angeles Arrien, in the book *The Four-Fold Way: Walking the Paths of the Warrior, Teacher, Healer, and Visionary*, explores indigenous wisdom traditions to articulate four central human tasks. Arrien asserts that, in order to live authentically with others, we must *show up, pay attention, tell the truth*, and *be open to the outcome*. Perhaps in no courses do these words ring more true than in community-based ones. Students entering a collaborative exchange with the world outside their institution's doors find that a dynamic experience awaits them, an experience that promises tremendous payoffs in personal growth, skill building, and understanding oneself and others in exchange for a commitment of time and follow-through.

As one of these students, you can use the material presented in this chapter to prepare you to show up and be fully present in the work that needs *you* to bring it to fruition; to learn all that you can through the experience of doing and reflecting on that doing; to articulate the meaning that the experience holds for you; and to deepen your capacity to understand that, in a true collaboration, no single person controls the outcome of the exchange. It is up to each of us to determine whether that is a frightening or an exciting proposition—and how to make our way through it as individuals connected through the bonds of community.

♣ Exercise 2.6: Exploring Breakdowns

Situation 1a

You are a student working with a community organization dedicated to welcoming refugees into your city by offering workforce training and tutoring in English. For your service-learning course, you have committed yourself to meeting with a tutee every Tuesday afternoon at the public library for a two-hour tutoring session. Your tutee showed up for the first scheduled session, missed the second session entirely, and came for the third session but indicated that he could only stay for an hour. While he was there, he told you that he might be moving out of town next week.

Situation 2a

You are part of a team of students developing a public relations campaign for an organization that provides free health care to persons experiencing homelessness in your community. Your team has been very excited about diving into this project after listening to a panel of persons who had received care from this organization talk about the difference it made in their lives. In order to complete your project, you need concrete information from your community partner, but in the past week you have sent three e-mails to your team's contact person, none of which have been answered.

Situation 3a

For your service-learning class, you are interviewing senior citizens at a local nursing home for a compilation of oral histories about the experience of living through the Depression. After your second day of interviewing, your contact person, the director of recreational programming at the nursing home, compliments your work with the seniors and suggests having a beer together over the weekend so you can get to know each other better.

Situation 1b

You are a student working with a community organization dedicated to welcoming refugees to your city by offering workforce training and tutoring in English. For your service-learning course, you have committed yourself to meeting with a tutee every Tuesday afternoon at the public library for a two-hour tutoring session. Everything went fine for the first two sessions, but your car broke down on the way to the library for the third session, and you had a dentist appointment scheduled during the fourth. You aren't sure where things stand with your tutee at this point.

Situation 2b

You are part of a team of students developing a public relations campaign for an organization that provides free health care to persons experiencing homelessness in your community. Your team has been very excited about diving into this project after listening to a panel of persons who had received care from this organization talk about the difference it made in their lives. You are the designated contact person for your team, but you just moved into a new apartment and haven't hooked up your e-mail yet. You aren't sure whether or not you gave your new phone number to your teammates or your community partner.

Situation 3b

For your service-learning class, you are interviewing seniors at a local nursing home for a compilation of oral histories about the experience of living through the Depression. Since you're considering changing your major, you ask your contact person, the director of recreational programming at the nursing home, to have a beer with you over the weekend so you can get to know each other better.

Reflect on the previous scenarios. How would you describe the communication breakdown in each of these situations? Who do you imagine is responsible for the breakdown? How does the "you" of each situation perceive the breakdown? How might the other person(s) involved perceive the breakdown? How are the perspectives in each of these situations impacted by the context of that situation? How might you choose to act in each of these situations to heal the breakdown and put the partnership back on track, and what choices might you make if the other person chooses to keep the partnership off course? If you really *were* the "you" of these situations, what would you do?

Now return to the list of principles of good practice found on page 22. Read this list and the previous scenarios again. Where do you find a breakdown between these principles and the situations? How could you make choices in these situations that would line up with these best practices?

Key Concepts

assets	impact	project-based
community partner	intent	responsibilities
contact person	interests	rights
direct-service	needs	

Key Issues

- How do students benefit through engaging in community-based learning?
- What are the different types of community-based learning a student might participate in?
- What are the characteristics of a successful community-based learning partnership?
- What are some of the basic responsibilities and rights of student-learners in community-based settings? What are some of the basic responsibilities and rights of community partners?
- What is the difference between *intent* and *impact* in communication, and what are some examples of the breakdown between these factors?

✸ Exercise 2.7: Action Learning Plan for Serving (ALPS)

This first ALPS worksheet asks you to consider what the purpose of this community-based learning experience is from the perspectives of all who are involved. To continue orienting yourself to your community partnership, answer the following questions, and keep your responses to refer to as your service-learning experience progresses. If you don't have responses to some of these questions, return to this worksheet when you have developed them out of your experience.

1. Review your course syllabus and recall the ways that your instructor framed this service-learning experience. From your instructor's perspective, what is the purpose/what are the purposes of this collaboration?

    •

    •

    •

2. From your community partner's perspective, what is the purpose/what are the purposes of this collaboration?

    •

    •

    •

3. What are your individual learning goals for this collaboration? At the end of your time in this experience, what do you expect to have learned?

    •

    •

    •

4. What are your individual service goals for this collaboration? At the end of your time in this experience, what do you expect from its service component?

    •

    •

    •

5. What is the final product, if any, for this collaboration, and how will the final product be evaluated?

6. What are the main components of the final product for this collaboration?

    •

    •

    •

7. What are the deadlines for the project and its components, as you know them so far?

ADDITIONAL EXERCISES

♟ Exercise 2.8: Which Type of Community-Based Learning Is Right for Me?

Reflect on the following questions to help you clarify which type of community-based learning to choose.

- What is the nature of the direct-service work I might take on? What kinds of projects might I complete? If there is not a preselected set of options, is there an office on campus that can help me identify my choices for community-based learning? Does my college/university offer an orientation to community-based learning, or will I get that in the course itself? Can I do a site visit with possible choices?
- As I consider my options, what kind of training, supervision, and feedback is available to me for each? How do these kinds of support fit with the type of support I think I will need?
- As I consider each option, do I understand the range of activities I'll be expected to complete? Am I willing to do these activities? Do I know where to get support for my work?
- What are the logistical considerations for each of my options? Will I be traveling to the partner's site or working from another location? Will I be alone or working with other students or employees of the partnering organization?
- How much time will I need to devote to this project in order to satisfy my community partner, my instructor, and myself? Am I prepared to dedicate this amount of time and rearrange my schedule as necessary?
- Will I be able to feel physically and emotionally safe enough in this environment to serve and to learn? What do I need to feel physically and emotionally safe? Are those factors present in the environments I am considering?
- What are my past experiences of working in a direct-service capacity? In a project-based capacity? What are my greater and lesser strengths working directly with others? What are my greater and lesser strengths in managing and completing projects?
- What are my personal/academic/professional goals for this experience? When I complete this experience, what do I want to have accomplished?

♟ Exercise 2.9: As Time Goes By . . .

Start by taking a large sheet of paper (at least 11 × 14 inches, if possible) and creating seven columns, each of which will be labeled at the top with the days of the week. Across the left side of the sheet, make twenty-four rows and label them for each hour of the day. Begin to block off time for the activities that fill your time in a typical week at this specific point in your life: sleeping, eating, classes, employment, homework, travel, free time, and so on. Be sure that every hour of every day is accounted for with some activity.

After you have finished labeling all of the hours in your week, use colored pencils to lightly shade in each block. Use one color for activities that absolutely cannot be moved to another time in your week (e.g., classes); use a second color for activities that are fairly firm but that could be moved around if absolutely necessary (perhaps your work schedule); and use a third color for the activities that are least fixed in your week (maybe free time or meals). Be sure that every block of time in your week has now been shaded in.

Now take a look at your week and use this visual representation of your time to help you make decisions about how you might commit yourself in this project. As you move more deeply into your project this term, you might repeat this exercise to reflect the changed nature of your schedule.

Note: This activity may also be used to guide teams in their negotiation of time responsibilities or as a template for scheduling with the community partner.

❓ Exercise 2.10: Pre-Service Checklist of Student Responsibilities

As a means of facilitating a practical consideration of the roles and responsibilities you have in working with your community partner, complete the following checklist prior to your first actual workday. Read the following statements and initial on the line adjacent to the statement, indicating that you understand and have received adequate information about that item. If you have not received adequate information, put an asterisk (*) on the adjacent line and inform your instructor or appropriate college administrator.

1. Students should clearly understand the requirements of their community project:

    ____ I have a clear understanding of both my instructor's and my community partner's expectations of me.
    ____ I understand my parameters (I have thought of the consequences of performing actions beyond my agreed-upon responsibilities).
    ____ I have identified the skills needed to carry out this project, and I feel comfortable with those skills.
    ____ I have identified the skills needed to carry out this project, and I have devised specific plans for strengthening skills with which I am not comfortable or familiar.
    ____ I know my client population and am making every attempt to understand their needs from *their* perspective.
    ____ I know what to do in case of an emergency.

2. Students need necessary legal documents:

    ____ If I will be driving, I have a valid license and liability insurance.

3. Students should take responsibility for their behavior throughout the community-based project:

    ____ I understand that I am responsible for my own personal health and safety.
    ____ I have insurance (if agency requires specific coverage for volunteers).
    ____ I understand the waivers I sign.
    ____ I have thought of risks involved in this community-based project. For example:

    • What are clients' special needs?
    • In case of accidents, what is unsafe?
    • What can I do to reduce risks by my own behavior, clothing, and preparation?
    • What behaviors fall outside my job description? (Example: Is it okay to transport clients?)

4. Students should understand these legal issues:

    ____ **Negligence** involves a mistake, lack of attention, reckless behavior, or indifference to the duty of care to another person. A reasonable person should have been able to foresee the possibility of injury (e.g., a wet spot on the floor, a child climbing on top of a table).
    ____ **Intentional or criminal misconduct** involves potential harm caused by a volunteer. A volunteer is responsible for any harm caused to an organization or individual if the harm resulted from intentional or criminal misconduct on the part of the volunteer.
    ____ **Invasion of privacy** involves confidentiality. I know and understand what the confidentiality policies of my partnering organization are. (e.g., Client histories and personal records are confidential.)

⚲ Exercise 2.11: Pre-Service Checklist of Student Rights

As a means of facilitating practical consideration of the rights you have in working with your community partner, complete the following checklist prior to your first actual workday. Read the following statements and initial on the line adjacent to the statement, indicating that you understand and have received adequate information about that item. If you have not received adequate information, put an asterisk (*) on the adjacent line and inform your instructor or appropriate college administrator.

____ I have received a description of the work I am expected to perform and have committed to doing that work.

____ I have received or am currently receiving proper training for the work I've committed to doing, or I understand that my training is on-the-job and will be supervised as I go.

____ I understand how I will receive supervision and feedback for the work that I do.

____ I understand the channels of communication through which I should express my concerns about the work I am doing, the ways I am being treated, or breaches of my service plan or other agreements.

____ I understand that I may expect to work in an environment that is reasonably safe and free from sexual and other forms of harassment.

____ I understand that I may not be discriminated against on the basis of race, ethnicity, gender, age, religion, ability, sexual orientation, and/or other protections offered by my college/university and/or community partner.

CHAPTER 3

Becoming Community

Moving from I *to* We

VICKI L. REITENAUER

The Low Road

> What can they do
> to you? Whatever they want.
> They can set you up, they can
> bust you, they can break
> your fingers; they can
> burn your brain with electricity,
> blur you with drugs till you
> can't walk, can't remember, they can
> take your child, wall up
> your lover. They can do anything
> you can't stop them
> from doing. How can you stop
> them? Alone, you can fight,
> you can refuse, you can
> take what revenge you can
> but they roll over you.
>
> But two people fighting
> back to back can cut through
> a mob, a snake-dancing file
> can break a cordon, an army
> can meet an army.
>
> Two people can keep each other
> sane, can give support, conviction,
> love, massage, hope, sex.
> Three people are a delegation,
> a committee, a wedge. With four
> you can play bridge and start
> an organization. With six
> you can rent a whole house,

> eat pie for dinner with no
> seconds, and hold a fund raising party.
> A dozen make a demonstration.
> A hundred fill a hall.
> A thousand have solidarity and your own newsletter;
> ten thousand, power and your own paper;
> a hundred thousand, your own media;
> ten million, your own country.
> It goes on one at a time,
> it starts when you care
> to act, it starts when you do
> it again after they said no,
> it starts when you say We
> and know who you mean, and each
> day you mean one more.

Marge Piercy, from *The Moon Is Always Female*

SERVICE-LEARNING invites you to bring who you are, what you know, and what you can do into the classroom and the world beyond (the *wall-less classroom*) in applying your whole self to creating community change. In the process, what you discover in the intersection of "you" and "not-you" will shape and transform your understanding of yourself and your place in the world, if you let it. Putting who you are and what you know into practice will change who you are and what you know and enlarge your understanding of yourself and the world of others who are both different from and similar to you. In forming a community with others (other students, the instructor, the individuals who comprise your community partner),

---

⁂ Exercise 3.1: Defining Community

How do you define "community"? Have you experienced yourself to be a member of a community in any way before? In what ways have you experienced belonging in a community? Are there communities to which you could belong, but choose not to? If so, why?

---

you increase the possibilities for creating transformation, as you experience deeply the principle of the whole being more than the sum of its parts. You are welcomed into a learning experience in which a community addresses real-world challenges in a way that an assortment of individuals cannot, and "it starts when you say *We* / and know who you mean, and each / day you mean one more."

Putting "Community" into a Community-Based Learning Course: A Case Study

One April morning, a group of students found their way to a large room on an extension campus of Portland State University (PSU) located in the city's western suburbs. I was the instructor for the course, and I arrived early, influenced by stories of the horrendous traffic jams I would likely encounter and by my own desire to have plenty of time to get lost in the confusing building. There turned out to be very little traffic and I managed to find the classroom pretty easily, and then there I was, where the students would soon be as well: in a big room rich in technology but short on the kind of setup that allows for full participation and interaction by both students and instructor.

I spent my extra minutes shifting the movable tables into an approximation of a circle that we could all sit around. Then, one by one, the students made their way in: ten in all, participants in a degree-completion program (a program in which students returning to the university while working full-time can accelerate the completion of their education). Most of the students were familiar with each other already. Throughout their time in the program, many had taken the same classes or, at the very least, had taken classes with someone who was now enrolled in this class. There were hellos and some hugs, there was catching up to do (*What did you end up getting in that soc class?*), there were the attempts at connection where hints of it existed (*Weren't you in that history class that I dropped last*

term?), articulations of the threads binding us together and the spaces where those threads would be attached. That is to say, some of us knew each other, some of us knew *about* each other, and all of us would find out a whole lot more about each other in the weeks ahead.

Coming into that first class, the only thing these students knew for sure was that they had to be there (or at least in another course similar to this one, as PSU requires most of its undergraduate students to complete a service-learning course in the junior or senior year) and that their being there would involve stepping out of the classroom in some way to work in their community. They didn't know what the work would entail, or what it would look like, and neither did I. In a course called Change for the Common Good, I believed it would be important to figure out first what those terms meant to all of us in this context. In other words, how would we, students and instructor, define "common," articulate "good," and see ourselves as agents for positive change within that shared understanding? Essentially, I was teaching the course as an exercise in collaborative group process. The syllabus contained objectives and course assignments designed to deepen our capacities as a collective decision-making body. Also, rather than being from a single disciplinary major, these students represented academic programs in science, social science, arts, and humanities. The course was truly multidisciplinary. We would collectively have to determine how best to apply our individual skills and knowledge to effect change for the common good.

So we began, with activities and exercises and readings and multiple conversations intended to bring us together, to attach and tighten the threads that bind, to move all of us from *I* to *We*: that is, from experiencing ourselves solely as individuals to understanding that, in community-based learning, the success of any one student is connected to successful engagement with others—other students, faculty, community partner. How might we experience and act from this place of shared investment in and responsibility for our learning? One early activity helped each of us investigate our own preferred learning environments, so that we might intentionally cocreate a class that included all of us (exercise 3.2).

Identifying Group Action for the Common Good

Since the students themselves were charged with identifying and pursuing a community partner with whom to work, we then turned our attention to the community outside our classroom and our perception of its needs. It didn't take long for a few proposals for our service project to surface. Someone had a contact with the Boys and Girls Club, which needed some painting and cleanup done at its site. Another student knew someone with the Latino Family Services Coalition, which had been approached by the City of Hillsboro and the Hillsboro Police Department to engage young artists to create a mural celebrating the growing Latino population in the county. Guests from both potential community partners visited our class and discussed the ways we could make a difference in the community it served, ways we might create change for the common good.

After the visits, a definite enthusiasm emerged about the mural project. We imagined how powerful and satisfying it could be to mentor a group of artists who would transfer their private visions into the public view. We thought about all of the persons who ride the commuter train into Portland every day—from which they would be able to see the mural in its home on the wall of the police station—and how the results of our hard work would live on in the community. We considered how the project would require an extensive range of skills—from art and design to marketing and public relations—and how we believed that those skills were represented in our class. While this project seemed to outshine the others that were under consideration, there was by no means immediate consensus that we should proceed in this direction. Some students expressed worry that the project was enormous in scope and impossible to complete in the weeks we had available to us. Others felt reluctant to enter into such potentially intense relationships with the young artists. Still others had concerns that they would not be able to work effectively with others who were so different in many ways from themselves, especially with respect to culture and language.

We talked about the project. We dialogued—passionately yet civilly—remembering our earlier discussions about the need for all of us to "practice active listening," "agree to disagree, using 'I think' and 'I feel' statements," "solicit others' opinions," and "practice the Platinum Rule of treating others how *they* want to be treated." We dialogued and dialogued. Many students said that they did not want to move forward until everyone was on board with the project. We listed the pros and cons; we mocked up a timeline and a detailed task list (led by two of the students well versed in project management); we did "go-arounds" (during which the students took turns speaking with no interruption) of our thoughts and feelings about the project.

Ultimately, a clear path emerged: Although not everyone was equally enthusiastic about the mural project, everyone agreed to work on it. And so the consensus decision was made: The students would indeed work with the group of young artists to guide and mentor them through the completion of a mural on the theme "Latino Heroes." After articulating this shared goal—the completion of a fifteen- by forty-foot

---

💡 Exercise 3.2: My Ideal Learning Environment

Complete a 7- to 10-minute freewrite on the theme "In my ideal learning environment . . ." What qualities are present in those learning environments in which you thrive and experience a sense of inclusion?

When you think about service-learning in general and your current experience in particular (as you now understand it), in what ways do you see the qualities of your ideal learning environment represented? What about this experience will suit your preferences well, and what will be challenges in this kind of course?

mural—we set about figuring out how to use our wisdom, experience, talents, and gifts to get the job done. We also discussed how students might choose to engage with the project so that their academic skills and knowledge would grow and expand during their time in the class. Students created an ALPS (Action Learning Plan for Serving) for themselves, and then we collectively developed a class ALPS. While the ALPS was modified over the course of the project, this strategy helped us to define common goals, timelines, and responsibilities.

Moving from *I* to *We*

We next deepened our conversation about what it would mean for a predominantly female, non-Latino class to work with a group of predominantly male, Latino artists. In our class two of the ten students were Latino and spoke Spanish; eight were non-Latino with a range of fluency in Spanish. Eight of the students were female, two male, and the instructor was a non-Latino female. Eight of the nine artists were Latino and six were male, including the non-Latino artist. The artists, who generally were referred to as "at-risk youth" in their

schools and the social service agencies of which they were clients, were more positively called "at-promise" by our community partner, who described how terminology and labels can put artificial psychological and sociological limits on individuals.

Before taking on the question of how to relate in an encouraging, non-oppressive manner with those we would serve, we first had to understand what each of us would bring into our learning community. We needed to more fully explore the *I* in creating the *We*. We needed to know: How had each of us been influenced to become who we are? How were we similar to each other, and how were we different? How might that affect our work with the Latino Family Services Coalition and especially the young artists with whom we had committed to work? How might we understand our own histories more deeply so that our preferences, our biases, our gifts, and our ways of being might be made more available to us to be used in the service of others and for our individual and collective learning?

The reflection exercise (exercise 3.3) helped us move more intentionally into the kinds and ways of knowing that most powerfully affect our ideas of ourselves and our relationships with others. First, each student wrote a reflection journal entry responding to the

---

✶ Exercise 3.3: Who Am I and What Do I Bring?

First, describe your background or identity on the basis of:

- Race/ethnicity
- Gender
- Spirituality
- Ability (physical/mental/emotional)
- Socioeconomic class
- Age
- Physical appearance
- Sexual orientation
- Other identifier(s)

Second, answer the following questions based on your background and identity description.

- What have been some sources of strength for you growing up?
- What have been some difficulties for you growing up?
- How has your background or identity affected your fit in this university, and how do you imagine it will affect your fit in this classroom and in the work we're doing with those we are serving?

Adapted by Laura C. Engelken from "Who Am I, What Do I Bring?" developed by Dr. Jamie Washington (2001).

assignment's prompts, and then we practiced active listening in class during a "go-around" to hear a part of each student's story. Each student was free to share any portion of his or her story in an uninterrupted way; the listeners' job was simply to hear each speaker's understanding of him or herself, without response.

Learning through the Service Project

With the insights gained through these activities and a plan to meet the artists interviewed and selected by our community partner, the students moved forward. Nico headed up the student team that would work directly with the artists to help them translate their visions onto the mural, while David designed and built the massive, movable mural structure. Susan and Sandra first helped assemble the structure, primed the wood, and created a studio for the artists in a county-owned warehouse, and then made sure that a steady supply of drinks and food was available for all. Carmen and Lydia offered their project management skills in the form of a tracking device for the tasks involved before turning their attention to winning publicity and additional funding for the project. Tracie inspired the artists by talking with them and picking up a brush when needed to move the painting along. Mercedes, Linda, and Julia interviewed each young artist, wrote biographies, and created a memory book of the experience for all participants.

We worked long hours through a hot summer. The mural evolved from an idea to a design to a pile of boards and metal to an enormous expanse of canvas ready for the application of paint and sweat. Over the weeks of our course, we all watched the shared vision of a group of artists emerge in vibrant colors and heroic shapes. Some newspapers and television news reporters came out to the warehouse to interview artists and students. As a result, how much this project mattered to us increased exponentially, a fact expressed in students' weekly reflection papers. Many students reported eagerness to return to the artists and the project at hand and a desire to impact the artists positively beyond the completion of the mural.

Even though I'm a history major with a focus on Latin American history, Miguel has taught me a lot about popular folk heroes in Mexican history. I

never expected to have such a great connection with him. And while we've painted together, I've been able to encourage him to think about attending the Art Institute in the future. He's just contacted an admissions counselor there to talk about his options.

The artists, too, asked about absent students, checked in if someone was late, and sought out conversations about a range of issues such as painting, family, finishing high school, or dreaming about college. It mattered that this work was being done. And it mattered that this particular group of people were doing it together. In many ways, the unfinished mural was already creating a common good by connecting us across gender, age, language, ethnicity, and culture.

Then one night, just a week before the scheduled public unveiling of the mural in a ceremony that Carmen and Lydia had helped to organize and publicize, a representative of the Hillsboro Police Department (the non-Latino male assistant chief of police), which had originally commissioned the mural from the Latino Family Services Coalition, visited the warehouse when several students and artists were working together. When he saw that there were various religious figures on the mural—the Virgin of Guadalupe, Jesus, Padre Miguel Hidalgo, Mother Theresa—he demanded that the artists paint over them. The assembled group didn't quite understand what he meant; wasn't the original idea that these artists were free to paint their vision of their heroes in whatever way they chose, so long as they did not use gang imagery in that depiction? Yet here was an official telling them, essentially, that their choices had been wrong. Their vision must be changed.

Conflict within the Community

The assembled group thanked the assistant chief for his input, asked him to allow them to get back to their work, and continued. They resisted. No one wanted to stop painting what was becoming a masterwork of culture, history, and the human possibilities of all who were involved with it.

There were plenty of upset feelings about the incident across the community: the artists felt manipulated and misled, the students felt angry, the instructor felt concerned, the community partner felt betrayed,

---

> ★★ **Exercise 3.4: Situation Analysis**
>
> Consider your responses to the following questions. If possible, discuss them with others in your class.
>
> - Why, in your view, did the assistant chief of police insist that the religious images in the mural be painted over? What factors may have motivated his demand? How should the persons affected—the artists, the students, the community partner, the instructor—respond to this demand, ideally?
> - Taking a broader view, how do you perceive the "I" of individuality intersecting and overlapping with the "We" of community? How are the "I" and the "We" separate and separable? How do you understand the multiple levels and layers of "I" and "We," using this incident as an example?
> - Considered in the light of this situation, do you think anything might have been missing from the course-constructed ALPS? How might the ALPS be modified now, as a result of this situation?

the police department personnel felt worried about public reaction. Through discussions inclusive of all those working on the project, it was decided that the community partner, the Latino Family Services Coalition, would talk with the police department regarding their concerns about the mural. The Coalition was the community organization directly connected to both the police department, on the one hand, and to the group completing the mural, on the other.

The students and artists took their collective anger and indignation and put it right back into their work. If the mural was impressive before, it became spectacular in the days that followed. The artists created on canvas what their heroes—the original figures as well as the Aztec snake and eagle, artists Frida Kahlo and Diego Rivera, the local school counselor and teacher Luz Maciel Villerreal, the actor Cantinflas, Emiliano Zapata, Cesar Chavez—had lived their own lives to foster: the enactment of social justice in the world, the practice of putting who we are and what we know into action on behalf of others, and then letting our knowing be, in turn, enhanced and changed by that practice.

The mural was finished without compromising the original artistic vision of the painters. The images that the assistant police chief objected to were still there to be revealed in the unveiling, during a community celebration that took place on a beautiful day in mid-August, with all of the artists and all of the students present to witness the appreciation of the gathered crowd. The press was there, too, lured by

the way the mural had turned from a feel-good story into an "issue." The assistant police chief also appeared, thanking everyone for their effort while explaining that a final decision about the future home of the mural had not yet been made. After speeches and the buildup of anticipation, the cloth covering came off and there it was: a testament to the power of individuals to come together into more than the sum of their parts, to render what was believed to be impossible not only possible, but necessary and human and real.

Getting to *We*

The mural example exemplifies the complex dynamic of moving from *I* to *We* in the midst of creating change that can also raise controversy. The service-learning course certainly tested students' knowledge and skills in new and unanticipated ways. Students learned that being a leader in the community is not as easy as reading books and taking exams.

A framework that was helpful to us in reflecting upon our experience and that may be helpful to you is the *Social Change Model of Leadership Development* (Astin & Astin, 1996). The authors examine factors that, when present, help individuals to develop into transformational leaders, that is, persons who are able to create positive change in the world through collaborative interaction. By this definition, all students in community-based learning classes are poised to learn and practice **leadership** in service-learning classes, as these classes are opportunities to positively impact others.

According to Astin and Astin (1996), a leader is

> one who is able to effect positive change for the betterment of others, the community, and society. All people, in other words, are potential leaders. Moreover, the process of leadership cannot be simply described in terms of the behavior of an individual; rather, leadership involves collaborative relationships that lead to collective action grounded in the shared values of people who work together to effect positive change. (p. 16)

A leader is a ***change agent*** (one who creates change) working in an active, collaborative process with others. More than likely, you will find yourself being a change agent as you engage in the community-based learning experience on three levels of involvement: the individual, the group, and the community. If you consider the course just described, we all came to the class as individuals. As we began to formulate course goals and identified our collective talents, we became members of a group cocreating a shared learning environment with common objectives and strategies. Finally, we engaged as a class community with the ***community*** outside the university's walls, a community in which we were all asked to apply our talents, skills, and capacities to the express task of making positive change.

Each level of leadership informs the others: that is, individual students impact the group dynamic and process, and that dynamic and process affects each individual; the group works in concert to effect positive change in the community, which then in turn affects the group; and each individual connects with the service activity in the community and is then shaped by that direct experience as well (figure 3.1).

Let's further explore this model as a method for reflecting on service-learning processes. Within each of the spheres, particular values, understood and practiced by participants, enhance the potential for individuals to bring about positive change. These elements are the "Seven Cs" of leadership development:

- ***Consciousness of self***, in which an individual is aware of his or her own beliefs, values, attitudes, and emotions that motivate the individual to action.
- ***Congruence***, or thinking, feeling, and behaving with consistency, authenticity, and honesty toward others.

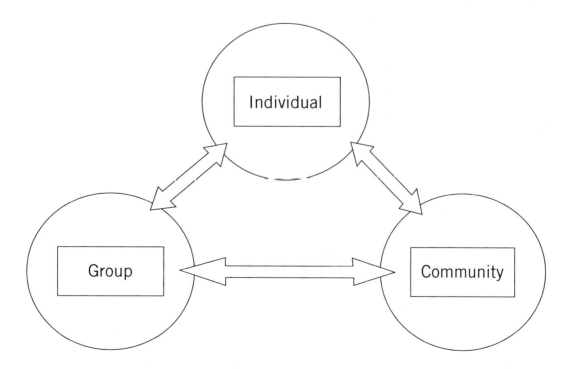

Figure 3.1.   **Levels of Leadership**

- ***Commitment***, the psychic energy that motivates the individual to serve and that drives the collective effort.
- ***Collaboration***, to work with others in a common effort.
- ***Common purpose***, which involves performing that collaborative work with shared aims and values.
- ***Controversy with civility***, which recognizes two fundamental realities of any creative group effort: that differences in viewpoint are inevitable, and such differences must be aired openly but with civility if the group is to accomplish its task effectively while honoring individual group members.
- ***Citizenship***, or the process whereby the individual (a ***citizen-learner***, in the case of service-learning) and the collaborative group become responsibly connected to the community through the service activity.

Each of these seven values can be placed in the sphere in which it operates (figure 3.2):

Notice how each of these values, practiced within its sphere of influence, both enhances and is enhanced by the practicing of the values in the other spheres; in other words, the arrows connecting the individual to the group to the community point in both directions. A service-learning course asks that its participants learn through serving on multiple reinforcing levels, and it promises that one's ability to lead will be expanded if that work is done in authentic collaboration with others, producing collective action for change.

Helping, Fixing, or Serving?

If we are to build genuine community partnerships in which reciprocal relationships described by the Seven Cs can thrive, we must look deeper into our motivations for serving and the varieties of ways we might choose to act for positive change. Just as we read in chapter 1 about the differences between charity and solidarity work, Rachel Naomi Remen (1999) articulates three different modes of service interaction for us to consider: helping, fixing, or serving.

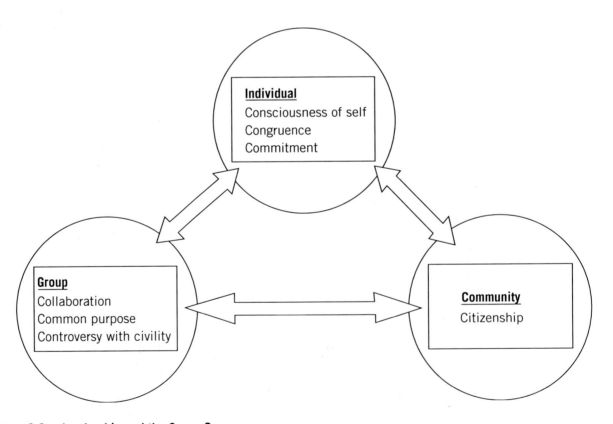

Figure 3.2. Leadership and the Seven Cs

✯✯ **Exercise 3.5: Identifying the Seven Cs**

Reread the case study that opens this chapter. Identify those elements of the narrative that speak to each of the Seven Cs: *consciousness of self, congruence, commitment, collaboration, common purpose, controversy with civility, citizenship.*

- Outline in writing where you find evidence of these values in action in the case study. What specific activities supported the development of the values, and in what ways?
- Conversely, how did the development of the values inform the continuing work and decision making on the part of the community involved in the project? From this case study and from your reading about the Seven Cs, what information seems immediately applicable to your own work as a citizen-learner?

"Helping, fixing and serving represent three different ways of seeing life. When you help, you see life as weak. When you fix, you see life as broken. When you serve, you see life as whole. . . . Serving is different from helping. Helping is not a relationship between equals. A helper may see others as weaker than they are, needier than they are, and people often feel this inequality. The danger in helping is that we may inadvertently take away from people more than we could ever give them; we may diminish their self-esteem, their sense of worth, integrity or even wholeness. . . . Serving is [also] different from fixing. In fixing, we see others as broken, and respond to this perception with our expertise. Fixers trust their own expertise but may not see the wholeness in another person or trust the integrity of the life in them. When we serve we see and trust that wholeness. We respond to it and collaborate with it. And when we see the wholeness in another, we strengthen it. They may then be able to see it for themselves for the first time." (Remen, para. 1)

✯✯ **Exercise 3.6: Helping, Fixing, or Serving?**

If possible, read Remen's (1999) entire article which is accessible online. Then, consider the ways that you have "helped" or "fixed," rather than "served." Reflect on these differentiations in order to investigate potential impacts on your motivations and the effects on those you serve. Note your responses in a reflection journal or share them with a classmate.

- Remember back to a time when someone sought to assist you with something by "helping" or "fixing" you (as Remen describes those terms). What was it like to be on the receiving end of those efforts? How did it feel before you were helped or fixed? How did it feel as it was happening? How did it feel afterward? What long-term impacts, if any, came from the interaction?
- Now remember back to a time when you felt genuinely "served" by another person (again using Remen's definition). What was it like to be on the receiving end of those efforts? How did it feel to you before you were served? How did it feel as it was happening? How did it feel afterward? What long-term impacts, if any, came from the interaction?
- What connections do you see between your experiences of being helped, fixed, and served, and your current service opportunity? What insights can you draw from to illuminate your continuing work as a service learner in this current context?

When, in a service-learning context, we operate from a position in which we see ourselves as the "experts" coming in to "fix" the community, we not only miss the opportunities we have to learn from others, we insult those who are bringing their own gifts to the table (as well as *assets* and *interests*, as we read in chapter 2). The "learning" part of the term *service-learning* suggests that we have powerful opportunities to learn and to grow—otherwise this course probably wouldn't be part of your institution's curriculum. When we recognize others as whole human beings, like us, who are bringing their own *assets* to the table, and when we operate from that conviction, true **reciprocity** can result from our interactions. This means that all of the constituents in the service-learning environment (students, faculty, and community partners) receive mutual benefits from the exchange.

Reflecting on Individual and Group Change

It took all the members of the community service project Change for the Common Good—students, instructor, and the community partner and its individual participants—to envision, create, and complete a compelling physical representation of the strengths of community. In addition to the literal figures represented in the painting, there is also invisibly present the process that the class went through to decide on the project. There is the particular grouping of artists selected to share their visions and the work they did first to bring these visions into single focus and then to apply them to massive boards. There is the assistant chief of police and the department he represents, acting out of his interpretation of the common good. There is the crowd of family and friends and neighbors watching a mural unveiled on a beautiful Sunday. None of us knew that would be where we were headed when we began, but we took one step and then another, committed to knowing ourselves and each other, and ended up in new and exciting territory, each of us changed and each of us having effected change. The end point could not have been reached with any other configuration of persons making their human choices in a collective way. This outcome required that all those persons be there, in it, watching the change that resulted from that effort and simultaneously being changed.

In the very beginning of this project there was no doubt that I really did not see how doing a community service project was going to be the culmination of my college career. So, I entered the project somewhat angry at the hoop I had to jump through for my degree. Then Carmen and I decided to help the group process along by offering to do a presentation on planning projects. This was a real shift for me. I could see the connection between my business major and the course. But even more of a shift was when I finally met the young artists. I felt my heart connect to the project. I then understood how I could help to create community change.

When I reread my reflections I could see myself changing as the project evolved. I found that at the beginning I was not sure of myself, the kids, and the team. In my computer science courses we have worked as teams on programming problems, but technology is a completely different environment. And I chose my major partially because you get to work alone a lot. Now I had to be a mentor, with kids totally different from me. But I found myself really wanting to know more about them and their family and culture. I saw myself listening to their stories, giving them advice, phone numbers of people they could contact for work and school. I even spent a Saturday at Raymo's house getting his computer connected to the Internet. He told me I'd inspired him to consider pursuing a career in graphic design.

In hindsight, there are definitely some things we could have done better. Perhaps most importantly, we should have included the police department on initial discussions and kept them posted on progress. I assumed the community agency would do this. But I think that this should have been a part of our rights and responsibilities discussion, and a part of our ALPS. I really think that if we had formed a dialogue with them earlier on, they would have been open to understanding the cultural importance of the figures instead of being reactive. As a communications major, this lesson will stay with me. Being a leader means fully collaborating even as you hold to a community vision.

========

In the spirit of the previous quotation, it seems fitting to end this chapter with another student reflection that aptly captures how a typical university classroom became a launching pad for a wall-less classroom where university meets community, where a blank canvas takes on color and form, where *I* becomes *We.* May your own learning and serving experience be just as rich.

Remember, this is the greatest project you have ever done.
Remember your passion.
Remember the look on the students' faces every day we worked together.

Remember the handshakes that turned into hugs by the end of the project.
Remember the stress you felt, and the joy of your accomplishments.
Remember the love and spirituality the mural represented.
Remember the hurt feelings you had by the words that came from your mouth and the mouths of others.
Remember the bonds that grew between so many people, so many people from different places in their lives.
Remember your heart both soaring and breaking as you walked away from the warehouse for the last time.
Remember the pride in our work and the pride in the community.

Key Concepts

change agent	commitment	consciousness of self
citizen-learner	common purpose	controversy with civility
citizenship	community	leadership
collaboration	congruence	reciprocity

Key Issues

- In what specific ways is the service-learning "classroom" different from those in traditional courses?
- Why is it important for students to develop the Seven Cs in a community-based learning environment?
- How do service-learning experiences exemplify the phrase "the whole is greater than the sum of its parts?"
- What are the possible gains that an individual student might take away from a learning and serving experience?
- What are the possible gains that the community receives?

PART TWO

Learning the Landscape, Learning the Language

As you participate in your learning-through-serving experience, you will come to understand yourself and others in new ways. In this section of the book (chapters 4 and 5), we provide you with information and exercises for interacting with diverse groups of individuals in order to maximize your effectiveness and empathy as a learner and server.

KEY SYMBOLS

 Exercises of utmost importance to complete (working either on your own or in a group)

 Optional exercises (strategies for gaining deeper insights into the issues)

 Exercises that provide further resources and information in your quest for understanding community problem solving and change

CHAPTER 4

Groups Are Fun, Groups Are Not Fun

Teamwork for the Common Good

PETER J. COLLIER AND JANELLE DeCARRICO VOEGELE

MOST SERVICE-LEARNING COURSES involve some level of group work. In this chapter we will examine several aspects of group dynamics, particularly as they relate to "getting the work done" in service-learning experiences. We also include two "Spotlights on Service" sections which highlight the challenges of bringing your teamwork into collaboration with a community partner, and we offer strategies for addressing these challenges in your collaboration. Even if you are engaged in a service project alone, you will still benefit from the information in this chapter, since work in almost every volunteer organization or employment situation requires you to collaborate with others. The ideas outlined here will assist you to be as successful and effective as possible.

"Good Groups" / "Bad Groups"

Professor (reviewing the syllabus on the first day of class): ". . . And 50 percent of your grade in this class will be based on a group project . . ."

Students (collectively): "Urgh! Oh, no, not another group project!!"

Professor (with a smile): "It's great to see the group has already reached consensus and it's only the first day of the term."

You may relate to the reaction of the students: You just don't trust group projects. Even though most students say that they do not "hate" all group projects, many are still leery of these assignments because they have had a wide range of experiences in them—with the "bad" tending to be much more memorable than the "good"!

This chapter explores the value of group work, particularly as it relates to service-learning. Why do professors assign group work? What makes for a productive group experience? What causes a group project to "go sour"? To prepare you to engage with these questions, reflect for a moment upon your own previous experiences in groups using exercise 4.1.

As part of a service-learning project exploring college student adjustment issues (Collier & Morgan, 2003), Portland State University students participated in a series of focus groups in which they were asked about their group experiences in college. The following are some of their responses; see if you recognize any similarities to your own.

Personally, I don't mind group work. In some cases I actually prefer it, but it all depends on the nature of the class.

I don't like group projects if you have too many group leaders, because some people are very task-oriented

---

✿ Exercise 4.1: How Am I in Groups?

On one side of a sheet of paper, describe a positive experience that you have had working in a group trying to solve some problem or accomplish a task. Then, on the other side of the same sheet of paper, describe a negative experience that you have had working in a similar group. Ideally, these should both be experiences working with school-based groups, but if that is not possible, any relevant group experience will do. If you need more room for your answers, use another sheet of paper. For each experience, answer the following questions:

• What was the nature of the group?
• How big was the group and who was in it?
• What was the problem or task the group was trying to address?
• What was the final outcome?
• Were you satisfied with the outcome? Do you think other group members were satisfied?

Finally—and this is the "one-million-dollar question"—What part did YOU play in each of these groups with regard to bringing about the final outcome?

After you have finished this exercise, take a minute to read over your answers and think about your responses. Do you tend to act the same way in most of the school-based groups you participate in? Why do you think you have acted in the ways that you have?

---

self-starters, and then you have those that are just lackadaisical.

You want to be able to expect that every other student in your group is going to contribute and is going to do their part and have respect for each other, but that

does not always happen. A lot of times one or two people end up carrying the whole weight of the group.

Sometimes I'll get stuck in a group for a whole term. And then my grade is dependent on somebody else and what they do. I hate that.

💡 Exercise 4.2: Connecting to Your Own Experiences

The student focus group participants, quoted previously, identified three issues that sometimes arise in group experiences:

1. Managing roles within the group (. . . *too many group leaders* . . .)
2. Equity and fairness concerns (. . . *one or two people end up carrying the whole group* . . .)
3. Individual evaluation based on group product (. . . *my grade is dependent on somebody else* . . .)

Think back to your earlier responses about your own group experiences in exercise 4.1. Do you see these concerns reflected there? Did you identify any additional group issues? List them in the space provided.

1. _____

2. _____

3. _____

Despite the difficulties, researchers have also identified several benefits of working in groups, including increased productivity (Eby & Dobbins, 1997), access to a wider range of information (Liang, Moreland, & Argote, 1995), and better decision making (Stasser, 1992). An old adage asserts that "two heads are better than one." In your reflection, were you able to identify this benefit—the ability to combine multiple perspectives on a topic to solve problems—in your previous group experiences?

Recent research suggests that faculty and students often enter learning environments with divergent learning goals—that is, the outcomes the faculty believes to be important, as compared to those that students value. There are two different types of goals related to student learning. ***Content goals*** have to do with completing specific assignments (for example, a term paper or an essay exam) and earning a grade in a course while developing knowledge about the particular course content addressed in that class. ***Process goals*** have to do with acquiring high-order skills (for example, critical thinking and interpersonal skills) that can be applied by the student in a range of other contexts beyond the immediate course.

According to Collier and Morgan (2003), students typically focus exclusively on content goals; as a result, they may see group projects as barriers to realizing their individual goals, such as getting a good grade in a class. Professors, on the other hand, believe that both levels of learning goals can be realized through group projects. They often view the ability to work successfully in groups as an overarching skill that students can apply across situations beyond any single course (and in a variety of work environments). Professors identify enhanced problem-solving abilities, increased appreciation of multiple perspectives on issues, and a greater likelihood of becoming active learners as benefits to students from participation in group projects.

As you progress through this service-learning experience, think about the ways in which your own skills are developing precisely because of the collaboration you are engaged in with others. How are your communication skills improving? What insights about the course content are coming from your peers instead of your professor? How are you collectively pooling your talents and knowledge to meet community needs?

So far, you have identified qualities that distinguish a good group experience from a poor one (through reflecting on past group experiences) and gained insights into what professors are trying to accomplish when they assign students group projects. In the next few sections, we explore how groups develop, as well as some of the issues that groups must address in order to be successful. To illustrate key issues, we will follow the development of two hypothetical groups from the same service-learning course, groups we call the *Mudslingers* and the *Visionary Skeptics*.

✤ Exercise 4.3: Marshmallows and Spaghetti

If you are working in a group as part of a class, request that your instructor allow you to have fun with the following activity. If you are working on your own, consider getting a group of friends together for some friendly competition.

Create teams of students (no more than five per group). Each group receives one package of spaghetti and one package of marshmallows. (You may also want to cover the floor with newspaper). The goal is to build the tallest tower possible out of the marshmallows and spaghetti. Allow 15 to 20 minutes for the exercise.

Afterward, explore the following questions together:

• How well did the team work together?
• What helped the group pursue its goal?
• What roles did you observe group members playing as you constructed your tower?
• What would you do differently if you could begin again?

The Development of a Group: Getting Started . . . and Beyond

The kinds of groups that are formed as part of a service-learning experience are generally task-oriented groups in which members begin interacting with each other as strangers and go through a series of identifiable stages to form a working team. Researchers like Tuckman (1965) and Fisher (1970) initially identified these stages and developed what is called the ***Phase Model of Group Development***.

Let's explore this model by beginning with our two groups on the first day of their service-learning class.

Phase 1: Forming
The first stage of group development, ***forming***, describes the beginning of a group's process, in which the primary goals are to get to know the other group members and to clarify the group's task. Members of a "forming" group have to make several major decisions:

- What is this group about? What is the task to be accomplished?
- Does each person want to be a member of this group?
- Who are the other people who make up the group?
- What is each person's place in this group?

At this stage, each person is checking out the other group members, trying to determine if he or she can count on the others and how it will be to work with each of them. Conversation among group members in the forming stage tends to be polite and not too revealing, because members of the newly formed group do not have a great deal of shared history to build upon. One way that forming groups can start to develop the closeness and interpersonal trust that will be needed to successfully realize the group's goal is by doing some kind of activity together—like getting together after class for a cup of coffee, going to a movie, or even just talking with each other about personal interests.

Mudslingers	*Visionary Skeptics*
On the first day of class, when the instructor assigned students to work together on a team project, two of the students in this group—Mandy and Julian—tried to get permission to work individually. When the instructor denied their requests, Julian picked up his books and walked out of class. Mandy sat with the group, but she spent her time working on her homework from her previous class. None of the other group members—Natasha, Angelo, or Jorge—had any ideas about what the group was supposed to do next. When the class was over, everyone left, without making a plan for when the group would meet again.	On the first day of class, when the instructor assigned students to work together on a team project, two of the students in this group—Bill and Anita—initially complained that they hated group projects. When the other students in the group—DeWayne, Maria, and Tiffany—started kidding them that "we're all in this together," both Bill and Anita laughed and agreed that, since the instructor was not "caving in" to requests for individual projects, maybe it was better to get busy on this team project. Maria suggested that the group get to know one another by having each member share one "unusual" thing that he or she liked to do for fun. Everyone cracked up when DeWayne talked about his pet boa constrictor that he liked to take to the mall. After the initial sharing, Bill suggested that everyone come to the next group meeting with ideas for how best to organize their project. The group agreed to meet the hour before the next class. When the class was over, they all went out for coffee, and to talk some more about DeWayne's snake.

Phase 2: Storming

In many ways, the ***storming*** phase is the most complicated stage in the development of a group. Conflicts surface in this stage that were not apparent during the introductory, forming stage. Issues of power arise within the group, and personality clashes can occur as the members focus their attention on the details of interaction within the group as well as the task at hand. One of the reasons that conflicts start to emerge visibly during this phase is that group members are becoming more comfortable with each other. With this increased comfort comes a greater willingness for individuals to express their true feelings and views compared to the polite, relatively nonconfrontational communication of the forming stage. Members of a group in the storming phase must address a new set of questions:

- What is the best approach for completing the group's assigned task?
- What are the different jobs that need to be done to accomplish the group's task?
- Who is doing what in the group?
- How can we make sure the workload is divided equitably?

A group's ability to successfully resolve the initial conflicts that arise during the storming phase has been identified as essential to developing subsequent group feelings of cohesion and cooperation (Whelan & McKeage, 1993). In some group situations, members may feel they are helping the group develop by avoiding the conflict that seems inevitably to occur during this phase. This is actually a serious mistake. Successful groups—that is, groups that work together to realize their shared goals—are those that are able to weather the "storm" and emerge intact on the other side of this stage.

Phase 3: Norming

The ***norming*** phase represents a shift from the earlier emphasis on competition and the presentation of diverse perspectives in the storming phase to an emphasis on trying to reach consensus on rules to govern how the group operates. Much more attention is paid to group *processes* (as opposed to group *products*). The norming phase reflects the group's willingness to regulate itself and to establish specific guidelines for how discussions will proceed and how decisions will be made. When a group progresses to the norming stage, it does not mean that all conflicts and issues that arose during the storming phase have been resolved. One of the defining characteristics of a group in the norming stage, however, is a noticeable increase in the levels of cooperation and willingness to compromise in order to help the group accomplish its goals.

Phase 4: Performing

The ***performing*** stage is when the real work of the group starts getting done. A set of working guidelines for how the group will operate is in place, and attention now shifts to accomplishing the assigned task. Of course, as a group moves more deeply into completing tasks, challenges to accomplishing the group's work often present themselves. Harris and Sherblum (1999, pp. 60–61) identify a four-stage problem-solving process that they suggest helps a developing group accomplish its goals effectively.

1. Defining the problem
   Do:
   - make sure pertinent information is shared among group members.
   - make sure that everyone is clear about the nature of the task to be completed.

   Don't:
   - assign blame or try to determine who is at fault regarding problems that arise.
   - discuss solutions at this point.

2. Generating possible solutions
   Do:
   - brainstorm solutions, no matter how "off the wall."
   - encourage participation by all members of the group.
   - set a time limit and stick to it.
   - generate as many possible solutions as the time allows.

   Don't:
   - edit, evaluate, or criticize any of the solutions.
   - settle on the first good idea that surfaces.

- spend too much time on any one person or good idea.

3. Evaluating solutions

   Do:
   - review a list of potential solutions and eliminate any that now have no support within the group.
   - anticipate the consequences of each potential solution.
   - encourage members to combine solutions.

   Don't:
   - let the discussion get sidetracked into debates about the pros and cons of a single solution.
   - assess value too quickly.
   - quit until you have clear consensus.

4. Creating an action plan

   Do:
   - generate some alternative "how-to-do-it" scripts before choosing an action plan.
   - make sure specific tasks are assigned within the group.
   - make sure that time frames are set up.

   Don't:
   - state roles and tasks in general, unmeasurable terms.
   - forget to include some method of follow-up so that the task actually gets completed.

One way to increase the likelihood of this happening in your group experience is by continuing to develop your individual Action Learning Plan for Serving (ALPS) that you began in chapter 2. If you haven't already done so, compare your personal ALPS (exercise 2.6, from page 31) with those of the other members of your group. Make sure you all agree on your understanding of the community partner's goals for this project, even though you each may expect to have different individual learning and serving goals.

After the group is clear about what the task is and what the group hopes to get out of the project, use **Exercise 4.4: Jobs List** to help divide the work equitably, and **Exercise 4.5: Timeline** to ensure that the project is completed within the allotted time frame.

In chapter 11, you will revisit and build upon these worksheets to help you evaluate the impact of your service project.

You might also use these exercises directly with your community partner and/or its clients. For instance, you could use the same set of worksheets that you have employed in this service-learning course to assist high-school students to create a new community recycling program. Remember, you may be forming groups on multiple levels in multiple locations during your service-learning experience. Check with your instructor, and/or decide as a group what action plan strategy works best for you. Just make sure to create a plan!

In addition, exercise 4.9 on page 73 will provide you with a tool to facilitate your group's evolution through the four stages of the model. Starting with your initial meeting, use the checklist often to identify the steps your group takes in this class as you prepare to engage in your service project.

Let's revisit our two groups from earlier in this chapter in order to see how their group formation is progressing.

Who's Doing What?: Group Norms and Group Roles

At this point, you have completed several group exercises. You may have noticed that your group has developed some basic guidelines for working together, such as not interrupting each other, making decisions by majority vote, and encouraging everyone in the group to participate. These are examples of **norms**, or guidelines for interaction in a group, that let group members know how they are expected to behave. Group norms don't come about because one person wants things a certain way. Group norms are developed based on agreement within the group and are maintained and enforced by the group as a whole.

While norms delineate expected behavior within a group, a **role** refers to the part a specific group member plays within the group. Robert Bales (1950) was one of the first to systematically examine the different roles that people play in groups, and how certain combinations of roles were essential to successful group functioning. He divided group roles into two general

Mudslingers	*Visionary Skeptics*
When the next class began, it didn't take long for this group to figure out they were already behind schedule. All the groups had met once since the last class except their own. When the instructor gave the groups the last half of the class period to work on their projects, Julian immediately began by blaming Jorge, Natasha, and Angelo for not having started on the project. Natasha reminded him that he was the one who had walked out of class without participating last time. Mandy said that if the two of them would stop arguing, she would tell the group the best way to complete their class project, an oral history of the neighborhood around the university. Jorge wanted to know why Mandy appointed herself leader of the group; he had his own ideas about how to complete the project. Mandy laughed and asked the group why they would listen to Jorge, because he was just a sophomore and had only recently transferred to the university, while she was a senior who had been here for five years. Julian said he thought they were both lame, and he wished he didn't have to be part of the group. Angelo told Julian that if he didn't stop his whining he'd take him outside and bring some sense to him. By that time the class period was over. As everyone grabbed their books, Mandy told them to come ready to work next class. Jorge tried to get the rest of the group to stick around long enough to schedule a meeting before the next class, but they all left, saying, "send me an e-mail and maybe we can set something up." Jorge picked up his backpack and left the classroom, muttering under his breath.	When the group got together before class, each member came prepared with some ideas about how to organize the group's project, an oral history of a neighborhood in their city, which was about to be dramatically changed by the construction of a massive housing project. When DeWayne reached to get his notebook out of his backpack, Tiffany and Bill started joking with him, asking if he'd brought his snake to school along with his books. Everyone, especially DeWayne, cracked up. Anita asked what the group thought about designating one person to start the meetings. Maria remembered reading that every group needed people to do three jobs—someone to run the meetings, someone to take notes, and someone to make sure that things got done on time. De-Wayne suggested that Anita be the one to run the meetings, since she had raised the point that the group needed someone to do the job. Everyone else agreed. Bill volunteered to take notes since he always had his laptop computer with him. Tiffany reminded the group that Maria had done a great job getting the Math Club's fund-raising project finished on time. Everybody looked at Maria and waited. After a minute, she agreed to take on that job for this group too. DeWayne started joking with Tiffany that they had managed to avoid taking any of the jobs. That's when Anita asked him to keep track of the time to make sure that the group didn't spend more time on a topic at a meeting than they had planned. He agreed, and Tiffany said she'd help him. When the instructor gave groups the last half of the class period to work on their projects, Anita had them get out their ideas for organizing their project, and they spent the rest of the time listening to each other share ideas.

categories: roles that help the group accomplish a task and roles that contribute to the social and emotional well-being of the group. ***Task roles*** have to do exclusively with getting the group's work done. ***Maintenance roles*** promote solidarity and help maintain good working relationships within the group. (See appendix

4.1 on page 75 for a description of specific task and maintenance roles.)

In addition to both task and maintenance roles, there are also ***organizational roles*** within any group. In order for you to successfully complete your service-learning project, there are a certain number of critical

⁂ Exercise 4.4: Jobs List

What are the key components of this project? List all the jobs that need to be done to complete the project. Be as specific as possible. Divide big jobs into smaller components. Link each specific job to the partner, learning, and serving goals from **Exercise 2.7: Action Learning Plan for Serving (ALPS)**, from page 31. Plan on returning to and revising this list as your project progresses.

Don't forget that you will also need to assess your achievements. Decide now on some ideas and processes for determining the success of your service efforts.

> ### ✳️ Exercise 4.5: Timeline
>
> Every project has deadlines. It is critical to the success of your service-learning project that you finish each step of the project in a timely manner. One way to ensure that things get done on time is to construct a project timeline.
>
> **Note:** Whether you are working alone or in a group, feel free to customize this activity to fit your particular project.
>
> *Step 1:* Take a large sheet of paper and draw a horizontal line across the page, dividing it into the days or weeks that correspond to the time you have to complete your project. On the extreme left side of your sheet of paper, list all of the subtasks that make up the project in the order they will have to be addressed.
>
> *Step 2:* Next, for each of the subtasks, draw a horizontal line representing when the subtask will start, how long it will last, and when it will end.
>
> **Tip:** It is a good idea to start with the total project deadline and work backward. You will probably have to modify your timeline several times before you have a project schedule that works. Not all subtasks are the same. You will find that it is sometimes possible to work on more than one subtask at the same time. Other subtasks can be started only after preceding ones have been completed.

functions that must be performed. You may notice that when individuals successfully fulfill these different organizational roles, they tend to utilize several of the task and maintenance roles. Among these organizational roles are the following:

- **Leader:** In order to get started, a task group (like the ones in the Mudslingers and Visionary Skeptics service-learning experience) needs a leader to get the process going, someone who will take responsibility for chairing the meetings. The leader's job is to make sure everyone in the group is clear about the aim of the current meeting, to introduce each topic the group is to work on, and to summarize discussion or decisions. This can be a difficult job. It is *not* the leader's job to try to get the group to do what she or he wants done.

- **Notetaker:** The group needs someone to keep a record of what goes on and what is discussed in meetings, who is supposed to do what tasks, and the time and place of the next meeting. This person should also produce an outline of the meeting notes and distribute them to the rest of the group. It is essential to have written documentation of your group's activities; if the notetaker is absent, someone else must step up and take notes for that meeting.

- **Progress tracker:** Your group will need someone to keep track of how different parts of your group project are progressing. This person makes sure that each group member is keeping to the agreed-upon timeline for her or his part of the project. This person also keeps track of the overall progress of the project.

- **Timekeeper:** In class-related group projects, there are almost always time limitations. It is critical for the success of the group that someone keep track of the time. Before the group begins a new task or starts a new discussion, the timekeeper asks "How long should we allow for this?" The leader or the whole group decides how much time is appropriate. The timekeeper then tells the group when that amount of time has passed. It is also useful for the timekeeper to point out when the allocated time is *almost* finished ("We've used 10 of the 15 minutes we said we'd use to talk about this, so we've only got five minutes left to wrap things up").

• **Process observer**: This person pays attention to what is going on (the process) as opposed to what is being talked about (the content). If the group starts drifting away from agreed-upon norms of respect and civility, the process observer's job is to bring this to the attention of the group so that they can change the way they are working. It is very important that this person avoids seeming critical or judgmental and concentrates on describing what he or she observed as well as offering positive, constructive suggestions for change. (Gibbs, 1994, pp. 21–22)

These organizational roles do not necessarily have to stay the same for the duration of your group project. In the beginning, one possibility is to allocate the different roles to the individuals who want them. A second approach would be to assign the roles to specific group members based on who seems best qualified from past experience. You may also feel more or less affinity with some of these roles based on personality and learning style differences.

Remember, if you do not assume one of the organizational roles, there are still task and maintenance roles for you to play within the group. It is essential to the group's success that each member take on one or more of those roles in contributing to the group process and project.

To further explore your own part in exercise 4.6, see **Exercise 4.10: How Am I in *This* Group?** on page 74.

We have seen how groups require their members to play a wide range of roles in order for the group to function effectively. One positive consequence of a smoothly functioning group is that members start to appreciate and feel closer to each other. That closeness is called ***group cohesion***, and it is the focus of the next section of this chapter.

Group Cohesion

In most of my group projects I usually take the role of smoothing things over when something goes wrong.

✸✸ Exercise 4.6: Group Roles

Your group should discuss how best to approach the service-learning project connected with your class. To do so, follow these four steps:

1. Make sure each person has read the descriptions of the different organizational, task, and maintenance roles. Decide who is going to play each organizational role in your group.
2. Go ahead with the discussion of your service-learning project. The people who have taken on organizational roles should try to perform their roles well without disrupting the meeting.
3. Each member of the group should take notes about how well each of the roles was performed. Jot down instances when you recognize yourself and other group members demonstrating different task and maintenance roles.
4. Have a post-meeting discussion where you talk about how the meeting went with group members performing the needed organizational roles. As a group, come up with at least three suggestions for how you will make sure these functions are performed even more efficiently at the next meeting.

- _____
- _____
- _____

> **Spotlight on Service: Connecting with Community**
>
> When community members begin working with your group, additional issues may arise concerning who performs which roles.
>
> **Situation 1:** Community members may be unclear about the group norms and expectations for group member contributions.
>
> **Tip:** Offer community members an overview of your group's development and working style, using the worksheets and activities you have completed as a guide. In addition, get feedback from all group members (students *and* community partners) at the end of every meeting regarding each member's perceptions of group effectiveness. Ask for suggestions for future meetings.
>
> **Situation 2:** Established roles and working dynamics may be temporarily interrupted; for example, task leaders may find themselves sharing their role with a task-oriented community member.
>
> **Tip:** Review and summarize the results of **Exercise 4.6: Group Roles**, on page 60. Ask community members if they would like to add their perspectives on the usual roles they take in groups. See if the group needs to build in some flexibility (for example, multiple task leaders who need to play other roles occasionally). If appropriate, alternate roles at each meeting (by taking turns being task leader, timekeeper, note taker, process observer, and so forth).

Actually, though, we were pretty lucky in this class because I think most of the people in our group knew what they were doing when it came to getting things accomplished in groups. We had the attitude that, how can we go out in the community and work with kids on things like following through, when we can't even work on it in our own little group?

For group cohesiveness to develop, individuals must first experience a sense of belonging to the group. *Group cohesion* refers to a variety of factors that encourage members to remain united and committed to group goals. Luft (1984) suggests the following characteristics as differentiating a collection of individuals from a group:

- Group members share a common goal or goals.
- Regular interaction takes place among group members.
- Individuals perceive value in their group membership.
- Differentiation of tasks emerges with time.

One of the most important ingredients for developing solid group cohesion is trust. During the normal ups and downs of group work and problem solving, members must be able to trust that their colleagues will work in the best interest of the group, even during (and, some would argue, *especially* during) times of conflict and disagreement. The following actions increase trust in groups:

- Openness to others' views, even when those views are not initially understood
- Flexibility in the face of rapidly changing conditions and different working styles
- Willingness to take responsibility for group goals and tasks
- Ability to endure times of ambiguity and frustration with the group
- Capacity to disagree while maintaining loyalty to the group

If this suggests to you that work is involved in building and maintaining group cohesion, you are correct; cohesive groups don't happen by accident. Research on

> ### 💡 Exercise 4.7: Revisiting the Seven Cs
>
> Chapter 3 introduced the Seven Cs of leadership development: *consciousness of self, congruence, commitment, collaboration, common purpose, controversy with civility,* and *citizenship* (pages 43–44). You've already reflected on opportunities in which you have been supported to develop the Seven Cs. Now focus on one or more of the actions that increase trust, as outlined previously. Recall a previous group situation in which those actions did *not* manifest themselves within the group. What about the group process prevented their development? How might the actions and behaviors that increase trust be supported by the values of the Seven Cs? How, specifically, might you as an individual implement the Seven Cs in this group experience? What are the implications for trust and group cohesion when each of the Seven Cs is consistently practiced within the group?

group cohesion demonstrates that this kind of work is well worth the effort. For example, some positive outcomes associated with group cohesion include group member satisfaction, increased motivation, heightened perseverance toward accomplishment of group goals, cooperation, open communication, and more effective listening (Donelson, 1999). Additionally, the more you learn about yourself and others and the more you are able to increase appreciation for diverse working styles, learning styles, and experiential and cultural perspectives, the more prepared you are to engage in the community.

Group cohesion can also result in less positive outcomes, however. Irving Janis (1983) developed the term **groupthink**, which he defined as "a deterioration of mental efficiency, reality, and moral judgment that results from in-group pressures" (p. 322). Janis originally used the term to explain major fiascoes in group decision-making processes. As he analyzed several cases of major policy decision making in U.S. history, he found that concurrence-seeking behavior in cohesive groups can become so dominant that members fail to adequately consider alternative courses of action. Group interactions become increasingly characterized by muddy thinking, poor decision making, and carelessness. Symptoms of groupthink include the following:

- Collective rationalization: Warnings and negative feedback are discounted.
- Perception of group morality: There is an unquestioned assumption that what the group does is right, good, and moral.

- Stereotyping other groups: An inaccurate and negative view of "the adversary" is created.
- Pressure to conform: Group members are pressured to conform to group opinion, and dissident views are discouraged.
- Mind-guarding: Group members actively protect the group from outside ideas that may contradict the group opinion or ideas.
- Surface agreement: There is an illusion of agreement, but individual doubt is not voiced to other group members.

Building a cohesive group pays big dividends when it comes to group performance. Even more important, cohesive groups are better able to deal with the problems that can tear other groups apart. When a group is experiencing difficulties, these issues can often be traced to some form of communication problem. Let's check in on our two groups of service-learning students and see how they are dealing with some of these issues.

Communication in Groups

At the beginning of this chapter (exercise 4.1, p. 52), you reflected on positive and negative experiences that you have had in task or problem-solving groups. Take a look at your responses to that activity: How many are related to communication in groups? For example, did any of the issues involve negotiation of conflicting perspectives, approaching another group member about his or her group behavior, assumptions about

---

Spotlight on Service: Uncovering Assumptions

Situation: In service-learning courses, groups might experience pressure to engage in *group-think* behaviors when community perspectives and student perspectives on issues clash, when the pressure to meet community project deadlines becomes overwhelming, or when the students feel unclear about or removed from community partners' expectations.

Tip: Include *assumption chaser* as one of your group member roles. This group member should routinely ask questions such as "What are we assuming?" and "Have we considered enough alternatives to this before we make our final decision?" Consult experienced outsiders (on and off campus) who are impartial and have a background in the subject area of your service experience. Finally, set time aside routinely during meetings to briefly reconsider your working notes from previous group meetings, with special attention to decisions that have been made.

Mudslingers	*Visionary Skeptics*
The deadline for presenting a final project draft is swiftly approaching, and all five members of the group are able to attend the group meeting for the first time in three weeks. "Okay, so last time Natasha said that we should just divide up the work into pieces and so we did," begins Angelo.	The deadline for presenting a final project draft is swiftly approaching, and the group is feeling some stress. Lately, disagreement has surfaced over some of the project content, and two group members had been out with the flu for a week. When the five members finally met, Tiffany began by asking DeWayne and Maria whether they were feeling any better.
"That isn't what I said," interrupts Natasha.	"Not completely," replied Maria, "but we need to get this back on track."
"Yes, you said that whoever wasn't here would just have to take what they got," said Angelo.	DeWayne agreed. "Why don't we go back over where we left off," he suggested. "The e-mail update was helpful, but we can't decide just based on that. Maybe someone could read the notes about the different ideas we had when we last met as a group, and then the other three of you can let us know what you did while we were gone."
Natasha, red-faced, replied, "No, I meant that we would all have to just get going on it whether we could talk about it or not."	
"Look, you've been trying to take over this project all term, so why don't you just admit it?" shot back Angelo.	
Mandy, Julian, and Jorge sat silently. Mandy was staring out the window and appeared uninterested in the conversation.	"So DeWayne," said Anita, "Are you saying you want to make sure we understand the different ideas and people's reasons? Then Tiffany, Maria, and I can show you the web material we got last week. After that, I think we'll need to make some decisions one way or another."
Finally, Julian broke the uncomfortable silence. "Did everyone else read that e-mail that you, I guess it was Angelo, sent out? Because I didn't get it. It was totally unclear what we are supposed to be doing."	
Natasha flashed back, "It wasn't unclear to me, but then I've been committed to making some progress during group meetings."	Everyone laughed when Maria suggested that DeWayne's snake could decide which direction to take. Finally, though, the group decided to compare the content areas to the original project goals to see whether some ideas made better sense than others.
"Hold on," Julian broke in. "Let's not rehash the past, let's just figure out what we're supposed to do and just do it. Get it over with."	
Mandy continued to stare out the window.	

others' intentions, or working across different communication styles?

More than likely, communication was central to many of the issues that you identified in that exercise. When group process breaks down, it is often blamed on a "lack of communication." We often assume that, if communication was happening as it should have been, then problems with group process could have been avoided. Yet it is more often the case that a great deal of communication was occurring, but perhaps not in a manner that contributed to group cohesion. Some communication habits that have served well in other contexts may need to be reconsidered in the context of problem-solving groups. In service-learning courses, we may need to expand our group communication skills to include ongoing contributions from other groups in the class, as well as perspectives of multiple constituencies on and off campus. In the context of service-learning, it is important to consider that awareness of communication dynamics (and the resulting impact on group process) has implications not only for the group itself, but for potential community partners who are depending upon the commitments you have made to the project. Therefore, adopt the notion that mistakes in communication will be made by all; this is to be expected as skills are expanded and tested. Remind the group that "competence is what you do when you make a mistake" (Smith, 1995).

Although we often picture speaking skills when we hear the word "effective communication," one of the most important group communication skills can be practiced with the mouth shut. Listening actively and respectfully to others is itself an important contribution to effective group functioning, yet it is very difficult to do consistently. One reason is that **_active listening_** is hard work. To illustrate why, consider the difference between active listening and other kinds of listening in the following box.

In any given situation, we move from active listening to minimal and inefficient listening and back again without awareness that we are doing so. Successful group process often depends upon group members' commitment (remember the Seven Cs!) to the focused efforts of maintaining open and active listening. This requires a heightened awareness of the kind of listening going on throughout group meetings.

Timmons (1991) suggests some additional ideas for improved listening:

- **Reduce distractions.** We often have more control over distractions than we know. Bring yourself back to the group discussion when you begin to drift away. Commit yourself to being _fully_ present for the next five minutes (and when five minutes is up, recommit yourself for the next five, and so forth). Tell yourself that what the speaker is saying is absolutely necessary for the group's success. (This may not always happen, but you never know until you hear the whole message.)
- **Write down questions you have as you listen.** Rather than interrupting before the

Active Listening	Minimal Listening	Inefficient Listening
Listening for main and supporting ideas; giving appropriate feedback; checking the accuracy of your inferences and assumptions; listening for content as well as intent and feelings; attempting to understand from the other's point of view.	Listening to words and sounds but not actively trying to understand beyond surface meanings; "tuning out" after hearing just enough to grasp main ideas; attempting to understand in the context of your own point of view, or in order to get your needs met.	Listening now and then; mentally composing a response while others are speaking; waiting to take control of the conversation; thinking of other things besides the current conversation; offering little or no feedback; attempting to confirm a preconceived idea of others' messages, feelings, or intent.

speaker has finished, jot down notes about anything you don't understand. For example, "What did she mean by community awareness?"

- **Set aside time in the group where listening, by itself, is the end goal.** This is a special time when group members can speak without censure or interruption. At this time, the purpose is not to discuss agreement or disagreement over ideas, nor is the purpose to debate or convince others of the merits of particular ideas or issues. Rather, the primary purpose is to listen appreciatively for an understanding of another's experience, ideas, or points of view (regardless of whether you agree or disagree). The increased understanding and group awareness often results in improved decision making when the group turns its attention to other forms of listening, such as listening for the purpose of evaluating various proposals for action.

- **Regularly discuss what you have heard and learned during group meetings.** We retain more when we confirm what we have heard with others. We also organize and process information more effectively by collaboratively summarizing with others.

- **Keep track of your own contributions to the group.** When you have commented two or three times, decide to listen for a while *even* if you have a pertinent comment (write it down if you are afraid you will forget). Chances are, someone else has a pertinent comment as well and may need the "space" to step in. If you must comment, phrase your comment as a question to invite contributions from others: "I'd like to know what others in the group think about . . ."

How well are our two groups practicing these techniques? (See page 63.)

Free-Riders and Other Equity Issues

Earlier in this chapter, students commented about possible issues that can arise in group projects, often emphasizing task equity and other concerns related to fairness. One student directly expressed this in the statement, "One or two people end up carrying the whole group." Perhaps you have experienced this challenge in previous group work. One consequence of having one or two persons feel like they are carrying the entire group is the deterioration of relationships within the group, which causes a marked decrease in group cohesion. Another consequence is that the project might not get finished with the level of quality originally anticipated due to a loss of buy-in from the overworked members—not to mention the loss of the perspectives of the absent group members. Overworked students may reach the point where they will no longer compensate for the lack of work (or the inferior quality of work) they perceive coming from other group members who are not "pulling their weight." Absent group members may pull away from the project even more as they feel ostracized and undervalued by overfunctioning members. In order to successfully complete your service-learning project, you'll need strategies to deal with *free riding*—the dynamic in which some group members are not doing (or are not perceived to be doing) their fair share of the work.

One tool that will help you identify individual contributions within your team is **Exercise 4.11: Group Member Work Tally**, located on page 74. You might use **Exercise 4.4: Jobs List** from page 58 to fill out the work tally. You may note that the reason the tally sheet distinguishes between "Who initially agreed to be responsible for the subtask?" and "Who actually did the task?" is that, as we know, plans often change over the duration of a long-term project. While there is generally no problem with group members swapping one task for another, using a tally sheet helps give all members of the group an accurate picture of who *actually* completed which project tasks. Not only will using tools such as the "Jobs List" and the "Group Member Work Tally" make clear the specific steps necessary for successful subtask completion, but it will also provide the group with more accurate information about individual members' contributions to the total project. To ensure that all members invest in the idea that the group must work equitably together to accomplish its goals, it is essential to address the issue of work equity. In order to discourage

Mudslingers	*Visionary Skeptics*
Angelo sent out an emergency e-mail to everyone in the group to meet on Monday for a work session, as the instructor would not approve the group's final project draft until it was rewritten. Only Natasha showed up to help, so the two of them rewrote it. On Wednesday during class, the instructor approved the final project draft. Natasha reminded everyone in the group (except Julian, who skipped class that day) that this weekend would be their last real chance to collect the neighborhood residents' stories for the oral history. They agreed to meet at the neighborhood community center on Saturday morning. Angelo said he would make sure that Julian got a message as to when and where the group was going to meet. On Saturday morning, Angelo, Natasha, and Jorge showed up at the community center, but there were no signs of Mandy or Julian. Angelo and Natasha started arguing over whether Julian ever got the message that Angelo left for him Wednesday night. Finally, because the residents were waiting for them, the three students started the interviews. Neither Mandy nor Julian ever showed up. After they finished the interviews, Jorge, Natasha, and Angelo had a meeting of their own. "What are we going to do about the final report?" asked Jorge. "I think we should make Mandy and Julian write the entire report. They haven't helped us with any of the other steps in the project," Angelo grumbled. "No way I'm counting on them," said Natasha. "My grade in this class depends on finishing the project. I think we have to just suck it up and finish it ourselves." The others agreed, but no one seemed very happy about being "dumped on" by Julian and Mandy.	Once the final project draft was approved, everyone got busy compiling the different parts of the neighborhood oral history. It was agreed that all the members of the group would meet at the neighborhood community center to talk with longtime residents and collect their stories about "the old days" in this neighborhood. When Anita, Bill, and Maria arrived at the community center, neither Tiffany nor DeWayne were there. Since all the residents were waiting, the three students got ready to start doing the interviews. Anita's cell phone rang. It was DeWayne; his cold had worsened, and he was "sick as a dog." He told Anita, "I don't think I should come out there today; all that would happen is that I would get a bunch of other people sick. Tell the rest of the group that I'll be responsible for the graphics and drawings to illustrate the final report, since I couldn't help today." When Anita told the rest of the group DeWayne's idea, they thought he was smart to have stayed away instead of spreading his cold to everyone else. They were actually happy with the plan; DeWayne's illustrations were always well done. Just then Tiffany showed up, about 15 minutes late. She started right into doing an interview. No one said anything about her being late, but Tiffany volunteered to stay after the rest of the group had finished to complete the last couple of interviews. Later that evening, Anita sent everyone in the group an e-mail reminder that each person had agreed to have his or her section of the final report ready for the next meeting.

"free-riders," incorporate discussion and acknowledgment of group members' individual contributions, and develop a shared understanding of the project's **performance standard**, as an ongoing part of your group's process.

Why Did He Do That?: Attribution and Communication

In the discussion of differences between active listening and inefficient listening in the previous section,

Mudslingers	*Visionary Skeptics*
Neither Mandy nor Julian was in class on Monday. Angelo, Jorge, and Natasha worked late to get the final report ready for the class project presentation on Friday. On Wednesday, both Julian and Mandy were in class, but Angelo, Jorge, and Natasha were still very angry and initially gave them both the "cold shoulder" for not helping with the community interviews. After the instructor reminded all the groups that it was required that each member of the group present some part of the final report, Mandy and Julian acted as if nothing was wrong and asked Natasha, "Which part of the report do you want me to present?" She assigned Mandy the introduction and Julian the neighborhood history sections to present, while Angelo fumed. The final in-class presentation was a disaster. Mandy read the introduction from the folded page of notes that Natasha had given her on Wednesday. Julian kept mispronouncing the street names in the neighborhood. The community partner looked very unhappy, and the instructor seemed to be embarrassed. As class ended and everyone was leaving, Natasha said to Jorge, "I pray that I will never again have to do another group project with any of these losers." Angelo turned in one copy of the final report to the instructor—without any graphics or illustrations—on the following Monday.	The group was working smoothly as they wrapped up the group project assigned in their service-learning class. Maria made sure the group stayed on the timeline. They finished the oral history of their neighborhood and put all the stories together in a final report, complete with DeWayne's drawings. At the final in-class project presentation, Tiffany introduced the project, and then each of the other group members told one of the neighborhood stories. At the end of the presentation, Bill and Anita made sure that the community partner got a copy of the final report. The following Saturday, all of the *Visionary Skeptics*—DeWayne, Maria, Tiffany, Bill, and Anita—met again in the neighborhood in which they'd done their oral histories and distributed copies of the report to the residents who were part of the project, and then sat down at a local coffeehouse to discuss their experiences. Bill said to the group, "you know I was not down for doing a group project when the instructor assigned it, but working with you has been a pretty good experience." The rest of the group agreed. Then Anita added, ". . . especially since DeWayne left his snake at home." The group had a good laugh and continued reminiscing about their experiences with this project.

one characteristic of inefficient listening was "attempting to confirm a preconceived idea of others' messages, feelings, or intent." In contrast, active listening was characterised by "checking the accuracy of your inferences and assumptions."

The process underlying both of these types of listening—one associated with negative and the other with positive communication styles—is attribution. **Attribution** involves trying to uncover the reasons and motives that explain why a person says (or does) what they've said and done. The attribution process can occur at any time, but it is more likely to occur in response to a direct question or unexpected event (e.g., "What are you doing here?"), when we fail to perform a task properly (e.g., "I dropped the ball because the sun was in my eyes"), or when we depend upon others for important outcomes (e.g., "I only got a C– on my essay because the teacher doesn't value creativity").

Heider (1958) initially identified two types of attribution for any given behavior. A ***dispositional*** or ***internal*** attribution explains the behavior in terms of some cause within the person (e.g., ability, personality traits, or mood); while a *situational* or *external* attribution explains behavior in terms of a cause outside the individual (e.g., environmental circumstances, luck, or fate). When an act is freely chosen and goal-directed, or when a great deal of effort is exerted to perform the act, observers conclude that an act is intentional, and usually attribute it to personal disposition rather than to the situation.

More recent work (Weiner, 1985) identified two additional dimensions—*stability* (i.e., is this a temporary or reoccurring situation?), and *controllability* (i.e., perceived level of personal control)—that interact with the original dispositional and situational dimension to produce greater differences in attribution. Weiner also proposed that a person experiences different emotions depending on the attribution she makes to explain a particular outcome.

For example, someone who makes the attribution that her grade on an exam is due to an internal quality such as "effort" or "intelligence" will feel pride at receiving an A on an exam, while a second student earning the same grade but attributing her performance to luck might feel relieved at her good fortune. Attributions impact the amount of effort a person puts into subsequent efforts to complete the same task. Depending on which attribution for the good test grade is made, an individual may work harder and raise sights toward higher achievement, or count on being lucky again. Similarly, if a person fails, she or he may be encouraged to try harder next time, or she or he may give up and not try at all.

Attribution Biases

The attribution process is very susceptible to biases. One is the ***fundamental attribution bias***; a tendency to easily accept dispositional attributions while overlooking or underestimating the importance of situational factors. A service-learning example would be immediately getting angry at adults for missing a GED tutoring session without realizing that they were working two jobs to pay their family's bills.

Another version of this, the **actor-observer bias**, occurs in situations where individuals must make attributions to explain their own and each other's behaviors in on-going interactions, like those between you and your community partner. When both parties engage in the same negative behavior (e.g., interrupting someone else before they have finished speaking) the tendency is to attribute other's actions to dispositional factors (e.g., as a personality trait, "the person is rude") while attributing one's own action to situational factors (e.g., the stoplight changed from red to green so I had to interrupt you and tell you to go"). With both these biases, the consequence

of making an attribution of internal causality allows the "attributer" to block the other person's attempts to deny responsibility for negative acts with which they are associated.

Impact of Attribution/Misattribution in Service-Learning Projects

Misattribution, a situation when someone makes an incorrect attribution in accounting for another's actions, can have serious consequences in service-learning experiences. As described previously, it could lead to a college student deciding to skip the GED tutoring session because they think the adult doesn't care or isn't serious about getting their degree.

One idea from attribution theory—that different emotions are associated with different attributions—also holds true in regard to explaining the words and actions of others. Misattributions by college students of community members' actions, or vice versa, can result in the alienation of a community partner. Misattribution within service-learning classes can lead to decreased individual participation and buy-in to the group's goals, decreased group cohesion, and, consequently, decreased productivity.

Attribution and the Mudslingers and Visionary Skeptics

To gain insight into how differences in attribution can impact group cohesion and productivity, let's reexamine the most recent vignette about the mudslingers and visionary skeptics. For the mudslingers, when Julian and Mandy did not show up on Saturday morning to help conduct interviews at the community center, Angelo, Natasha, and Jorge made an internal attribution that Julian's and Mandy's motivation for not attending the group's interviews was something "controllable"—they were trying to avoid doing their share of the group project. As a consequence the rest of group felt "dumped on" and shared feelings of anger and resentment toward the absent members.

Interestingly, the visionary skeptics also faced a situation where a group member, DeWayne, unexpectedly did not show up for an important meeting with the community partner. When DeWayne called Anita,

Exercise 4.8: Actors and Observers

Read each of the following vignettes. In the space that follows each story, explain the reason why you think the person in the story acted the way he or she did.

Vignette 1

1. Your service-learning class group decides to meet outside of class for a project planning session at a local coffee house at 11 a.m. Everyone is on time for the meeting except one student. No one in the group knows any reason why he may be late, and no one received a call from him, though another student mentions that he told her he did not have a cell phone. After about five minutes, the group decides to start the planning meeting, which includes dividing up the specific tasks that need to be completed for the next step in your service-learning project. The group finishes all the necessary work by 11:25 a.m. You wait around until 11:30 a.m. in case he shows up late, then everyone leaves.

What attribution did you make for why the student from your service-learning class did not show up for the agreed upon planning meeting on time?

Was this an internal/dispositional attribution (e.g., any references to self or personal variables as well as the types of things a person has control over) or an external/situational attribution (e.g., references to other people; special circumstances that limit the person's choices; and luck, chance, or fate)? Explain your choice.

Vignette 2

2. Your service-learning class group decides to meet outside of class for a planning meeting at a local coffee house at 11 a.m. You estimate that it will take you 20 minutes to drive to the meeting place and you allow 10 minutes to find a parking space. You start to leave your house at 10:25 a.m. Just as you're about to leave your house, you get a telephone call on your home (only) phone. It's your brother, calling from the East Coast with an important relationship problem that he needs to share with you and get your advice on. You finally get off the phone with him, but the call lasts 15 minutes—now you may be a few minutes late for your meeting. When you get down near the coffee house, you can't find a place to park. You circle around a municipal parking structure only to discover there are no available parking spots. You finally find a spot to park on the street, but by this time you are 30 minutes late for your meeting. When you get to the coffee house, the class group is not there. When you get home, you call one of the other students in the group and try to explain.

What attribution did you make for why you did not show up for the agreed upon planning meeting on time?

Was this an internal/dispositional attribution (e.g., any references to self or personal variables as well as the types of things a person has control over) or an external/situational attribution (e.g., references to other people; special circumstances that limit the person's choices; and luck, chance, or fate)? Explain your choice.

Review your attributions for the two vignettes. Discuss any differences between the two explanations you came up with for why each person acted as he or she did.

while the group was at the neighbourhood center, and explained that his cold had gotten worse and he was not joining the group because he was concerned that he "would get a bunch of other people sick," Anita and the rest of the group made an internal attribution—DeWayne's not here because he is sick. However, this was seen as something that was uncontrollable; getting sick was something DeWayne had not planned on. The emotions the group felt about DeWayne's situation were concern, empathy, and gratitude, particularly after he volunteered to do the graphics and illustrations for the final report. In the end, DeWayne did his fair share of the group work, while demonstrating consideration for the group and the community partner by not exposing others to his cold.

Cross-Cultural Differences in Attribution

People from cultures other than the United States demonstrate differences in the attribution process, particularly in regard to understanding achievement and individuals' motivations for achievement. In Weiner's model of stability and controllability the concept of achievement is connected with a person reaching some standard for excellence in a competitive context, such as earning high grades, winning athletic contests, answering more questions correctly on a cognitive test. Yet in studies of Navajo and Anglo youth, Duda (1986) found Navajo youth were more likely to emphasize self-referenced and mastery conceptions of achievement (i.e., success equated to personal improvement) than competitive-based criteria like high grades. In a second study, Chilean students perceived external causes as more external, stable attributions as less stable, and controllable attributions as less controllable than American students (Betancourt & Weiner, 1982).

How Might Cultural Group Differences Increase Unintentional Misattribution?

When researchers examine multi-cultural material on *fundamental attribution bias*, they find it is much more likely to happen in individualist cultures than collectivist ones. One possible explanation is that members of collectivist cultures seem to be more aware of the im-

pact of situational factors on individual decisions. Morris and Peng (1994) analyzed newspaper articles about two mass murders committed in the United States—one by a Chinese graduate student, the other by a White postal worker. Both stories ran in English in the *New York Times* and in Chinese in the *World Journal*, a Chinese language newspaper printed in the United States. The researchers found that the articles in the *Times* attributed both murderers' actions to internal/dispositional factors while the articles written in *World Journal* placed greater emphasis on external/situational factors.

A second possible explanation has to do with differences between individualist and collectivist cultures in how each view the self. Individualist cultures share an *independent* view of the self in that individuals are seen as self-contained or autonomous, whose behavior is primarily determined by internal attributes (e.g., motives, values, and traits). On the other hand, collectivist cultures favor a more *interdependent* view of self in that the self is seen as more dependent on relationships with others and social groups. As a result individual actions are more likely to be influenced by social obligations. These differences in self-conceptions impact the attribution process (Markus & Kitayama, 1991).

For example, Miller (1990) asked Americans and Indians to explain the actions of individuals involved in a motorcycle accident in India. An attorney was driving a motorcycle on his way to work, with a passenger on the back. The back tire burst and the passenger was thrown off of the motorcycle, striking his head on the pavement when he fell. The driver took the passenger to a local hospital and left for work without consulting with doctors as to the severity of the accident. The passenger ultimately died. Respondents were asked to explain why the driver left the passenger at the hospital without staying to consult with physicians. Thirty-six percent of Americans made internal/dispositional attributions (e.g., the driver was irresponsible or focused on his career) and 17 percent made external/situational attributions (e.g., he had a duty to appear in court). Among Indian respondents only 15 percent of made internal attributions, while 32 percent referred to external/situational factors. For Indians, the social role of the driver was very important; as an attorney he had a responsibility to others to perform his job. Individuals from collectivist cultures are more likely to explain an individual's actions as the product of responsibilities or commitments to others.

These culture-based differences in attribution are important to keep in mind when college students interact with community members in service-learning projects. Consider the vignette in exercise 4.8 where you were asked to explain why the student from your service-learning class did not show up for the agreed upon planning meeting. If the situation was changed so that the person who missed the meeting was a community member from a collectivist culture (e.g., a recent immigrant from Asia or Africa) instead of another student, students making an "automatic" internal attribution that the community member's absence reflected negative personal qualities such as laziness or irresponsibility not only may be incorrect from the community member's perspective (e.g., he attributed his absence to having to deal with unexpected family obligations), but could lead to future problems in the service-learning project due to the erosion of trust and commitment from the partner. In a similar manner, students in service-learning projects also need to be aware of different situational factors that affect outcomes in a community setting compared to the university, and, even when dealing with similar situational factors, the relative strength of influence that those factors have in each context may be different. A good piece of advice when dealing with community partners is: "before making an attribution, ask the person to explain why he acted as he did."

Groups Revisited

Before concluding, let's take one more look at our two groups of service-learning students.

Throughout this chapter, we have examined multiple aspects of working in groups in community-based learning settings. We hope you have gained insights about why instructors assign group projects; the potentially positive and negative outcomes of group projects; how groups develop; the importance of group roles, group cohesion, group communication, and group equity of tasks; and means of evaluating group work.

Completing service-learning experiences, however, does not just mean forming connections with other students. You will be (or already are) interacting with community members. To complete a project successfully, it is necessary for all students to understand their relationship with the community from both their own and the community's perspective. The next chapter explores multiculturalism, intercultural communication, the politics of difference, and the implications for community engagement.

Recommended Readings

Duda, J. L. (1986). A cross-cultural analysis of achievement motivation in sport and the classroom. In L. VanderVelden & J. Humphreys (Eds.), *Current selected research in the psychology and sociology of sport* (pp. 115–132). NY: AMS Press

Harkins, S. G., & Jackson, J. M. (1986). The role of evaluation in eliminating social loafing. *Personality and Social Psychology Bulletin, 11*, 457–465.

Miller, J. G., Bersoff, D. M., & Harwood, R. L. (1990). Perceptions of social responsibilities in India and in the United States: Moral imperatives or personal decisions? *Journal of Personality and Social Psychology, 58*, 33–47.

Moorhead, G., Ference, R., & Neck, C. (1991). Group decision fiascoes continue: Space shuttle challenger and a revised groupthink framework. *Human Relations (44)*, 539–550(6).

Tuckman, B. W. (1965). Developmental sequences in small groups. *Psychological Bulletin, 63*, 384–399.

Key Concepts

active listening
actor observer bias
attribution
content goals
forming
free riding
fundamental attribution
    bias

group cohesion
groupthink
maintenance roles
norming
organizational roles
performance standard
performing

Phase Model of Group
    Development
process goals
role
social loafing
social thinking
storming
task roles

Key Issues

- Why do instructors assign group projects? What is the value of group work?
- How do groups develop?
- How does work get done in groups?
- What must be done to keep a group together?
- How can we make sure each member does a fair share of group work?
- How might cross-cultural differences affect the attribution process?
- What can be done to minimize the possibility of misattribution?

ADDITIONAL EXERCISES

☙ Exercise 4.9: Facilitating the Development of Your Group

Refer to this checklist often to keep track of your group's progress.

FORMING: Getting off to a good start.

_____ We have taken some time to get to know each other as individuals.
_____ We have clearly communicated our expectations of how the group should operate.
_____ We have a clear idea of each group member's expectation for commitment to the group and have developed guidelines for dealing with any barriers to getting work done.
_____ We know something about each member's preferred method of working in a group.

STORMING: Using strategies to promote productive (not destructive) conflict.

_____ We have done at least some of the activities to facilitate forming.
_____ We acknowledge that we do not all share the same perspective on issues, but, even when we disagree, we are able to articulate our disagreement while treating other group members with civility and respect.
_____ Whenever possible, we try to resolve disagreements face-to-face, rather than by e-mail.

NORMING: Reaching consensus as to how we will operate as a group.

_____ We have devised mutually acceptable, effective guidelines for running group meetings and decision making.
_____ We have established a "Jobs List" detailing what needs to be done and who will do it.
_____ Each group member has clarified with the instructor, the community partner, and other group members answers to the following questions:

What are the steps in my part of this project?
What are the deadlines?
What should my piece of the project look like in the end?
What resources are needed to complete my part of the project in a timely way?
How will I know if I have met the community partner's expectations?

PERFORMING: Getting the actual work done.

_____ We have gone through the problem-solving process and developed an action plan to accomplish our group's assigned task.

_____ We have clarified with our instructor the expectations for the format and content of our group product.

_____ We are clear as to how the grade for this project will be determined, as well as who will assign the grade for the group product (instructor, community partner, or both).

☀ Exercise 4.10: How Am I in *This* Group?

Whether you played one of the five organizational roles (leader, notetaker, progress tracker, timekeeper, process observer) or not, reflect on your own actions in the group discussion. Answer the following questions, referring to **Exercise 4.6: Group Roles** (p. 60) as needed.

• What task roles did you play in the group discussion?
• What maintenance roles did you play in the group discussion?
• Were there any times during the discussion when you thought "someone should do something" (a specific task or maintenance role), but you hesitated to do what was needed? Describe those moments. Why do you think you hesitated?
• If this group was having another discussion on a related topic, which task and/or maintenance roles do think you would play? Why?

☀ Exercise 4.11: Group Member Work Tally

List all the jobs that need to be done to complete this project based on your group's earlier Jobs List (exercise 4.4 on page 58).

Task/Subtask	Who initially agreed to do it?	Who actually did it?	How long did it take?

Appendix 4.1: Group Roles Checklist

Task Roles	*Examples of behaviors*
Creating	Initiates plans, proposes new ideas or goals, defines group's position
Elaborating	Expands on ideas of others, provides examples, clarifies and develops earlier points in the discussion
Integrating	Organizes and coordinates the group's work, puts together parts of different members' ideas into something new
Reviewing	Summarizes the group's work or discussion to the current point, reminds group of previously mentioned items
Evaluating	Critiques ideas, suggestions, or action plans; proposes standards by which to evaluate information
Documenting	Keeps records of the group's work, prepares reports, serves as secretary or group historian
Consensus testing	Seeks verification that a group decision has been reached, makes sure an apparent group decision is acceptable to all
Information sharing	Presents data, facts, and other evidence relevant to the group's task; seeks additional information as necessary
Opinion giving	Expresses personal beliefs, provides an interpretation of the facts from a personal perspective

Maintenance Roles	*Examples of behaviors*
Encouraging	Expresses appreciation for others' contributions, shares positive feelings about other group members
Reinforcing	Expresses support for another group member's idea or suggestion, agrees to follow another's lead
Mediating	Promotes harmony within the group, reduces tensions, suggests a compromise
Gatekeeping	Suggests taking turns in a discussion, gets the floor and makes sure less outspoken members are heard
Process observing	Points out the ways in which the group is or is not working together
Tension relieving	Breaks tension within the group through the use of humor, encourages informality, helps new members feel at ease

print gvn control article

Creating Cultural Connections

Navigating Difference, Investigating Power, Unpacking Privilege

VICKI L. REITENAUER, CHRISTINE M. CRESS, AND JANET BENNETT

To be honest, I didn't think I had a lot to learn about diversity from taking a service-learning course. I'm a business major, and we work in teams all the time. I've had lots of experience working with people who are different from me.

Truly, though, I am amazed at what I learned. Before, we'd get some random assignment to complete as a team, and we'd finish it, one way or another. In this class, though, we were doing something real for the community. It was a much bigger proposition than just doing something for a grade. I had to figure out how to work well with people whose experiences and perspectives were totally different than mine. I had to figure out the differences between what it means for me to work collaboratively and what it means to others. And I was surprised to find that I had a lot to learn from the practice of joining with others to address a community problem.

The biggest surprise was the basic realization that recognizing and respecting our differences actually helps collaboration. We were all far more creative in this course. What I mean is, before in groups we usually competed with each other, but it doesn't make very much sense to compete with each other in a situation like this, because competition gets in

the way of using all our skills and different ways of looking at things to get the job done.

—Michael, community-based learner, working on a marketing plan for a Meals on Wheels program

---

PERHAPS YOU ARE like the student quoted here, engaging in this service-learning environment with a lot of prior experience working with other students in team settings. Even if your only team experience has come through the work you are currently undertaking in this class, after reading the last chapter you have begun to think about the diverse roles and responsibilities that exist within a group, and you have practiced some strategies for working effectively with others. At the very least, you have probably started to think about the many factors that affect group dynamics; clearly, any collection of people yields lots of differences in personal preferences, styles, and ways of being and doing in the world.

Where do these differences originate? Is there a deeper, more meaningful way to think about both the differences and similarities that exist among people that can offer clues to greater understanding of yourself as an individual student? Might these insights further your own knowledge base and skills for operating in a diverse world, for connecting with team members and classmates in your course, and for positively impacting the larger community you are serving?

Service-learning experiences are opportunities for bridging a variety of cultural ways of being and doing. This chapter offers resources to frame your experience in order to expand your capacities for working effectively with those who are different from you, and to recognize how to act on commonly held desires for creating positive change in the world. Further, we explore how our different perspectives are actually keys to maximizing the innovative problem-solving capacities that exist in any community setting. We look at the ways that our notions of "service" are culturally based and seek a common language for serving and learning with respect and integrity.

What's Culture Got to Do with It?

Culture is the creation of learned and shared values, beliefs, and behaviors in a community of interacting people. Each of us constructs a multicultural identity from the many cultural influences that impact us, including nationality, ethnicity, race, age, gender, physical characteristics, sexual orientation, economic status, education, profession, religion, and organizational affiliation.

In your service-learning experience, you may be working shoulder-to-shoulder with people who are culturally different from you. When we talk about cultural differences, we don't simply mean varieties of art and music, but rather different ways of thinking, of communicating, and of applying our distinct values to our actions. In our multicultural world, it is virtually impossible to work side by side with classmates and a community partner and not encounter differences related to culture. In other words, community-based learning is an *intercultural* context.

Sometimes this means collaborating with an intercultural team, a group whose members are quite diverse. Other times you may be working alone but engaging with persons from backgrounds so different from your own that you may not be able to comprehend their perspectives. You may find that you are the only person from your own culture present in a given situation, and you might experience a sense of isolation as you immerse yourself in this new environment.

Each of these scenarios requires *intercultural competence*, the ability to communicate effectively and ap-

propriately in a variety of cultural contexts. To be interculturally competent, you need to cultivate a *mindset* (analytical frameworks for understanding culture), a *skillset* (interpersonal and group skills for bridging differences) and a *heartset* (motivation and curiosity to explore cultural variables). These three essential components of competence support your learning with others in the community (Bennett & Bennett, 2004).

The *mindset* gives you knowledge and academic understanding of other cultures through information about attitudes and behaviors. The *skillset* builds on that knowledge base by enhancing your intercultural abilities, including your capacity to listen, to solve problems, and to empathize. And the *heartset*, the interest and concern for others, provides the motivation to continue the effort even when things get complicated and challenging.

As you ponder your own cultural background and that of others, the main characteristic needed to guide your learning is *cultural humility*, that is, respect for the validity of other peoples' cultures (Guskin, 1991). We are frequently tempted to see the perfectly obvious superiority of our own way of looking at the world, of conceptualizing a task, or of resolving a conflict. Cultural humility instead requires us to recognize that diverse worldviews are equally legitimate. It suggests that we suspend our value judgments, question the primacy of our own orientation, and realize that we may not even know what is really going on in an intercultural context. While this can be a major challenge, it is a prerequisite for getting along with other cultural groups.

A second step in becoming interculturally competent is to develop *cultural self-awareness*, the recognition of the attributes and patterns of your own culture. Each of us processes many layers of cultural patterning. At one level, you belong to a national culture, or what some call a "passport culture," referring to the country of your citizenship. For some individuals, this is easy to identify. However, if you grew up in Mexico, moved to Canada, and now live in the United States, this becomes a more complicated aspect of your cultural identity.

As part of your developing cultural self-awareness, you may become more conscious of your ethnic heritage, including your relationship to the geography and history of the place your family originated, and how much of that culture they (and you) continue to identify with. Ethnic heritage is often more important than national culture, since so many countries consist of powerful groups with unique identities, groups that may resist assimilation into the dominant culture. Some of these groups are pan-national, such as Arabs, Kurds, and Roma, whose communities stretch across borders; some of them are within a national border, such as groups within the United States, including African Americans, Latino Americans, Native Americans, Asian Americans, and European Americans. Each of these designations suggests the ethnic background of the individual, as well as the national culture. Particularly notable in the United States is the designation of European American, a group that frequently forgets that it has an ethnic identity.

Stop and think for a moment: What is your ethnic identity? It may seem—particularly to those of European American heritage—that European American patterns are, well, *just the way things are done.* Only by bringing ethnicity into consciousness can we become aware of that bias.

There are other levels to cultural identity. Regional cultures influence our communication interactions. For example, those from the southern United States may use speech patterns and behaviors dissimilar to those who grew up in New England. Socioeconomic class and education impact our values and beliefs as well. Gender culture, the many ways we are acculturated to our roles as men and women (and even the bi-nary description of that designation), affects our cultural beliefs and individual choices. Other cultural influences include religion and spirituality; sexual orientation; physical, psychological, and learning abilities; organizational culture; and, on college campuses, even departmental cultures.

Some aspects of your own cultural identity are probably more important to you than others, for example, your gender culture or your ethnic heritage. However, you create your multilayered, multicultural self through the choices you make about how these cultural influences affect who you are. Culture is not a "thing," but a dynamic process in which you interact with family and community influences to reflect the cultural being you choose to be in the context in which you live, study, and work.

Let's take a look at your concept and experience of "service" through the lens of culture with exercise 5.1.

What does all of this mean to you, as you work in a community to serve and to learn? It suggests that you have to understand who you are culturally before you interact *across* cultures. If your sense is that other individuals are doing things that are weird, indecipherable, or unacceptable, this feeling might be tempered when you realize that you are viewing the situation from your own cultural worldview and that the other persons' perspectives are entirely different

---

✯✯ Exercise 5.1: Cultural Dimensions of Service

In this activity, you will explore how you have come to define and understand what "service" means to you by examining your own cultural definitions. Begin by drawing (or otherwise indicating) yourself in the middle of a large sheet of paper. Around this figure, make notes about what service means to you and what kinds of service to others you have been engaged in, inside or outside a school setting.

Next, draw figures around you and connected to you, representing important persons in your life from whom you have learned about service. These could be parents and grandparents, siblings, other relatives, friends, mentors, schoolmates, teachers, professional colleagues, and others. What kinds of service have these persons been engaged in? What do you believe "service" means or meant to them?

Now, consider these persons and relationships through the lens of culture. Who among them shares one or more aspect of your cultural identity? How do those cultural groups to which you experience belonging understand "service"? How is that reflected in your drawing?

Conversely, who among these persons has had a distinctly different cultural experience from yours? How did these cultural differences affect your relationships with those persons and how they understand "service"?

from yours. Recognizing this, you can make a choice to practice cultural humility in order to learn more about the cultural worldview of those who are different from you.

Recall **Exercise 3.3: Who Am I and What Do I Bring?** on page 40. In this activity, you explored your current understanding of your identity in relation to a variety of racial and cultural factors (race and ethnicity; nationality; gender; language; spirituality and religion; physical, mental and/or emotional ability; socioeconomic class; age; physical appearance; and sexual orientation). These identifiers are lenses through which you perceive the world around you, which in this course includes your teammates and classmates and your community partner. Let's deepen your reflection on this theme with exercise 5.2.

🔑 Exercise 5.2: I and We and You and Us and Them

Step 1: Reflect

Reread your earlier reflection from **Exercise 3.3: Who Am I and What Do I Bring?** Think again about the ways that your current understanding of your identity positions you to experience this community partnership. Use the following prompts to focus your thinking about who you are in relation to the others with whom you are working.

- How do the multiple expressions of your identity impact the way that you perceive your community partner as an organization and the work that it does?
- How does your identity impact the way that you perceive other people, including your teammates and classmates, your community partner contacts, and the people served by your partner?
- How does your identity orient you toward effective interactions with others, and how does it challenge effective interaction?
- How might you use your perspective to further your investigations into creating effective working relationships with your team, your classmates, and your community partner?
- How might you learn from the perspectives of others? What particular perspectives would be most valuable for you to encounter?

In preparing your reflection, consider breaking out of the confines of the traditional narrative reflective form. Write a story or a poem or a dialogue. Paint, draw, or collage a picture. Compose and record some music. Choose to be as honest as possible in this reflection, which might mean that you record "negative" or contradictory thoughts and feelings as well as those that seem "positive" and clear.

Step 2: Step Back

After creating your reflection, take some time to review it and consider what it communicates to you. Then answer the following questions in writing:

- What is it like for you, this process of considering identity and its effect on your perceptions of others?
- What thoughts and feelings emerge as you consider these questions?

Step 3: Reflect Again

After your next service experience in the field or class session, reread your responses to the questions in both step 1 and 2. What does your reflection reveal about you as a person, a student, a community-based learner? How does this connect to your cultural background? How does it connect you to your team, your classmates, and your community partner?

With an ever-evolving understanding of yourself as a cultural being, it is important to be aware of the pitfalls of stereotyping others. A ***stereotype*** is a "hardening of the categories," a process of developing rigid ways of thinking about individuals from other cultures, as if those individuals represent some statistical "norm" of their culture group. We frequently base such unjustified ways of thinking on having met a single person from a culture or having been exposed to media representations of a culture's patterns.

A ***generalization***, on the other hand, is a lightly held hypothesis based on research about patterns of behavior in the other culture, a hypothesis that we never act on until we have confirmed that it is appropriate for the individual we have met. Thus, if we default to the notion that all men like sports or all Asians are quiet, we are simply stereotyping. However, in interactions across cultures, it is often useful to have hypotheses in mind that we hold tentatively until they are confirmed. In your community-based learning experience, it may have already proven useful to you to be exposed to some generalizations about the groups of persons and the cultural realities they embody to help guide your interactions. In another of his journals, Michael, our community-based learner from the opening of this chapter, described an experience he had of using generalizations to help him relate respectfully to the community he served:

I was riding with one of the Meals on Wheels volunteers on her rounds delivering lunch to persons who are elderly and disabled. I figured it was good to get hands-on experience of what they do before I started working on the marketing plan. I wasn't too nervous about dropping off food with the older folks, because I hang out a lot with my grandfather and his friends, but I don't know any people with disabilities. The last thing I wanted to do was hurt somebody's feelings.

I guess the volunteer must have sensed my nervousness. She said that generally the disabled people with disabilities she serves on this route seem to really appreciate it when she makes eye contact and connects with them. She said it can be helpful to be on the same level with people who are in wheelchairs, for example. Like everybody else on the route, they like it

when you can spend a few minutes talking, since we might be their only visitor for the day.

When we showed up, the lady there was very happy to see us. She was in a wheelchair, so I sat on a sofa facing her as I told her how I was a student from the university working on this project for the Meals on Wheels program. I have to admit I was surprised when she told me a little bit about the career she had had in advertising. On a whim, I asked her if she might be willing to give me some feedback on the plan before we turned it in, and she said she'd be happy to.

At our group session, I told my teammates about meeting this woman who is not only a client of our community partner but also has done the same kind of work we're doing. Now they want to meet her too. I think getting to know her is going to have a definite impact on our final product in a number of ways.

Conversely, you may have also experienced the negative impact of stereotyping, in which the unexamined views you have held about different cultures have worked against your successful interaction with others. Exercise 5.3 asks you to consider both generalizations and stereotyping in the context of your particular service-learning experience.

Building Intercultural Sensitivity

As each of us experiences cultural differences, we tend to react to those differences in fairly predictable ways. These reactions are based on our worldview and reflect how we think, feel, and behave in the presence of unfamiliar cultures. We can look at the typical stages individuals move through as they acquire cultural self-awareness, learn to identify and appreciate cultural differences, and, eventually, adapt to others as a process of building intercultural competence.

This process has been described in the *Developmental Model of Intercultural Sensitivity* (figure 5.1), a framework that explains the development of increasing sophistication in our experience and navigation of

✦✦ **Exercise 5.3: Deconstructing Stereotypes**

You may choose to complete this activity in a variety of ways: You might create a collage, using visual and/or word images clipped from magazines and newspapers to create a representation of those persons you are serving in your community partnership. Or you might pay particular attention to the ways that those you are serving are shown in the broadcast media, including film, television, and the radio, by watching and listening to several shows and making notes about what you see and hear. After you have spent some time intentionally engaging with the images in popular media that connect with the group of persons you are serving, respond to the following questions:

- How do these images represent stereotypes about the community you are serving?
- How are the stereotypes about this group reinforced in the media? How do the media negatively portray this group?
- How are the stereotypes about this group challenged in the media? How do the media positively portray this group?
- How do these images connect with your own experience of this group, and how are they different? When you look at these images, do they help you to see the faces of the individuals you are serving, or do they obscure the faces of those individuals? How?

differences (J. M. Bennett, 1993; M. J. Bennett, 1993; J. M. Bennett & M. J. Bennett, 2004). The model begins with three ***ethnocentric*** stages, in which our own culture is experienced as central to reality in some particular way. The latter three stages of the model are termed ***ethnorelative***, in which one's own culture is viewed in the context of other cultures.

Stage One: Denial of Difference
Individuals who view others through the denial filter either neglect to notice differences at all or think in extremely simple categories. Those who are just beginning to explore cultural differences are often unaware that they have a culture or that certain privileges exist in their world that don't exist elsewhere. They are per-

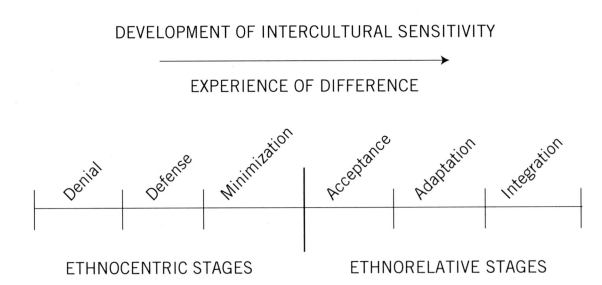

Figure 5.1. Developmental Model of Intercultural Sensitivity

From Bennett & Bennett (2004)

plexed when asked about their own cultural filters and are unconcerned about the impact of cultural differences on their lives. The following journal entry was completed by a student named Jennifer, whose service-learning experience involves working at a large family planning clinic in a multicultural community:

> *After learning about cultural patterns in the readings, I expected these patients to be really different from me, and so I'm quite surprised at how smoothly things are going. I've really not met anyone yet who seems that different from me. After all, healthcare is healthcare, no matter what culture you're from. And we all speak the same language, so I figure if I'm just myself things here will continue to be fine.*

Stage Two: Defense against Difference

When individuals become aware of cultural differences in more powerful and penetrating ways, they may slip into the defense posture, where their worldview is polarized into us/them distinctions. ("Now that I've noticed they're different, I recognize they're bad!") Individuals thinking in this way may criticize others or assert the superiority of their own culture. One intriguing variation on the defense perspective is what is called "reversal," which involves denigrating one's own culture and exalting some other culture's ways of being and doing. ("The Native Americans live in harmony with nature, not like us dominant Anglos," says the Anglo student.) While this may superficially seem to be more culturally sensitive, in fact it is nevertheless still dualistic and a defensive reaction to exposure to difference. The object of the defense has simply shifted.

The following journal excerpt is from Todd, a journalism major, completing his community-based project writing for an small alternative press that focuses on the needs of the Latino community. Although he is not a member of this community, he is deeply interested in the impact of addiction and is conducting a research project about heroin treatment in the community he is serving.

> *My visit to the treatment clinic went really badly. I ran into some super-defensive, antagonistic people who clearly didn't grasp why I was there. They were*

> *even hostile. I can't understand why they didn't see I was there to help. Man, when these people are angry, they really let you know it. If they had taken more time to get to know me, they would have realized I was on their side. I'm beginning to wonder if we ought to be helping them at all, if they're going to be so rude.*

Stage Three: Minimization of Difference

Those who have achieved the minimization worldview typically feel they have arrived at intercultural sensitivity, since, in most contexts, suggesting that we are all the same despite surface differences is a vast improvement over the cultural biases that normally exist. However, this is perhaps the most complex strategy for avoiding cultural differences. Indeed, if we believe that deep down, we are all alike, then we don't have to do the difficult work of recognizing our own cultural patterns, understanding others, and eventually making the necessary adaptations. This stage is thus characterized by the assumption that we are similar in some universal context, whether physical or philosophical. "It's a small world, after all."

Maria and her team from the business administration program are working to develop a database and website for a new minority-owned small business for their community-based learning project. In her journal, Maria writes the following:

> *It's so great to realize that the people here care about the same things we do in my culture. They want their businesses to make money, too! So values really ARE universal! They seem to eat different foods, and dress a little differently than I do, but deep down, we obviously share a common worldview. Partly this is technology that is bringing us all together, and partly it's basic human motivation. It sure makes the work easier this way.*

Stage Four: Acceptance of Difference

As we become increasingly aware of our own culture, we begin to recognize how truly distinct other cultures are from our own, and we understand this distinction as difference without judging it to be "bad" or "less developed." This movement into the stages of ethnorelativism reflects our capacity to acknowledge our own cultural filters and suspend our judgments temporarily in order to understand others. In a sense, for the first time, we may see the complexity and validity of the other culture's worldview.

Individuals who are operating at the acceptance stage are initially interested in behavioral differences ("They use chopsticks and we don't"), and move into more complicated observations ("I've noticed that Mariko observes our group conversation for a long time and thinks carefully before offering her comments"). Ultimately, those at acceptance are able to decipher—and accept—profound value differences. However, it is essential to note that this does not mean agreement or preference for those values, but rather acceptance of the reality of the other culture's worldview. In addition, people at the acceptance stage will not expect that people in other culture groups will share their worldviews.

In the community, therefore, those in acceptance do not assume they are bringing "answers" or "help," but are more likely to understand that they are operating as "colearners" in the community environment. For instance, as part of her service-learning requirement for her degree, Natacha is volunteering at her local AIDS hospice.

When I arrive at the hospice, I now know I am entering a different world. I realize, for the first time, that while I thought I was doing this work to help them, I'm the one who is learning, changing, growing. Sometimes it is really difficult for me, since some of the patients are gay, and I'm not really sure I understand everything I should about their culture. Still I try to be respectful of their strength, their humor, and, especially, their patience in teaching me how to be more useful. Sometimes it seems as if we are building a bridge between our ways of viewing the world.

Stage Five: Adaptation to Difference
The necessary motivation to move to adaptation occurs when we need to be effective in our interactions with others in order to get something done. It is no longer enough merely to have the mindset (to know *about* a culture). Adaptation requires the alignment of a mindset with a heartset (motivation to continue engaging with difference) and skillset (skills for engaging

with difference), as well. Bringing all of these elements together helps one develop **empathy**, the premier capacity of an interculturalist. Empathy is the capacity to take the perspective of the other culture, to shift frames of reference, and to act in the context of the other's perspective. Based on our appropriate frame shifts, we can adapt how we interact, a process called "code-shifting." We may adapt our greeting rituals, our problem-solving strategies, or our apology patterns as part of a reciprocal learning experience.

Those at the stage of adaptation may wonder: "Do I have to abandon who I am to be interculturally sensitive?" For instance, "Do I have to give up being a feminist while I work in a church-based soup kitchen?" It may help us to understand that intercultural sensitivity is an *addition* to your personal repertoire of behavior, not a subtraction. You are who you are, but with adaptive intercultural expertise. You maintain a commitment to your own values and strive to make personal decisions in accordance with them, while understanding that others do the same from within their own cultural perspective. And you take on the challenge of creating an intercultural context large enough for all of these perspectives to coexist.

Kichiro is part of a class team designing a community-based learning project. Not only is the project located in a multicultural area of town with which he is not familiar, but his team also includes members from six different ethnic groups:

This term I have been trying very hard to participate in class discussions. Although this is my third year in the United States, I never imagined how difficult it would be to get a turn in an American class discussion. The students always seem to be interrupting each other, so I have resolved to adapt and try to be more direct with them. It's quite challenging to do this. However, I think some of my classmates also realize how useful my more quiet style is when we go into the community, where it fits very effectively. So perhaps the adaptation is mutual.

Stage Six: Integration of Difference
The natural outcome of sustained, in-depth intercultural adaptation is *multiculturality*, the internalization of multiple cultural identities. This may result

> ### ☼ Exercise 5.4: The Competence Continuum
>
> Reread all of your own writings completed so far for this course. (These could be pieces that came from the reflection activities suggested in this book or other assignments you have completed.) Highlight passages in these writings that reveal one or more of the stages of the development of intercultural sensitivity. What do you notice about these statements? How is your awareness of your own ability to practice intercultural sensitivity impacted by your re-reading of your written work for this course? How has your capacity for working across cultures changed over the duration of this service experience? What specifically has facilitated that change? How have you been encouraged to practice cultural humility and intercultural competence, as revealed in your own written work?
>
> What do these statements suggest about the effectiveness of your work in the community so far? What information is present here that suggests areas for additional attention as you continue to work collaboratively with each other and with the community and develop your intercultural competence?

when individuals intentionally make a significant, sustained effort to become fully competent in new cultures. This adaptation may occur for nondominant group members to a dominant or colonial culture, or persons who grew up in multiple countries, or long-term sojourners who have lived for extended periods of time in other cultures. It may also occur for individuals who consciously live in ways that bring them into full participation in two or more cultures simultaneously.

This multicultural identity allows for lively participation in a variety of cultures but may result in an occasional sense of never really being "at home." Home has become everywhere: Your sense of who you are as a cultural being becomes quite complex. The multicultural person brings many perspectives to every task, numerous ways to solve problems, and multiple possibilities for shifting codes. While multiculturality is certainly not a prerequisite for deeply effective and respectful collaboration across cultures (which becomes increasingly possible as one develops one's mindset, skillset and heartset), engagement in such collaborations may ultimately inspire a person to desire and strive for this degree of intercultural competence.

Soraya is a chemical engineer who has lived in other cultures most of her life. For her senior seminar community-based project, she is working on an environmental task force dedicated to saving the local river basin. In her journal, Soraya wrote the following:

I enjoy this task force because I can use the many cultural frames I have to try to solve problems. In each culture where I have lived, people resolve challenges differently. While I can shift from one frame to another, I still know who I am. I feel most comfortable bridging differences and acknowledging all the parts of the multicultural me.

A Step Further: Investigating Power and Unpacking Privilege

Becoming both interculturally sensitive and interculturally competent is fundamental to working successfully with others who embody different cultural ways of being and doing. These differences may be clear and overt, or they may be quite subtle. Adopting a stance of cultural humility, as a preliminary step, allows us to remain open to the many expressions of human ways of being and doing that have their foundation in the rich diversity of cultural forces.

To go a step further, we may choose to investigate the ways in which some groups have historically been and continue to be disadvantaged both socially and politically. This is referred to as *marginalization*—the exclusion or separation of individuals and groups of people from access to power, opportunities, and resources afforded to others. As you consider your community partnership, think about ways that marginalization currently manifests within the community you are serving. In other words, how is the social and political reality you are engaged with in your community partnership informed by racism (exclusion based on race and ethnicity), sexism (exclusion based on gender), classism (exclusion based on socioeconomic status), heterosexism (exclusion based on sexual orientation), and other forms of *discrimination*? Further, what can each of us do about these social injustices, while we are members of this class community and after we leave this particular community setting?

Giroux (1983) and Solorzano (1997) claim that "marginalized" persons can become empowered agents for change beyond the boundaries of socially and politically imposed separation. This insight is especially important with regard to students' experiences in service-learning courses. In fact, marginalized persons—those who find themselves outside the centers of power—may be more likely to instigate change since these persons may have less to lose and more to gain by doing so. While systems and organizations may have historically disenfranchised and isolated some groups of people, true hope for improving social conditions resides (at least in part) in collaborating with those who best understand that isolation and exclusion through their own lived experience. For many of us as community-based learners, understanding how we may have experienced marginalization in some aspects of our lives as well as access to power in other aspects will help us understand more precisely how we may collaborate with others to bring about the change we all, as collaborators, desire.

In a well-known and widely available article, author Peggy McIntosh writes about her awakening to the fact that she experiences *privilege*, or unearned benefits, on the basis of her white skin (McIntosh, 1988). McIntosh writes that, although she did not ask for these benefits, she receives them simply because she is a member of a dominant group. Further, she was not taught to investigate these privileges or even to recognize that they exist, because, while we may understand that racism is something that puts others at a disadvantage, we are generally taught not to see that the privilege that stems from having white skin puts white people at a distinct advantage:

My schooling gave me no training in seeing myself as . . . an unfairly advantaged person. I was taught to see myself as an individual whose moral state depended on her individual moral will. My schooling followed the pattern my colleague Elizabeth Minnich has pointed out: whites are taught to think of their lives as morally neutral, normative, and average, and also ideal, so that when we work to benefit others, this is seen as work which will allow "them" to be more like "us." (McIntosh, 1988, p. 1)

In her article, McIntosh gives many examples of the ways she benefits by her membership in the dominant racial group in the United States. Among other things, she includes everyday benefits related to being and doing in the world, such as "I can go shopping alone most of the time, pretty well assured that I will not be followed or harassed," as well as deeper social issues, in that "I can be pretty sure that if I ask to talk to 'the person in charge,' I will be facing a person of my race," along with broader political issues like "I can remain oblivious of the language and customs of persons of color who constitute the world's majority without feeling in my culture any penalty for such oblivion" (1988, p. 1).

Because the way that privilege works is often so tricky to understand, so slippery, and generally so invisible and complex, it can be difficult for those of us who experience privilege to fully understand that we hold it and how it may act as a barrier to our successful work across cultures. Because of the complex nature of identity—the fact that most of us experience some degree of privilege stemming from some aspect of our identity that aligns with a dominant culture—we are all charged with investigating the ways that we do and do not have access to power, and how that power is connected to certain social and political benefits.

Take, for instance, a student of working-class background who is of the first generation in his family to go to college. Perhaps this student is you or sits beside you in your community-based learning course. Because he is the first among his family to attend an institution of higher education, in his first days on campus he may find it an enormous challenge to navigate the complicated systems in this new environment: how to register for courses, how to sign up for a library card or a meal plan, or how to approach a professor with a request to be added to a class. Given the lack of experience his family has had in this regard, he may have to do much more work to understand these systems than someone from a middle- or upper-class background who has been informed by her parents or siblings about what to expect and how to negotiate it. Not only is the first-generation college student disadvantaged in this scenario, but the student with a family history of college attendance holds privilege relative to that status. This student didn't ask for the benefit, most likely doesn't even know it exists, and certainly is not a bad person for holding this privilege, but the privilege exists and benefits her regardless of her awareness of it.

Another way to think about privilege comes from the work of sociologist Pierre Bourdieu (1977), who describes **cultural capital** as specialized or insider knowledge not available equitably to all. If we understand "capital" in the way economists do, as a synonym for "wealth," we begin to see how particular cultural experiences may become more highly valued than others, because these experiences transfer the kinds of attitudes and knowledge that give their owners greater access to power and resources. The first-generation college student described previously did not have the same cultural capital as his classmate to "spend" in his first days at school, and so had to extend additional amounts of his time and energy to figure things out. Similarly, we may think about cultural capital as it applies to the persons we are serving in our community partnerships, and how limited access to particular kinds of highly prized and useful information may keep entire groups on the margins.

As learners who are serving, we are charged with exploring the ways in which privilege attaches to membership in certain groups in order to better understand the cultural dynamics at play in our community partnerships and to continue to develop our intercultural competence. Helpfully, McIntosh (1988) offers a list of ways in which she has identified her white-skin privilege, which we will use in exercise 5.5 as a way to investigate privilege.

What We See Depends on Where We Stand

Now that you've explored the ways in which you experience and hold privilege, let's widen the frame to look at the bigger picture: the ways that we are all located within oppressive structures and systems, and how you might more thoroughly understand what that means for you as a service learner.

Kathy Kelly, a lifelong peace and human rights activist who was nominated for the Nobel Prize for her work in promoting creative nonviolence, asserts that "what we see depends on where we stand" (Kelly, 2011). For example, how someone might describe the

---

✲✲ Exercise 5.5: Investigating Privilege

Begin by reading Peggy McIntosh's article "White Privilege: Unpacking the Invisible Knapsack" (available free in abridged form through several Internet sites). After your reading, respond in writing to the following questions:

- What feelings emerged after reading this piece? Describe as precisely as you can the body sensations and emotions that you experienced. What information does this mix of feelings give you about your own experience of privilege or lack of privilege relative to race and ethnicity?

- How is your reading of this piece informed by your complex cultural identity? For example, are there particular ways you read this piece because of your socioeconomic class, nationality, native language, gender, sexual orientation, physical/mental/emotional ability, spirituality/religion, political views, or other identifiers?

- How does this piece connect for you to your experience of your community partnership? Adapting McIntosh's list to your own experience, are there points of intersection between your position relative to power and privilege and the positions of others served by your community partner? Are there dislocations between you and your community partner that you can identify through your adapting this article to your situation?

- What does your developing consciousness about power and privilege mean for your work with the others in your class and with your community partner and for your developing intercultural competence?

conflict in Afghanistan depends on whether they are a U.S. policymaker, a U.S. soldier, an Afghan fighter, or an Afghan child. Each would tell a different story from their individual view of the same situation.

This concept is a great definition of **standpoint theory**, which offers us a framework for understanding the ways that our memberships in various identification groups situate us to perceive the world. Standpoint theory allows us to deepen our understanding of the ways that we have been empowered and privileged through our memberships in certain groups, as well as the ways we lack privilege and access to power through our memberships in other groups.

In regard to those groups in which we hold power and privilege, we occupy **agent status**; through our memberships in groups that are societally and politically marginalized, we occupy **target status**. In the course of a lifetime, all of us will occupy both target and agent positions, and we often occupy both positions across all of our **social locations** at any given time. For example, in our family or cultural group we may still be seen and acted upon as a child, while at our workplace or school we occupy positions of leadership and influence. How we are empowered (or disempowered) in each situation contributes to the puzzle of our social location and the ways that we may occupy both agent and target statuses at any given time.

In her germinal work, "Toward a New Vision: Race, Class, and Gender as Categories of Analysis and Connection" (1993), Patricia Hill Collins offers a nuanced and powerful articulation of how we might begin to see the ways in which "our thoughts and actions uphold someone else's subordination" (p. 98) within the **intersectional** oppressions that exist on a societal level. In a service-learning context, it is essential to interrogate our positions of privilege so that we may be forces for nonoppressive interactions with others, or else we may easily do damage to those whom we are serving. When we operate from the unexamined position that our perspectives are correct and true and applicable to everyone in every situation, we fail to recognize that different societal forces operate differently in persons' lives, and we risk imposing our biased solutions on others, regardless of our differences.

With our widened frame, let's look at the intersecting systems of oppression that operate as societal and political forces in our world. For all of the gains that social movements (e.g., the labor, civil rights, women's liberation, gay and lesbian rights, and trans liberation movements in the United States) have made possible,

our world is still profoundly marked by racism, ethnocentrism, classism, gender oppression, heterosexism, ableism, adultism (age oppression which targets the young) and ageism (age oppression which targets the old), and religious oppression (Morgan, 1996). Our social locations position us differently in regard to these forms of oppression, such that all of us will both experience oppression and hold the power to oppress others across a lifetime.

Consider, for example, a male student who wants to teach children but may eliminate this as a career option because he doesn't want to be perceived as gay. In this example, the male student in question may or may not be queer-identified. If he does identify as gay, he occupies target status, and changing career plans is an adjustment to the oppression experienced by him as a member of a targeted group. If he identifies as straight, he is not the target of homophobia and heterosexism (and thus is not himself oppressed), but he is clearly impacted by the homophobia that calls into question his motivations for teaching.

Or think about a college student in a wheelchair who is approached on the first day of class by her service-learning instructor, who suggests that she could do an extra credit project instead of service because of her disability. This student, targeted by ableism, is being seen as someone who *can't* do things, rather than as someone who has particular skills and capacities, just like everyone else. Instead of engaging with the student to discuss how she might participate fully in her service-learning course, her instructor has instead targeted her for oppression by deciding for her what she can and cannot accomplish in the context of the course.

In other words, when we occupy positions with target status—that is, when we lack power and privilege relative to our membership in societal-level groups—we experience oppression, which manifests itself in a variety of ways on both the micro and macro levels. When we occupy positions with agent status and can *invisibly* count on the power and privilege these positions afford us (as McIntosh [1988] showed us earlier in this chapter), we are often unaware of our agent positionality. In fact, as McIntosh reflects from her own position of privilege as a White woman, she recognizes that it is a *manifestation* of privilege and that agents typically *don't* see these as privileges at all.

For McIntosh, owning her privileges—the unearned benefits she received simply by being a member of an agent group—included the realization that, as a White person, she can "invisibly" count on being able to shop at a store or a mall without being followed or harassed. Or take the example of Michael, the student whose words about creative collaboration across difference opened this chapter. In order to understand something about Michael's social location, we need to look more closely (with Michael's permission) at the identifiers that Michael holds: he is 22 years old, White, able-bodied, and atheist; he identifies as a cisgender man (meaning that Michael's sexed body aligns with his gender identification and presentation) and straight; and he was raised in a middle-class family.

Looking at the dominant culture in which Michael was raised and in which he currently lives, studies, and works—namely, the dominant culture in early twenty-first-century United States—we can see that Michael holds agent status through his social location in the **categories of difference** that mark race, class, sex, gender, and sexuality. Michael holds target status in the categories that mark religion, and is on the cusp between agent and target status in the category that marks age.

Understanding our social locations and how these positions both privilege and marginalize us is not about fixing blame on individuals—or, at least, it doesn't have to be an exercise in finger-pointing. Instead, in the spirit of true and meaningful learning through serving, investigating our social location and what that means for each of us as members of a collaborative learning experience allows us to know ourselves and each other and to leverage our power and privilege to make positive change in our communities; and, at the very least, understanding our social locations offers us information about where we stand, so that we might better engage our critical thinking abilities in the service of our learning.

We'll read more about this in chapter 13, and you'll hear again from Michael at the end of this chapter. In the meantime, we encourage you to complete **Exercise 5.6: Mapping My Social Location,** in order to reflect deeply about where you stand, what you see, and what that means for you as a student, a service learner, and a human being.

Conclusion

Let us return to our starting point: with Michael, our community-based learner, reflecting on how his collaborative partnership brought out more creativity than he had ever experienced in a group setting.

Asked to speak about the learning he gained around intercultural sensitivity, power, and privilege, Michael had this to say:

At first, I have to admit, I was defensive about all this privilege stuff. As a white male who grew up in a middle-class household, it seemed that this was about bashing me and people like me for having had a good upbringing. It seemed at first that I was supposed to pretend to be someone I wasn't, or apologize for who I am and be ashamed of it. After being in this course, though, I am gaining some new perspectives. It's not that I'm supposed to deny that I have access to privileges because of my position in the world, but that I should become aware of them so that I'm more effective at communicating with people from different backgrounds. I realize now that I can make a choice to use my privileges for the benefit of both myself and others. I realize that I'm privileged to be in college, and I have the opportunity because of it to connect this community organization up to new marketing strategies for their Meals on Wheels program for the elderly.

One thing in particular my professor said has really stuck with me. You know how we've all learned the Golden Rule, to treat others the way we want to be treated? She said that, in intercultural relationships, we should use the Platinum Rule [M. Bennett, 1979] instead: "treating others the way that they themselves want to be treated." To do that, we have to really get to know each other. And to really get to know people, we had better get pretty good at communicating despite our differences.

By looking at my own social location, I understand now that "the elderly" aren't just a monolithic group. They are persons who occupy different social locations based on a variety of factors—race, ethnicity, class, and so on—and if I want to be successful in developing a marketing plan to reach all of them, I need to understand "where they stand" so that my message can reach them and motivate them to act.

Like everything else, "service" as a concept and practice is informed by our complex cultural identities and the privileges we hold (and do not hold) relative to those identities. We end this chapter by asking you to go deeper still, into the heart of your motivation for doing service and the impact that motivation may have on others. Remembering McIntosh, who said that unexamined privilege may lead us to see our own positions as "neutral, normative, and average, and also ideal, so that when we work to benefit others, this is seen as work which will allow 'them' to be more like 'us'" (McIntosh, 1988, p. 1), be cognizant about how we may frame our culturally informed positions on service so that they may orient us to serve from a place of being agents for social justice and social change, for the benefit of us all.

Key Concepts

agent status	ethnocentric	mindset
categories of difference	ethnorelative	privilege
cultural capital	generalization	skillset
cultural humility	heartset	social location
cultural self-awareness	intercultural	standpoint theory
culture	intercultural competence	stereotype
discrimination	intersectionality	target status
empathy	marginalization	

Key Issues

- What is an "intercultural" context? How is it especially relevant in community-based learning?
- How do your mindset, skillset, and heartset orient you toward effective intercultural communication?
- How might generalizations help us familiarize ourselves with cultures that are new to us? How do stereotypes hinder our understanding?
- How do power, marginalization, discrimination, and privilege affect individuals, relationships among classmates, and community partnerships?

ADDITIONAL EXERCISE

✯ Exercise 5.6: Mapping My Social Location

First, read Patricia Hill Collins's (1993) essay (available in several anthologies and on the web at http://www.memphis.edu/crow/pdfs/Toward_a_New_Vision_-_Race_Class_and_Gender _._._.pdf). Then reflect on all of the information, reflections, and activities you have engaged with in this chapter. Now, create a map of your social location. You might start by placing yourself at the center of a piece of paper, and then indicating all of the identifications you hold in regard to the various categories of difference (race, ethnicity, social class, sex, gender, sexuality, ability, age, religion, nationality, language). Use different colors to code those memberships in which you hold agent status and those in which you hold target status. Then continue to fill in your map with issues and insights that are particular to your work as a service learner this term. Make your map your own: What has your service-learning been about for you this term, and how might you locate what's bubbled forth in your community work on this map of your social location?

Second, write a brief reflection that addresses the following questions: How do you "see" your service? How does that seeing connect to your social location as represented on this map? How might you intentionally engage with others who are both similar to and different from you in order to widen your frame and perform your role as a service learner with greater awareness, greater integrity, and greater effectiveness?

PART THREE

Facilitating Learning and Meaning-Making Inside and Outside the Classroom

The goal of part three (chapters 6–10) is to highlight multiple venues for understanding the community-based experience—when things are going well and when things are not going well. Specifically, how can you use reflection to construct meaning and knowledge from your experience, what can be done if the community interaction is a disappointment or is failing, and how can the context and content of the course itself provide direction and insight?

KEY SYMBOLS

 Exercises of utmost importance to complete (working either on your own or in a group)

 Optional exercises (strategies for gaining deeper insights into the issues)

 Exercises that provide further resources and information in your quest for understanding community problem solving and change

CHAPTER 6

Reflection in Action

The Learning–Doing Relationship

PETER J. COLLIER AND DILAFRUZ R. WILLIAMS

I have realized that it is often difficult for people to explain why they believe a certain way. What I have been forced to do in the writing assignments is just that. This process of writing down my views and patterns of thinking took nearly every drop of energy I had.

IN THE PRECEDING CHAPTERS, we have encouraged you to complete a variety of **reflection** exercises on a range of topics from "What Is Citizenship?" to "How Am I in Groups? What, exactly, *is* the process of reflection? How can you as a student train yourself to reflect at deeper and deeper levels in order to maximize your learning and the ways that your learning can inform and impact your life?

Several service-learning researchers (www.compact .org/disciplines/reflection/index.html; Eyler, Giles & Schmiede, 1996) have identified the characteristics of successful reflection:

- **Continuous**: Reflection must take place before, during, and after the completion of the service project to be fully useful.
- **Challenging**: Effective reflection involves pushing ourselves out of our comfort zones to make new connections between concepts and to think in new ways.

- **Connected**: Successful reflection can serve as a bridge between the service experience and our discipline-based academic knowledge.
- **Contextualized**: Effective reflection is framed in a manner that is appropriate for the context in which the service experience takes place.

We've designed the activities in this book to engage you in reflection that is *continuous, challenging, connected,* and *contextualized*. In this chapter, we'll take a closer look at the process of reflection and the necessary components of **deep reflection**.

Why Reflect?

Why is there so much emphasis on reflection in service-learning classes? Reflection serves as a bridge for the back-and-forth connecting between what you as a student learn in class and what you are experiencing in the community. Reflection, within the context of a service-learning class, helps you integrate what you have been absorbing through the course content with the community external to the college campus.

Engaging in reflective practices has been linked to other benefits for students. Mabry (1998) found that, for students in twenty-three different service-learning courses, those who participated in reflection exercises attributed more learning to the service experience than students who participated in the service project but not in reflection exercises. Eyler and Giles (1999) also noted the positive impact that reflection had on academic outcomes for college students. Furthermore, researchers have found that written reflection about emotional events can serve to reduce anxiety and depression (Bringle & Hatcher, 1999; Pennebaker, 1990). In an experimental study in which students wrote for four consecutive days on either traumatic events or superficial topics, Pennebaker, Kiecolt-Glaser, and Glaser (1988) found that students who engaged in reflection on traumatic life events had more favorable immune system responses, less frequent health center visits, and higher reports of subjective well-being. These researchers found that the most important factor that distinguished persons showing health improvement from those who did not was a greater ability to include causal thinking, insights, and self-reflection in their stories. Taken together, research studies suggest that activities that promote personally and academically meaningful reflection on service-learning experiences may result in both intellectual and health-related benefits.

Connecting Reflection to Service-Learning

Psychologist Irwin Altman (1996) identified three distinct kinds of knowledge: ***content knowledge***, which involves the rote learning of facts (for example, that the capital of the state of Oregon is Salem); ***process knowledge***, or skills that involve learning how to do something (like how to search a library database); and ***socially relevant knowledge***, which connects one's personal perspective with content within particular social contexts (for example, how to effect social change through activism). Traditional teaching methods typically produce content and, sometimes, process knowledge. Service-learning, however, involves a kind of teaching and learning that promote both content and process knowledge, as well as developing socially relevant knowledge in students. The key to making this happen is reflection.

I was extremely myopic prior to this class. I had no concept of any of the issues facing today's educator. Now I feel informed and knowledgeable and I believe that there ARE some contributions I can make

to society. I know that my work as a teacher is not only to educate the particular class that I am working with at any given time, but to model excitement about learning and a real passion to be of use in the world.

Building upon ideas originally developed by the pragmatist philosopher John Dewey (1933), within the context of service-learning classes we define "reflection" as "a person's intentional and systematic consideration of an experience, along with how that person and others are connected to that experience, framed in terms of particular course content and learning objectives." Successful service-learning involves reflection—again, an "intentional and systematic consideration of an experience"—before, during, and after the actual service experience. Toole and Toole (2001) posited reflection as being a central feature of the ***Service-Learning Cycle***. As you read about the stages of this cycle, think about how your service-learning experience and the reflection you have done throughout the experience fits into these stages. You might thumb through the previous chapters of this book to match the exercises you've already completed to the stages. Figure 6.1 illustrates the stages.

Pre-service reflection: Reflection plays a critical role in the initial steps of a service-learning project. Already, you have engaged in reflection on your own (and possibly as part of a group) as you identified your service-learning experience and planned for its accomplishment.

1. **Identifying a project**: You completed reflection exercises to increase awareness of important community issues in order to provide a useful frame for determining which community concern you would focus on and which specific project you would undertake.

2. **Planning and preparation**: You completed reflection exercises to try to imagine all the potential problems that could arise with the project as well as possible solutions to each problem that could serve as contingency plans for dealing with unexpected issues related to the project, thus aiding you in the planning and preparation processes.

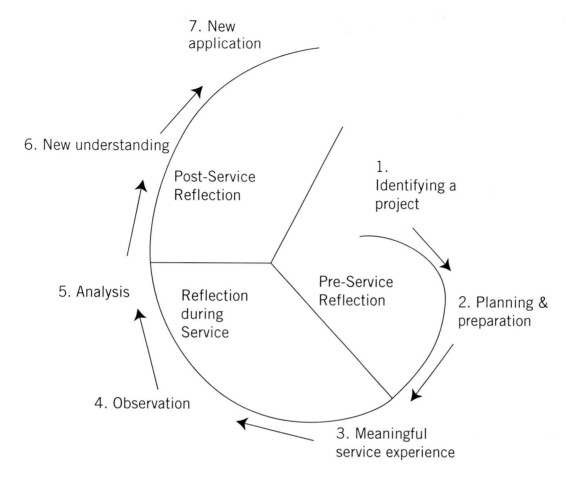

Figure 6.1.   Reflection and the Service-Learning Cycle

From Toole & Toole (2001)

Reflection during service: Reflection will continue to be crucial for the success of your service-learning experience.

3. **Meaningful service experiences**: You will have opportunities for reflecting on how to connect course concepts and academic discipline knowledge with the service experience, along with your own personal reactions and insights.
4. **Observation**: During and immediately after the service experience, you will be guided to describe the project in its social context, as well as your personal reaction to being part of the service experience.
5. **Analysis**: Additional reflection assignments will help you go beyond description and reac-

tion, to applying academic knowledge and course concepts as a means of better understanding the service experience.

Post-service reflection: Reflection will help you further your analysis of the current situation and make larger assessments of what you have accomplished.

6. **New understanding**: You will complete reflection exercises that promote an increased sense of self-awareness about how your understanding of community issues has broadened and deepened as a result of the service-learning class.
7. **New application**: Reflection exercises will encourage you to assess and evaluate the accomplishment of your learning and serving

goals and to review the lessons of your service experience with a "bird's-eye view" perspective. These then will lead you to the identification of issues and/or social contexts where the lessons of your current service-learning experience can be applied to other community engagements to produce positive results.

edge as a means of achieving a desired goal. That goal may be as fundamental as trying to make a more informed decision about whether and how to best offer your services to communities in the future.

Reflection, for Dewey, goes beyond experience. He believed that to really understand an experience, it is imperative to understand how you were connected to or affected by it. As you reflect upon your service-learning experiences, it is important that you place yourself in the middle of the process of connecting the current situation with past experiences and knowledge as a means of achieving a desired goal.

Models of Reflection

As we noted earlier, reflection is the means by which your service experience is linked to learning and learning is manifested as meaning. John Dewey was one of the first thinkers to recognize the important role that reflection plays in learning. Dewey argued that reflection, or reflective thinking, is the key to whether any experience is "educative," meaning that it involves learning (1933). Reflection connects the world of observations and facts with the world of ideas. For Dewey, reflective thinking is what moves a person from mindlessly drifting through life to connecting the current situation with past experiences and knowl-

Kolb (1984) built upon the foundation of Dewey's work on reflective thought in developing the *Experiential Learning Model* (figure 6.2). Experience is the cornerstone of this model, and learning is viewed as a process by which knowledge is created through the transformation of experience. Kolb developed a cyclical model of experiential learning that involves a repeated pattern of "grasping" or comprehending an experience followed by "transforming" that experience into knowledge. This model provides us with a conceptual framework for understanding the organic process of learning through serving.

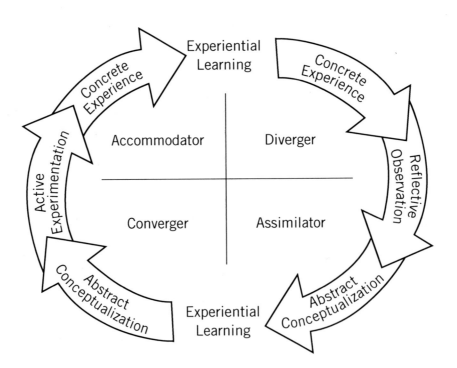

Figure 6.2. Kolb's Experiential Learning Model

Adapted from Kolb (1984)

The stages of Kolb's Experiential Learning Model can be explained using the example of Tina, a student engaging in a hunger awareness publicity campaign at her local food bank. As Tina first begins to spend time at the food bank, she realizes that this service experience is different and distinct from other school or everyday occurrences. In what Kolb calls the **concrete experience** stage of the model, Tina comprehends that this is something fundamentally different from anything she has ever experienced before. If we were to read Tina's journal, she might write an entry like the following:

I never imagined I could have an experience like this as part of a class. My time working at the food bank is drastically different from writing a term paper in another class or even just watching people shop at the food bank on the weekend.

Next, Tina enters the **reflective observation** stage of the model, as she begins to reflect upon her personal reactions to the concrete service experience.

I'm getting more used to it now, but sometimes working at the food bank and seeing so many people come in day after day after day—many of whom look a whole lot like me and my friends and family—is pretty overwhelming. I always assumed that people who didn't have enough to eat simply weren't working hard enough to earn a living or were spending their money stupidly. That just doesn't seem to fit the people I'm meeting.

The initial observation and description of the service experience has now been transformed into something that is personally relevant through the intentional process of reflection.

In the third stage of the model, **abstract conceptualization**, Tina ties in course-related and other previously acquired knowledge and theories to redescribe the service experience from a conceptual rather than a descriptive perspective. Tina might write,

Based on the materials we studied in class on social inequalities and political issues within our state, my service experience at the food bank is more than just a field trip; it is an opportunity to examine firsthand how what appears to be an individ-

ual social issue—for example, hunger—is really the result of societal-level structural inequalities. To think that individual people going hungry in my state is connected to political decisions that have adversely affected independent farmers in our region—frankly, I never understood or really cared about that before.

Finally, during the **active experimentation** stage, Tina uses her new understanding of the service experience developed during the abstract conceptualization stage to stimulate an application of her new understanding of this situation within the context of a set of options for her personal choices in the world.

If hunger in our state is better understood as being caused by societal, rather than individual-level factors, can this same perspective provide me with insights into understanding other problems, such as homelessness and illiteracy? What are the connections between these issues? How might I make sense of these things too?

This experimentation in new settings leads the student back to the beginning of the model—a new concrete experience—and the cycle begins again.

The different aspects of the learning process that make up the four stages of Kolb's model have also been linked to four different learning styles. Each learning style is defined by the stages of the learning process that immediately precede and follow it, and each represents a different set of skills that a student may acquire.

Before we go on, let's take a minute and revisit **Exercise 4.3: Marshmallows and Spaghetti** (p. 53). As you recall, in this exercise each group received a package of spaghetti and a bag of marshmallows. The goal of the exercise was for the group to build the tallest tower possible out of the marshmallows and spaghetti. Now we will illustrate the different learning styles associated with Kolb's model by linking them to the different roles team members may have played in the exercise. (If you didn't complete this exercise, try to imagine what type of learning style most resembles yours.)

Diverger: Kolb describes this learning style as emphasizing *concrete experience* and *reflective observation*. A diverger's strengths include imaginative ability and awareness of the meaning of a situation. A diverger is capable of viewing a problem from a variety of

---

⚡ Exercise 6.1: Reflecting on Community Partnerships Using Kolb's Experiential Learning Model

The following reflection exercise uses the stages of Kolb's model to frame your service-learning experience and help you better understand your interactions with your community partner.

Concrete Experience: Typically, in service-learning classes, the kinds of community partnerships that you experience will involve multiple constituencies—your university, local government and nonprofit agencies, citizen groups, and students. First, think about a situation from your current service-learning class involving other "players" from your community partnership. Next, describe an interaction between yourself and at least one other player from that partnership. As you describe the interaction, make sure to include what you observed, what you and others said, and any nonverbal behaviors that you noted. Try to reserve judgment and be as neutral in your description as possible.

Reflective Observation: How do you feel when you reflect upon the interaction you described? Did the interaction turn out the way you expected it to? If not, what was different? What do you think the community partner expected from the interaction? Reflect upon the assumptions you brought with you about the other people in this relationship before this interaction occurred. What assumptions do you think the community partner had about you?

Abstract Conceptualization: Using materials from this service-learning course and knowledge gained from your academic major, how would you explain the nature of this community partnership? What concepts or theoretical models might help explain both the outcomes of this interaction, as well as the underlying processes? Specifically consider the following:

• What influence does culture have on this interaction?
• What influence does power have on this interaction?
• How does your understanding of service impact this interaction?

Active Experimentation: How have your plans for relating to future community partners changed as the result of your current service-learning experience? Has the experience changed your personal understanding of "service?" If so, how? How will your current understanding of "culture" and "power" impact your interactions with community partners in the future? What would you do differently next time?

---

personal perspectives and then organizing these multiple views into a meaningful description of what's going on. In the exercise, a student who favors a *diverger* learning style might be very active early in the process, coming up with multiple ways that the team could approach the problem—for example, the team could stack marshmallows on top of each other like a tower, or it could connect pairs of marshmallows like tinker toys using a piece of spaghetti, or it could build a pyramid by constructing a wide base of marshmallows supporting vertical pieces of spaghetti that would then support a smaller second story platform of marshmal-

lows with more vertical pieces of spaghetti that finally reach a point. Divergers tend to excel in situations that call for brainstorming and the development of alternative ideas and strategies. Divergers possess good data-gathering skills, tend to be sensitive, and are interested in people.

Assimilator: The emphasis in this learning style is on *reflective observation* and *abstract conceptualization*. An assimilator is very comfortable using inductive logic, in which one works from observations to make theory. In the exercise, a student who favors an *assimilator* learning style might take a more active role in determining which of the various alternatives makes the most sense for the group to pursue. For example, after comparing the different possibilities from a theoretical design perspective, the assimilator might declare that the pyramid structure is the most architecturally sound and therefore should provide the team with the best chance of creating the tallest structure. Assimilators are particularly valuable in situations that call for the development and creation of theoretical models. Assimilators tend to be more interested in ideas for their own sake than the application of those ideas to practical situations.

Converger: The emphasis in this learning style is on *abstract conceptualization* and *active experimentation*. A converger's strengths include the abilities to problem-solve and make decisions and the willingness to search for the practical uses of ideas and theories. In the exercise, a student who favors a *converger* learning style might focus on the question, "What is the best way to put a pyramid together?" and would be actively involved in construction decisions with the project. The converger will wonder if it will provide more support to use two pieces of spaghetti rather than one to connect the marshmallows on the larger base level to the marshmallows on the smaller second story. A student favoring this learning style tends to perform well in situations where there is a single correct answer and the group task is to identify the "best" solution for a particular problem. Convergers are comfortable using deductive logic, in which they use theory to explain real-life occurrences; they prefer dealing with technical tasks and problems rather than social or interpersonal issues.

Accommodator: The emphasis in this learning style is on *active experimentation* and *concrete experience*. An accommodator's strengths lie in doing things, carrying out plans, and getting involved in new experiences. A student favoring this learning style will do well in situations that require a willingness to adapt to circumstances in order to successfully complete a task. In the exercise, a student who favors an *accommodator* learning style might become active only at a late stage of the actual building process as the exercise time limit is approaching and the team is struggling to make the pyramid design stay together. The accommodator might help modify the pyramid by putting in additional stability supports to prop up the structure so that, while it no longer looks like a pyramid, it is fairly tall and stays together until the assignment is "judged" by the instructor. Accommodators learn best from hands-on

experiences. These individuals are pragmatists—concerned with what works—and are willing to throw away a theory if it means a better way can be found to address a problem. Accommodators tend to rely on people much more than on analysis, but are sometimes perceived by others as pushy because of their focus on getting things done.

We should note that, while Kolb recognizes that individuals typically prefer one learning style over others, he also proposes that, to achieve real learning, students should develop some competence with all four styles. In most traditional learning experiences (such as lecture-format classes), students with assimilator and converger learning styles—styles that emphasize "thinking" activities—seem to be most comfortable. Interestingly, one of the strengths of service-learning classes is that they provide students preferring accommodator and diverger styles—styles that emphasize "doing" activities—with a more compatible learning environment. Kolb maintains that experiential learning involves both "thinking" and "doing," and, regardless of where you "start" (in terms of your preferred learning style) and which teaching approach is used (such as experiential activities in community collaboration), it is imperative that you visit all the stages in the cycle in order to fully integrate the learning experience.

Deep Reflection

You may already have had many course experiences in which you have been asked to reflect. Many instructors assign journals, for example, as a tool for students to record their thoughts and feelings about what they are learning or to write less formally about various subjects. Effective reflection in service-learning classes, however, needs to go deeper than most traditional notions of reflection, beyond a surface description to what anthropologists call a "thick" description (Geertz, 1973). *Thick descriptions* capture the richness of detail in what is observed, as well as the personal connection between the individual and the experience. We propose that deep reflection in service-learning experiences is composed of three components: *observation*, *personal relevance*, and *connection*. To practice deep reflection, you will need to pay attention to all three elements; no one component alone or pair of components is sufficient to connect "thinking" with "doing" in the service experience.

> ☀ **Exercise 6.2: What Is Your Preferred Learning Style?**
>
> Think about the different experiences you have already had in this service-learning course, such as class exercises, working with community partners, group projects, and the contributions that YOU personally made to each of these elements. Which of Kolb's four learning styles—*diverger, assimilator, converger, accommodator*—best describes your preferred style?
>
> To investigate your preferred style, choose a specific example of an element that you have used in this course. Briefly describe the activity or event, and then itemize the ways you participated in it. Looking back on this experience and the learning styles described previously, which learning style did you most fully work from? How has your preferred learning style impacted the collaboration you are part of in this class? What can you learn from others' preferred learning styles to more fully develop your capacities as a learner and a doer?

In 18 years of schooling, I have never really questioned events around me, how I fit in, and how those events affect the way I fit in, until now. Now it seems like that is the major work of this course: to make connections, to understand how one thing is related to another, and how I am related to all of it.

The following descriptions offer ideas for how to practice reflection that is deep and thick. The students represented here were part of a service project to weatherize the homes of low-income and elderly residents. In the quotes that follow the descriptions, listen to how the students have articulated their own deep reflection:

Observation: Describe what you experienced—the setting, the community agencies, and the individuals with whom you interacted:

First off, I found it weird to winterize at the beginning of summer. Our class is meeting during the hottest time of the day, so it can be pretty brutal to be stuck in some attic feeding insulation into the wall. And it takes a good long while, too. But I guess with 200 homes to weatherize a year, the Community Energy Project must spread out the projects throughout the year in order to finish them. Yesterday we helped an elderly woman in a trailer park in Northeast. She and a friend of hers went on

and on about how fortunate she was to have these services for free and how we were a wonderful gift.

Personal relevance: Connect the service experiences to your own reactions and responses. How did you feel? Use "I" statements when talking about your feelings:

It was great for me to see the elderly woman's appreciation for our team and to have her say such nice things to us. I think she appreciated having young people around for a while. I realized that until I volunteered my time with the Community Energy Project, I didn't really have an understanding of what it feels like to make a difference in somebody's life, so that's good. But to be completely honest, as good as it was to have somebody appreciate our work, I just wanted to get out of there, to cool off and take a shower, and get back to my familiar life. I know I'll be ready to do some more houses next week, but for now I need some time to think about things.

Connection: Frame your observations and personal reactions in a context provided by relevant course readings, research, or other materials. How does the content of this service-learning class provide an interpretive lens through which you can better understand other persons' experiences and feelings and the social and political context in which your work was accomplished?

In this class we've been reading about the qualities of effective leadership. I never knew that many, if not most, of the most skilled leaders have made a dedicated commitment to volunteering at some point in their lives. I never thought that there might be particular things I can learn through sacrificing my own time to benefit others, and that this could benefit me in the future. I have been forced to do volunteer work for other leadership classes, but I never truly understood why. Now I know it's because it brings out our true leadership skills. It makes us learn to work with others to accomplish the same goals, and it helps us to learn how to be less selfish, which is a very important characteristic of leadership.

This class has exposed me to concepts that were not previously evident in my educational experience. They may have been present, but through ignorance, not caring, or whatever, I was not aware of them. Although my awareness of the issues presented in this class has developed over the years, never have I personally grown and become more aware of these issues than in the last 11 weeks. At times that growth has been exciting, at times frustrating and agonizing. This class has inserted so many questions into my mind.

The DEAL Model of Critical Reflection

Another framework for promoting deep reflection is the ***DEAL Model of Critical Reflection*** (Ash & Clayton, 2009). DEAL is an acronym for *Describing, Examining,* and *Articulating Learning.*

Building upon Bloom and his colleagues' (1956) ideas that critical thinking is a sequential process, the framework starts with primary responses to students' experiences by asking you to first *describe* what is happening. Once that is accomplished, the analysis process begins. This second stage, *examining,* asks you to think and view the situation from different perspec-

tives. Finally, since learning is assimilated when one shares it with others, the last stage is to *disseminate* your insights and next steps for action.

The DEAL model is especially useful if conflict occurs at a service site. This may be with another student, a client, an instructor, or a community partner. The truth is, serving is emotionally, psychologically, and interpersonally messy (we will deal with these issues even more in chapter 9, "Failure with the Best of Intentions"). Using a framework, like DEAL, can be helpful in understanding causes and possible solutions to conflict.

Consider an uncomfortable or "messy" event that occurred at your current service site. Or, if you have not yet begun one, think about a time when you performed any kind of volunteerism or service to others and things didn't go just right. Then, use the following DEAL model question prompts to help you make new sense of the situation.

(For those of who are doing global service-learning [in a country other than your homeland] or service-learning where you live at the site for a few days or a few weeks [such as Alternate Spring Break or J-term], you may want to review chapter 12, "Global and Immersive Service-Learning," that deals even more with intercultural conflict and reflection.)

Certainly, if you feel that any of the circumstances or events violates ethical, moral, or legal responsibilities then you need to take immediate action to resolve them. Normally, you should report these kinds of messy situations or uncomfortable activities to the community partner or a faculty member as soon as possible (see also chapter 2 for the Pre-Service Checklist of Student Rights). When in doubt, seek out authority figures since no one should feel unsafe.

Still, there is a difference between actually being unsafe and feeling uncomfortable. Certain levels and degrees of being uncomfortable may be a necessary part of the service experience (such as being too hot because you are not used to high levels of humidity if you traveled to a new part of the country or another country).

Also, some mental uncomfortableness (known as cognitive dissonance) may be necessary for learning. Vygotsky (1978) called this the zone of proximal development; if situations are too familiar (or comfortable) we may take them for granted and not learn anything. If situations are too frightening (or uncomfortable) we will reactively try to escape or flee from them and also

Exercise 6.3: The DEAL Model: Reflection to Action

Follow the three sequential steps in the model and specific prompts associated with each step. Write down your responses for later sharing with others.

1. Describe your experience in an objective and detailed manner. (Do not underestimate the importance of details.)

   • Where and when did the incident occur?

   • Who was present, what did they say, what did they do?

   • Who wasn't present, and what wasn't said or done in the way that you expected?

2. Examine these experiences using a "frame" provided by your service-learning class instructor. For example, you might use an academic discipline frame such as psychology, sociology, or women's studies in which to re-review the details you described previously. Do certain elements of the situation now appear different or hold more or less importance?

   You might try using a frame like critical theory, social justice, or issues of privilege and empowerment. You might also apply other conceptual ideas like competition theory, free market capitalism, socialism, maturation theory, cause and effect, trickle-down, diminishing returns, supply and demand, or even the notion of "the path of least resistance." All of these are different frames from which to reexamine what you experienced or encountered.

   If none of these frames seem to work for you, use the assertion that civic engagement is a higher education responsibility. Most colleges have civic engagement as a mission statement or initiative. This may be why your service-learning course exists. So, using civic engagement as frame, consider the following:

   • Who are the different stakeholders involved in regard to this community issue? What is each stakeholder's position in regard to this issue? What coalitions or alliances exist among stakeholders?

   • What efforts have been made to involve a greater number of community members in this issue/decision process? In what ways has your service-learning project impacted efforts to increase community participation in this issue?

3. Articulate your learning. What new insights have you gained about this situation? What can you apply to future actions? These actions include the next time you are at your current service site and goals for future action that you can employ in your next service-learning experience to facilitate subsequent learning.

   • What do you see or understand now that you didn't in the midst of the situation?

   • As you have reframed and reexamined, what new insights do you have about yourself? In general, but also specifically concerning your knowledge, skills, and abilities?

   • What will you do next at the site?

   • How can you apply this learning to future service-learning sites?

not learn anything. Therefore, we need an optimal level of "newness" to force us to think and act in different ways. Then, as we reflect on these new ways of thinking and acting, we begin to determine new future ways of being.

Indeed, it is often the uncomfortableness of service that opens our eyes and minds to learning about the new cultures in which we are engaged, but also our own culture, which we may not have previously reflected upon in a critical manner. This is often the case for students who perform global service-learning. Traveling to another country and the contrasting "foreignness" of that culture to our home culture can bring to light social paradoxes we never considered. Read and reflect on the Spotlight on Service: Blemished and Beautiful In India and America.

In both the Kolb and DEAL models, deepening our reflective capacities about our service-learning may leave us with even more questions than we had when we began reflecting. But that is the whole purpose behind reflection—to offer us a tool for making meaning of our activities so that we recognize and use the learning in future experiences. In other words, reflection leads us to an informed understanding of ourselves, others, and the world in which we are all called to participate as lifelong learners and doers.

We encourage you to discover your own best setting and environment for reflection and to develop your own best practices of reflection. The following is a list of tips, offered by service-learners, to help guide your reflective engagement:

Tips for Successful Reflection Experiences

- Seek out quiet moments. Talking—and being talked to—can be distracting.
- Be attentive to and mindful of the present moment.
- Practice acute observation. Work to decipher the clues in the world around you.
- Figure out what matters most for the task being considered.

Spotlight on Service: Blemished and Beautiful In India and America

At the evening reflection group, Jennifer shared portions of her journal with the class.

> I see extreme beauty in India's art, dress, historical artifacts, temples, and people. But I agonize over the fact that the streets and rivers are polluted and trashed. I am moved by the bright florescent colors of women's silk saris and jasmine scented flowers carefully pinned in their long braids, but am disturbed by the contrasting views of India's landscape filled with plastic and trash.

Jennifer's classmates nodded in agreement. Ramon, a fellow student gently reminded Jennifer, "Remember, our professor forewarned us that keeping an open mind would be difficult at times." Latesha, a third classmate admitted,

> It's hard to be open-minded when you think you're going to die on the rickshaw! For days I thought there weren't any driving rules with all the weaving traffic, no lanes, no blinkers, and constant honking. Then coming back from the market one day the driver swerved to miss a huge hole in the road and the other drivers don't crash into him. I realized then that these are expert drivers with their own rules. Our rules don't apply! It turns out that my initial interpretation was very short-sighted.

Jennifer smiled in appreciation and continued,

> It's true. The visual dissonance makes my head and heart spin. I am simultaneously filled with awe and react with repulsion. I need to learn how to accept and embrace the culture for its wholeness. After all, every country has its good and bad elements. Just think about Portland, how many of us walk down our beautiful tree-lined city streets passing dozens of those who are homeless and not even think about it.

- Make a conscious effort to focus on the experience you're reflecting on.
- Permit yourself to feel emotional.
- Go beyond your "self" and your personal perspective.
- Use the lens of your past experiences to make links to the present.
- Recognize—and think about—the tension between being attached and involved and then stepping back to gain a detached perspective of the situation.

Modes of Reflection

Now that you have read more about the reasons you are asked to reflect in service-learning courses and the ways that you may direct yourself as a reflective thinker, we offer ideas for different modes of reflection. Your professor may have already selected the type of reflection activities you will complete. If not, discuss with him or her the various options. The activities may also be used alone as you process your learning-through-serving experience. Figure 6.3 identifies four primary modes of reflection—telling, activities, multimedia, and writing—along with a few representative examples of each type.

Because each type of reflection exercise has different strengths, the decision about which mode of reflection to use should be based on two major factors:

- **What is the context of your current class?** Perhaps your instructor has very deliberately structured and assigned reflective activities for you and your classmates based on her expertise and experience with service-learning courses. Even if the benefits of completing the reflective assignment in the way she has indicated are not apparent to you, follow her guidelines. In fact, you might deepen your own reflection on the assignment by investigating your ideas about why the instructor chose to frame the assignment in the way she did. What impact does this framing have on you? What did you learn as a result of completing this reflection in this way? How might you use this particular reflective assignment to understand your experience more fully? What questions do you now have as a result of having completed this reflection?
- **What is the best means for telling the story of your service experience?** Whether or not your instructor has assigned reflective activities for you and your classmates, you may choose to practice reflection both formally and informally beyond the scope of those assignments. In creating your own reflective opportunities, you may experience greater freedom in using new and different modes of reflection than you

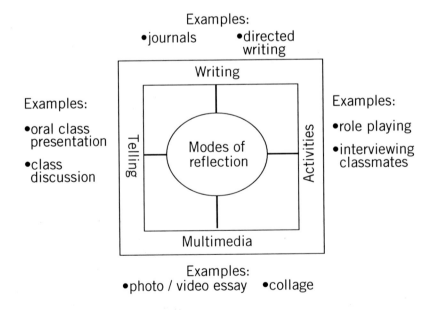

Figure 6.3. Modes of Reflection

have in past courses. Sometimes photos, drawings, collages, or videos may capture the essence of a service experience with much greater clarity than written words. Remember, whatever form your service-learning reflection takes, the underlying elements of deep reflection—observation, personal relevance, and connection—need to be present.

Telling

Reporting our insights orally to others is a great way to deepen our understanding of those insights. Storytelling remains one of the most important ways that humans transmit information to each other. The benefits of storytelling, however, don't only apply to those listening to the story; the teller, too, has his or her understanding enhanced through the act of communicating it to others.

In a formal way, oral presentations can offer several advantages in service-learning courses: providing students with opportunities to practice their public speaking skills, allowing the use of nonverbal behaviors to reinforce an emotional message, and providing the starting point for dialogue between different stakeholders in the service project. Other less formal examples of "telling" reflection activities can include talking casually about the service experience with classmates or with others outside the service-learning experience.

> ？ For an example of "telling" as reflection, see **Exercise 6.5: Telling the Tale**, on page 109.

Activities

Activities, projects, and other forms of "reflection through action" can also offer some specific advantages in meaning-making. Often, these sorts of exercises speak to a variety of learning styles, help to develop groups, and allow forward momentum to be built into the project.

If you are interested in exploring these experiential ways of reflecting, you might choose to spend time, on your own, in the environments experienced by the persons you are serving. For example, if you are tutoring refugees in basic English-language skills, you might spend a day attempting to read a newspaper or follow directions in a language you do not know. If you are writing grant proposals for a camp for stroke survivors and their families, you might spend time living as if you had limited use of language or movement. If you choose to reflect in this very experiential way on your role as a service-learner, remember chapter 5 and the importance of behaving and interacting with integrity around the differences between you and those your service impacts.

> ？ For an example of using activities as reflection, see **Exercise 6.6: Showtime**, on page 110.

Multimedia

Collages, drawings, photo or video essays, and other forms of multimedia reflection offer additional advantages for the reflector through incorporating multiple learning styles, serving as excellent tools for capturing subtle emotional truths, and providing great opportunities for creative expression. If you choose to explore multimedia reflection, you might collect objects from your service site to create a visual representation of your community-based experience. (Be careful about the use of confidential materials, making sure to get permission before collecting any items.) Consider writing a piece of music to capture the essence of your service to the community. You might also paint a picture that captures the community-based experience or that expresses your vision of how the community will be changed for the better by your collaborative efforts.

> ？ For an example of using multimedia tools as reflection, see **Exercise 6.7: Every Picture Tells a Story**, on page 110.

Writing

For many students in service-learning projects, the predominant form that their reflection takes is written. Written reflection techniques offer several unique advantages compared to other modes: They provide an opportunity to practice and refine writing skills, challenge us to organize our thoughts in order to make coherent arguments, and generate a permanent record of the service experiences that can be used as part of future learning activities.

Written reflection can take a variety of forms, including directed assignments, in which a writer responds to topics framed by an instructor; portfolios, in which a student compiles multiple pieces of evidence to demonstrate what he or she has learned; and journals, which might track the evolution of thought throughout a period of time. In this service-learning course, your instructor very likely has assigned you written reflections. In addition to these assignments, you might choose to engage in self-directed writing activities to fully mine the depth of your community-based experience.

> ✎ For an example of writing as reflection, see **Exercise 6.8: Newsflash**, on page 110.

While journals can take a variety of forms, certain types have distinctive characteristics and focus. For example, exercise 6.8 is a directed writing assignment and may be thought of as a **structured journal**, a format that most closely resembles a series of directed writing assignments. In assigning a structured journal, your course instructor or campus service-learning coordinator will provide you with topics or key questions to focus each specific assignment and may leave room on each journal page for her feedback.

A **critical incident journal** takes a completely different approach. Instead of the instructor telling you what the important topics are to reflect upon, you, the student, are asked to identify a "pivot" or "turning point" in your own service-learning experience. Reflection is focused on this key situation or event in which a decision was made, a conflict occurred, or a problem was resolved. This can help to focus your attention on the idea that not all events have equal significance in realizing the goals of a service-learning project and encourage you to identify those particularly meaningful events.

A **role-taking**, or **shift-in-perspective**, **journal** differs from either of the previous types because, even though you are writing in the journal, you are asked to take on the perspective of some other participant in the service experience. Instead of asking you to reflect on the meaning of the class service experience to you, this format encourages you to reflect upon key questions and aspects of the community issue being addressed from a different perspective—for example, community members or the director of the community agency you are partnering with—rather than as students. Such perspective taking can enhance compassion and acceptance of others.

Finally, a **triple-entry journal** (exercise 6.4) is a format that works very well for promoting "deep reflection." In it, you will reflect upon three distinct issues in each journal entry by (a) describing what happened during your service experience, including what was accomplished as well as things that puzzled you (*observation*); (b) analyzing how aspects of course content apply to the service experience and how these theories and concepts help you understand what occurred (*connection*); and (c) applying the course materials and the service experience to your own life, particularly with regard to how you will approach similar experiences in the future (*personal relevance*).

Why Reflect? Revisited

We reflect to understand where we have been, what we have experienced, and where we go from here. In this chapter, we went beyond a mere definition of "reflection" to investigate its theoretical underpinnings and underlying processes. You have learned why reflection may be especially important for community-based learners and have investigated multiple modes for practicing reflection. You have expanded (and will continue to expand) your reflective capacities by starting with the activities assigned by your instructor and developing a more fully self-directed and continuous commitment to practice reflection on your own.

While most reflection techniques focus on the positive outcomes of service experiences, others, such as the critical incident journal, draw attention to the fact that learning through reflection can occur even "when things go wrong" in a service-learning class. Chapter 9, "Failure with the Best of Intentions: When Things Go Wrong," explores the issue of dealing with unexpected challenges in the community setting in greater detail.

Exercise 6.4: Triple-Entry Journal

Use the format from the sample triple entry journal (appendix 6.1, p. 111) to reflect upon your next several experiences at your service project site. Make at least two complete entries during the course of the week, preferably directly after a meaningful interaction or event. At the end of the week, go back and reread your entries. Do they accurately capture what you experienced? How do these entries compare with your previous journaling efforts?

Key Concepts

abstract conceptualization	DEAL Model of Critical Reflections	Service-Learning Cycle
accommodator		shift-in-perspective journal
active experimentation	deep reflection	
assimilator	diverger	socially relevant knowledge
concrete experience	process knowledge	
content knowledge	reflection	structured journal
converger	reflective observation	thick description
critical incident journal	role-taking journal	triple-entry journal

Key Issues

- How does reflection promote learning?
- How do differences in learning styles affect learning?
- What is necessary to turn simple description into deep reflection?
- What are the strengths of different modes of reflection?
- How can reflection help you understand your service-learning experiences using new frames and perspectives?

ADDITIONAL EXERCISES

 Exercise 6.5: Telling the Tale

Pair up with another classmate who was not part of your team in "Marshmallows and Spaghetti." In two minutes, tell your classmate the story of your experiences building the marshmallow and spaghetti structure. In the next two minutes, answer any questions your classmate has about the story you just told.

Reverse roles. Repeat the process, with your classmate now telling you about her experiences.

For a final two minutes, discuss together how having to respond to questions about your story affected your own understanding of the experience.

☝ Exercise 6.6: Showtime

Have each team from "Marshmallows and Spaghetti" sit down together for 15 minutes to develop a five-minute skit about the group's experiences building the tower. Everyone on the team must have a role in the skit, and everyone must play another person.

When it is your team's turn, present your skit to the rest of the class. How is your own understanding of your experience affected by taking on another student's role? How is your understanding affected by observing other teams' skits? What insights have you gained by watching this reenactment of the activity?

☝ Exercise 6.7: Every Picture Tells a Story

Along with the other members of your team from the "Marshmallows and Spaghetti" exercise, gather magazine and newspaper photos, cartoons, advertisements, pieces of text, and even your own drawings that relate to your group's experience completing this building exercise. Put together a group collage on a large piece of poster board. When presenting the collage to your class, have each member of the team explain how at least one section of collage relates to his or her personal experience with this group project. How does the group's reflection on building the marshmallow and spaghetti structure, as shown in the collage, relate to your own understanding of your experience? Did the experience of making the collage itself reinforce any of the group's dynamics from "Marshmallows and Spaghetti"? If so, how?

☝ Exercise 6.8: Newsflash

Imagine that you are a newspaper reporter assigned to write a "human interest" article on your team's experiences completing the "Marshmallows and Spaghetti" exercise. First, come up with a headline for your story. Next, follow the steps of basic journalism as you answer the following questions: Who? What? When? Where? With what results? Finally, pretend that you, the reporter, are interviewing you, the student, and answer two final questions: "What did you learn from this experience?" and "How does this relate to the other material you've learned in this course?"

After asking yourself these questions, write that newspaper article. What new insights have you gained about your participation in this activity after interviewing yourself and crafting a news piece from that interview?

☝ Exercise 6.9: Reflecting on Reflection, Revisited

Take a moment and reflect on the process of reflection. From your own personal experiences as a reflective thinker, what, if any, are the benefits of reflection? How do you feel when you reflect upon your service-learning experience? How do you feel when you are able to connect course concepts with what has occurred at your service-learning project site? Which do you think is more important—"doing" the service project or being able to make the connection among course concepts, your personal values, and the service experience? Explain your position.

Appendix 6.1: Triple-Entry Journal

Section 1: Describe the situation.

Section 2: Connect course materials to the described situation.

Section 3: How does the combination of class materials and the service experience relate to your personal life and how you might approach similar situations in the future?

CHAPTER 7

Mentoring

Relationship Building for Empowerment

PETER J. COLLIER

MANY SERVICE-LEARNING experiences include tutoring, coaching, or assisting others with academic or personal challenges. Peer-to-peer relationships have been shown to positively affect college student learning in a range of areas, including interpersonal competence, cognitive processing, and humanitarianism (Kuh, 1995). In service-learning classes, peer-to-peer interactions can also serve as vehicles for empowering yourself and others in the community your project serves and as well as in your service-learning class. This chapter explores peer-to-peer relationships that are directly linked to empowerment and capacity building, specifically, mentoring.

Mentoring

Mentoring occurs when a senior person or mentor provides information, advice, and emotional support to a junior person or mentee over a period of time (National Academy of Sciences, 2008). **Hierarchical mentoring** occurs between two individuals who occupy different social positions or social locations (see chapter 5), for example, a senior manager and a junior manager, a faculty member and a college student, a college student and a high school student.

In contrast, **peer mentoring** occurs in a relationship where a more experienced student (mentor) helps a less experienced student (mentee) improve his or her overall academic performance by providing advice,

support, and knowledge to the mentee (Colvin & Ashman, 2010). Unlike hierarchical mentoring, peer mentoring matches mentors and mentees who are roughly equal in age and power to provide task and psychosocial support. While a peer mentor may be slightly older than a mentee, there is a considerable difference in each one's level of experience in the college context.

Dual-Function Model of Mentoring

Discussions of the benefits mentoring provides are based on Kram's (1985) work on mentoring relationships in a business context, where she proposes that mentoring relationships serve two primary functions: career development and psychosocial support. This **dual-function model of mentoring** is sustained in the higher education research literature with agreement that a mentoring experience may include both forms of support: career development (e.g., helping a mentee become a successful student) and psychological support (helping a mentee feel connected to the campus community).

Peer-to-Peer Mentoring in Higher Education

In higher education, peer mentoring has sparked significant interest among college and university administrators as an intervention to potentially improve the retention, academic success, and educational experience of their students. Among public four-year colleges and universities included in the ACT 2010 What

Works in Student Retention Survey, 65 percent of respondents reported peer mentoring programs. These programs, along with complementary enhanced academic support in other areas (tutoring, counseling, financial aid), are part of a coordinated effort to create campus climates that contribute to the retention and academic success of students, particularly those new to the campus and at risk of dropping out (Pascarella & Terenzini, 2005).

Peer Mentoring and the Career Support Function in Higher Education

Peer mentoring helps mentees learn how to be successful college students through role modeling, and in the process it promotes academic success. *Role modeling* involves mentors' demonstrating to mentees how to act in ways typical of successful college students. Mentors share time-tested strategies and practical advice for dealing with important college adjustment issues such as applying for financial aid, taking notes in lecture classes, or other college study survival skills. Not surprisingly, peer mentoring has been shown to have a positive impact on mentees' grade point average, yearly number of credits, and retention rates.

Pagan and Edwards-Wilson (2002) concluded that peer-mentoring programs are especially effective in improving retention rates of vulnerable first-generation (i.e., the first in their family to attend college) students who often are not familiar with the culture of higher education or the most effective ways to achieve their academic goals. For example, in the Midwest Campus Compact Citizen-Scholar Fellowship Program, 450 student fellows (mentees), supported by 150 peer mentors, provide direct service in multiple community projects. In addition to the valued service to the community they provided, the student mentees, many of whom are first-generation or low-income students, demonstrated higher retention rates and levels of academic success than a comparison group of similar (i.e., Pell Grant eligible) students (Cress, Burack, Giles, Elkins & Stevens, 2010).

Peer Mentoring and the Psychosocial Support Function in Higher Education

Further research indicates that college student mentees highly value the support provided by peer mentoring relationships. Interestingly, perceived mentor support can result in a range of different positive outcomes for mentees, including increased campus connection, higher levels of motivation, and improved mentee self-efficacy. In other words, it makes students like you feel differently and gain new meaning of the value of a college degree.

One way peer mentoring positively affects student retention is by increasing mentees' engagement with their own education. Astin's (1977, 1984) involvement model of college student success and persistence proposes that the extent to which a student is engaged and involved in the actual process of her or his education is an excellent predictor of academic success and degree completion. Peer mentoring promotes increased mentee involvement in learning through the combination of role modeling (e.g., demonstrating the positive effects of involvement) and increased campus connection (e.g., increasing awareness of opportunities for mentees to become more actively engaged in their own education).

Peer mentors provide mentees with strategies for college success (i.e., important information about how to successfully enact the student role) that the mentee was previously unfamiliar with. At the same time, by encouraging mentee reflection the mentor can help the mentee recognize that he or she may already have useful information about student success that the mentee does not realize he or she has. In a California Campus Compact Youth-to-College program that paired underrepresented disadvantaged high school youth with college students in service-learning projects, 90 percent of the students reported that through their service-learning experiences they had a better understanding of how a college education could help their future (Cress, Stokamer, & Drummond Hays, 2010).

In-Person versus Online Mentoring

Traditionally, college student peer mentoring programs have relied on in-person, face-to-face interaction to deliver support services (e.g., Hoffman & Wallach, 2005), though the number of **online** or **e-mentoring programs** is increasing (e.g., Bierema & Merriam, 2002). Is one approach necessarily any better than the other? As part of a year-long program to promote first-generation freshman student retention and academic performance, Collier, Fellows, and Holland (2008) tested the relative effectiveness of online and a combination of online and in-person peer mentoring and found that the kinds of information and support provided, rather than how it was provided, was most important to mentee success. Students in the online mentoring group earned comparable grade point averages, completed the same yearly number of credits, and demonstrated comparable retention rates as the in-person mentoring students; both groups of mentored students outperformed the average rates of all university freshmen.

One suggestion for improving the likelihood of success for online mentoring programs is to have an initial face-to-face meeting between the mentor and mentee to establish rapport and mentor credibility. Credibility has two components: expertise and trustworthiness. *Expertise* is the source's degree of knowledge of factual information associated with the issue in question, while *trustworthiness* is the degree to which the source is perceived as being likely to share this related factual information (Hovland, Janis, & Kelley, 1953). Mentors can establish their perceived credibility with mentees in several ways. Mentors demonstrate their expertise to mentees by sharing their own stories of successfully dealing with the same issues the mentees are facing. As the mentors and mentees are currently college students, there is a common perception of trustworthiness because of similarities between them.

Mentors can establish their credibility by helping their mentees realize the extent of their own knowledge. Even as they struggle to address important college adjustment issues, such as how to successfully approach their professors, mentees many times have more potential strategies available to them than they initially realize. The new Johari Window is a useful tool for mentors to help mentees develop their own successful problem-solving approaches.

The Johari Window

The Johari Window (named after its inventors, Joseph Luft & Harry Ingham [1955]) is a model for describing the process of human interaction. A four-paned window divides personal awareness into four types represented by the following four quadrants of the window (see figure 7.1):

- **Open**: something I know about me and you also know about me
- **Hidden**: what I know about myself that you do not know
- **Blind**: something you know about me that I am unaware of

Figure 7.1. The Johari Window

- **Unknown**: information I do not know about myself and that you do not know either

The lines dividing the four panes serve as window shades that can move as the interaction progresses and previously unrevealed knowledge of self is made public. The window is a metaphor to show how a person's self-awareness increases through interaction. The goal is to increase the size of the open pane of the window, thus increasing meaningful interaction with others.

Facilitating Self-Awareness

Several exercises from chapter 5 could be useful in facilitating your self-awareness before beginning the Johari Window exercise. **Exercise 5.5: Investigating Privilege**, and **Exercise 5.6: Mapping My Social Location**, can be helpful in understanding how social identity, based on the groups you belong to, affects how you perceive others.

Also, take a moment to review the material from the first step of **Exercise 5.2: I and We and You and Us and Them**. The first three prompts could be particularly useful to you as you try to make sense of your interactions with others in your community service site (see Luft & Ingram [1955] for more information about the Johari Window).

The New Johari Window: How Mentoring and Reflection Promote Mentee Success

The format of the **New Johari Window**, shown in table 7.1, is useful for demonstrating how the combination of mentoring and reflection can work together to increase mentee knowledge of how to be successful in the mentoring context (e.g., college track in high school, first year of college).

In this new model of the Johari Window, reflection has an effect on the open and hidden cells, while mentoring affects the missing and oblivious cells.

Open cell is information the mentee has that he or she is aware he or she possesses. To tap into relevant knowledge the mentee already has, the mentor encourages mentee reflection through direct questioning:

- "Could you tell me the kinds of things you will need to be able to do to succeed in doing X?"
- "How adequate do you feel your skills are in regard to each of the things you identified needing to be able to do to succeed in doing X?"

Hidden cell is information the mentee has that he or she is not initially aware that he or she possesses. To tap into a mentee's relevant tacit knowledge, a mentor should encourage reflection, which helps the mentee uncover knowledge and skills the mentee might not initially think he or she possesses. Two reflection techniques that promote the retrieval of tacit knowledge by mentees are **generative interviewing** and **thinking by analogy**. In generative interviewing (Peet, Walsh, Sober, & Rawak, 2010) the mentor/interviewer prompts the mentee to tell stories about specific learning and work or life experiences (the types of stories depend upon the purpose of the reflection). From these stories, the mentor/interviewer identifies an initial set of patterns and themes that reflect the

Table 7.1: The New Johari Window		
Who Knows What?		
Information	*Mentee knows*	*Mentee doesn't know*
Information mentee has	Open: things mentee knows he or she knows	Hidden: tacit knowledge; stuff the mentee does not realize he or she knows, either because the mentee "takes knowledge for granted," or because it is some key action that has become automatic because the mentee does it so often he or she has separated the instrumental function of the task—getting the work done—from the actual skills involved in doing the task
Information mentee does not have	Missing: things mentee knows that he or she does not know	Oblivious: information that is relevant to success in this domain or role that the mentee does not even include in his or her current understanding of the minimum level of competencies needed to be successful in this domain

mentee's tacit knowledge. These initial patterns and themes are shared with the mentee and validated, and then tested against additional stories.

Thinking by analogy is a reflection approach a mentor can use to help the mentee recognize that skills from an apparently non-related area could be adapted to address an issue in the current domain (e.g., college). The thinking by analogy process involves three steps:

1. Identifying the issue the mentee needs to address (e.g., how to approach different professors to get questions answered).
2. Asking the mentee to reflect on similar experiences from other areas of the mentee's life (e.g., family, work, team sports, socializing, traveling) that the mentor believes could be relevant in dealing with the current issue. This involves the mentor's *identifying the underlying process* involved in addressing this issue (e.g., different authority figures need to be approached differently) and then *identifying potentially relevant areas from the*

mentee's experience where issues involving this same process had to be dealt with (e.g., how to approach each parent differently, how to approach different managers at current job, how to approach different coaches on a sports team).

3. Probing (i.e., asking questions to help clarify problem-solving strategies) and connecting (i.e., explaining how using a similar strategy in the current situation might work) by the mentor helps the mentee realize he or she has viable tools for addressing an issue the mentee did not initially acknowledge. Potentially useful probes involve *requesting elaboration* ("Could you tell me a little bit more about that?"), *requesting a definition* ("What do you mean when you say X?") and *requesting clarification* ("Please explain your last statement.").

Missing cell is information the mentee is aware exists but he or she does not possess. Mentoring is

---

✵✵ Exercise 7.1: Thinking by Analogy

The thinking by analogy reflection technique involves three steps:

1. Identifying an issue. You can pick one of the following issues to use in this exercise or identify another issue related to your current mentoring project:

   - (for a high school student) how to identify and apply for college scholarships
   - (for a high school student) how to prepare to take the SAT or ACT
   - (for a new college freshman) how to figure out professors' expectations for assignments
   - (for a new college freshman) how to locate classrooms on new campus
   - (for a new college freshman) how to feel more connected to new campus

   Question 1: What is your issue?

2. Identifying other potentially similar experiences

   Question 2a: Explain the underlying process relating to the issue that must be addressed.
   Question 2b: Drawing from your own experience, explain how you see issues involving the same process playing out in one or more other areas of your own/the mentee's life.

3. Probing and connecting

   Question 3a: (probing) Drawing from your own experience, what problem solving strategies did you use in dealing with similar issues in the other areas you identified in Question 2b?
   Question 3b: (connecting) Explain how your problem solving strategies in other areas (response to Question 3a) could be used in trying to address your issue (from Question1).

the key to helping a mentee gain this information the mentee is already aware he or she does not have. For example, a mentee recognizes that the professor may be the best source of clarification on how to best prepare for an exam but at the same time not be clear about the best or most appropriate way to approach the professor. Because of the mentor's greater experience in the context, he or she has already worked out strategies that have proven effective in addressing this issue. By sharing these strategies, the mentor helps the mentee move from knowing there is important information missing and not knowing how to go about acquiring it to actually acquiring that information.

Oblivious cell, for example, is the successful college student role information the mentee does not possesses and is not even aware that it is important to student success. The mentee does not know he or she is missing key information that is very important to college student success. Because the mentee is oblivious to the importance of this information, he or she does not even include it in his or her current understanding of the minimum level of competencies needed to be a successful college student.

This is another situation where mentoring can help. The mentor not only identifies the issue as important but can also share appropriate strategies that have a high likelihood of success in addressing the issue, as well as any available resources for addressing the issue, all of which are based on the mentor's previous experience or expertise in this domain or role. Many times it is most helpful for mentees for mentors to share their own stories about how they learned to successfully address the same issue the mentee is facing. By accepting the mentor's advice, the mentee swaps a poor likelihood of success strategy (i.e., process of trial and error based on a minimal number of not necessarily good strategies known to the novice) for dealing with important previously unknown issues for a high likelihood of success strategy that has already been proven to be effective in how to address the issue. Through mentoring, the complex process of decision making involving multiple alternatives is replaced with simple judgment: Is the mentor trustworthy?

To illustrate how the New Johari Window could be used in a service-learning project, consider the following vignette about a college student mentor, Tamara, and her high school mentee, William.

Don't Forget the Next Step

As a mentor it is very rewarding to see the mentee's self-confidence and self-esteem grow as he or she recognizes capacities and problem-solving skills the mentee may not have, may not have had in the past, or even realized he or she had, but don't stop there. This is a golden moment, an opportunity to prime your mentee for even more growth through additional reflection. Encourage your mentee to consider how to apply the problem-solving approaches identified through the New Johari Window exercise to other situations, now and in the future. A useful set of prompts for encouraging this type of reflection in your mentee can be found in step 3 of exercise 6.3. Remember, a good mentor looks for any opportunity to facilitate mentee growth and learning.

Summary

Even though peer-to-peer relationships have been shown to positively affect college student success in multiple areas, many times students underestimate the positive impact they can have on other students. In this chapter, we have explored peer-to-peer mentoring relationships that are directly linked to empowerment and capacity building. Through your service-learning class, you have opportunities for empowering yourself and others in the community your project serves as well as in your service-learning class.

Recommended Readings

Cress, C., Burack, C., Giles, D., Elkins, J., & Stevens, M. (2010). *A promising connection: Increasing college access and success through civic engagement.* Boston: Campus Compact.

Kuh , G. D. (1995). The other curriculum: Out-of-class experiences associated with student learning and personal development. *Journal of Higher Education, 66*(2), 123–155.

Peet, M. R., Walsh, K., Sober, R., & Rawak, C. S. (2010). Generative knowledge interviewing: A method for knowledge transfer and talent management at the University of Michigan. *International Journal of Educational Advancement, 10,* 71–85.

Smith, B. (2007). Accessing social capital through the academic mentoring process. *Equity & Excellence in Education, 40*(1), 36–46.

Vignette: Mentoring, Serving, and Learning: Looking through the New Johari Window

William is part of a neighborhood improvement group that is trying to promote community empowerment and pride through a tree-planting project that will not only make the neighborhood look nicer but will also help cool houses in the neighborhood by increasing the amount of shade. His mentor, Tamara, is a college student who is part of a service-learning class whose members are mentoring neighborhood youth in getting the neighborhood tree-planting project off the ground. The mentor-mentee pair has been given the task of coming up with a plan to disseminate information on the project and its potential value to the neighborhood to residents. Tamara starts by asking William, "Let's think about what we're going to need in order to complete our task. What do we need to have set up before we even start to try and get information out to the community?" He thought for a minute and replied, "Seems like we'll need as much information as we can get about the value of tree planting for the neighborhood and what neighbors have to do to maintain the trees once they are planted; plus, we'll need some organized way to get that information out to the neighborhood. Those seem like such big tasks; I'm not sure what to do first." Tamara uses the New Johari Window to help her mentee figure out the best way to proceed with these tasks.

The mentor initially focuses on the *open cell*, information about solving the problem that the mentee already knows. Tamara said to William directly, "Imagine I am one of your neighbors, and tell me what you already know about why it is valuable to the neighborhood and me personally to participate in this tree planting program." William replied, "I know some things because of the training we received in our neighborhood group. One reason that planting a tree in front of your house will be valuable to you is that you will get to enjoy the beauty of that tree all year round. A second reason is that as the tree matures, the shade it provides will help cool your house in the hot summer months, so you won't have to spend money on electricity to run fans or an air conditioner. Planting a tree will benefit you and the entire neighborhood because a tree-lined block will increase the value of all the homes on the block. Also, if we could get each homeowner in the city to plant one tree, the overall air quality would improve because of the oxygen the trees give off."

Tamara then shifted her attention to the *missing cell* of the model, trying to identify information William knows is important to make a compelling argument for his neighbors to participate in the program but that he also knows he does not possess at this time. "William, that's a good list of reasons to participate, but can you think of any other information you know you'll need before you'll feel you're ready to explain the project to your neighbors?" William replied, "I'm worried people are going to ask me to provide details about how the trees are going to be planted, how they need to be maintained . . . gardening stuff. I don't know much about gardening, but I know that is going to come up." Tamara thought for a minute, then said, "I know a couple of the other mentors from my class who can help. Hector's family owns a nursery, and Cally's active in the community garden program. We can get the information we need about planting and maintaining the trees from them. Is there anything else?"

When William said that was all the information he needed, Tamara shifted her focus to the *oblivious cell* of the model, information that the mentee does not possesses and is not even aware that it is important. Tamara continued, "There are a couple of issues homeowners might raise that we haven't talked about. First, we'll need to reassure homeowners that we will have the city come out to identify power cables and water lines before we start any new digging project. Second, we'll need to get information from the city about the extent of the homeowners' responsibility for collecting and disposing of fallen leaves." William was surprised; initially he had not really considered either of those issues, though now he could see they were important.

Tamara continued, "One thing we haven't talked about is an organized way of getting this information out to the community." William replied, "I really don't have an experience with this community organizing stuff. It is all pretty new to me." Tamara shifted the focus to the *hidden cell* of the model, relevant information the mentee possesses but does not know he or she possesses it. "William, can you think of any time you did any fund-raising activities for your school, church, or sports team?" He replied, "Last year the members of our football team went around the neighborhood collecting empty pop cans and bottles for the return money so we could help buy uniforms. We raised a lot of money." Tamara pressed him a little," What were some of the things that made that project so successful?" William thought for a minute, "We divided up into groups of three because it's harder to say no to three kids than just one, and each team concentrated on the houses that were closest to where each player lived, so they were asking people who knew them to help. We all wore our football jerseys when we went door to door, so the people could see we were really football players." Tamara continued, "How can we use those strategies that worked so well in your football project, to help us get the information about the tree-planting one?" William immediately made the connection, "We'll divide up the neighborhood into three- or four-block areas and have pairs of kids—so it's harder to say no—from my youth organization concentrating on blocks of houses in the immediate vicinity of where the kids live, so they'll be contacting neighbors who know them. And we'll all wear our neighborhood tree-planting project T-shirts so everyone will know who we represent."

William met with Hector and Cally to get the information about planting and maintaining trees and contacted the utility company to get information about how residents could have the city come identify where buried power lines were on their property, and Tamara helped him get the information from the city sanitation department about residents' responsibilities in disposing of fallen leaves. He presented his proposed approach to the larger community improvement group, and they enthusiastically adopted his plan. When Tamara congratulated him on doing such a thorough job, William said, "You helped me realize I knew more about doing this than I thought."

✿ Exercise 7.2: You're an Expert . . . and You May Not Know It!

Just as mentee reflection is crucial for unpacking tacit knowledge the mentee already possesses in the *hidden cell*, mentor reflection is important in identifying knowledge and problem-solving strategies the mentor hopes to share with the mentee in the *oblivious cell*. You may be initially aware of some of your preferred problem-solving strategies, but others may only become clear after you unpack taken-for-granted assumptions.

Return to the issue you identified in **Exercise 7.1: Thinking by Analogy**. Based on everything you now know, what is the best strategy for addressing that issue? Why do you believe this is the best approach? What other approaches have you tried to best address this issue? Pull together a story (or stories) based on your experiences that illustrate why your chosen problem-solving strategy works better than some other approaches you have tried.

Do not underestimate the power of personal stories as a means of illustrating the advice you are sharing with your mentee. Many times mentees report learning as much about problem solving from more experienced students' stories of approaches that didn't work as those that did. As a mentor you are more of an expert than you may give yourself credit for.

Key Concepts

dual-function model of
   mentoring
e-mentoring

hierarchical mentoring
New Johari Window

online mentoring
peer mentoring

Key Issues

- What are some ways a mentor could build initial rapport with a mentee?
- What are some of the potential advantages of online mentoring? Are there any potential limitations?
- How would the dual-function model explain the positive impact of mentoring on college student success and persistence?
- How do mentoring and reflection work together in the New Johari Window model to increase mentee knowledge of how to be successful?

CHAPTER 8

Leadership and Service-Learning

Leveraging Change

PETER J. COLLIER

A S YOU MAY RECALL, the purpose of this book is to help you learn how you can best provide significant, meaningful service to a community group or organization while gaining new skills, knowledge, and understanding that you can apply to multiple situations beyond your current service-learning project. In chapter 3, we learn that leaders are change agents who apply their skills and knowledge to effect positive outcomes. In chapter 4, we explore group interaction and include tips on how to improve the functioning and productivity of groups through healthy interaction with others as well as identifying different roles within a group that are necessary for a group to succeed. Indeed, collaboration and motivating others toward common goals are hallmarks of the Seven Cs of leadership development (consciousness of self, congruence, commitment, collaboration, common purpose, controversy with civility, and citizenship), discussed in chapter 3.

Models of Leadership

While issues of leadership in groups have been important throughout human history (e.g., How did the Philistines determine that Goliath was the best person to lead them in their conflict with the Israelites?), understanding leadership as an empowerment mechanism

---

✯ Exercise 8.1: A Leader You Admire

We encounter leaders in many different parts of our everyday lives: family, work, politics, community groups, religious groups, sports teams, and social movements. We learn about famous leaders from the past in history books and about those from the present through news media. We value leaders for different reasons, including getting things done, promoting specific social values, and empowering others. For the first part of this exercise, pick a leader from any area of life whom you admire and answer the following questions:

• Who is the leader you most admire?
• How has this person demonstrated that she or he is an effective leader?
• What qualities does he or she have that you think contribute to the person's being an effective leader?

---

is particularly important in service-learning projects. Let's examine a number of different theories about how leaders come to be.

Some People Are Just Born to Lead
The **great person theory of leadership** suggests that some people, because of personality or other unique characteristics, are destined to lead. One of the first proponents of this model was the English essayist, Thomas Carlyle (1891). The kinds of characteristics first examined—physical attributes (e.g., size, strength, appearance), personality traits (e.g., adjustment, empathy, charisma), and cognitive abilities (e.g., ability to analyze, synthesize, or organize)—did not indicate conclusive findings or better predictions of who should emerge as a group leader. Yet while this model has fallen out of favor with scholars, we still can see examples of leadership decisions seemingly being made based on this concept, especially in U.S. political life (e.g., the Bush family, George H. W., George W., Jeb; the Kennedys, John, Robert, Ted, Patrick).

Being in the Right Place at the Right Time
The **situational model of leadership** focuses on how circumstances and the flow of events, as well as the structure of the physical and social world of the group, act to bring a particular individual, who may simply be at the right place at the right time, into the position of leader. Instead of claiming that great leaders cause great events to happen, this approach sees great events as the product of historical forces and that the great event was going to happen whether the great individual was present or not.

Structural elements of the situation can also influence who becomes the leader of a group. For example, in research on communication networks, it is agreed that since communication is necessary for leadership the person who can communicate most effectively tends to become the leader. In a communication network exemplified by the wheel where all information is channeled through spokes from group members to one individual at the center or hub of the wheel, that person is likely to become the leader primarily because of his or her position in the network (Leavitt, 1951). Place another individual in the key hub position, and the new individual should become the leader.

New Perspectives on Leadership

Because of the complex, diverse nature of the 21st-century world, traditional hierarchical leadership approaches such as the great man or the natural-born leader that may have worked in the past are no longer effective. Rather, community as well as global issues require leaders to include stakeholders and empower others. There is an increased premium on being able to build community and create environments where diverse groups of people can feel comfortable and benefit from membership in that community.

As part of her discussion on how concepts from the new science, that is, quantum physics, chaos theory,

---

Situational Leadership in Action: The Tank Man of Tiananmen Square

On June 5, 1989, in the midst of repeated efforts by the People's Republic of China military forces to break up two weeks of huge protests that had already resulted in hundreds of deaths, Chinese security forces moved a column of 15 tanks into Beijing's Tiananmen Square to disperse an ongoing sit-in of as many as one million Chinese. As the armored column bore down on the seated demonstrators, a single man wearing a white shirt and carrying what appeared to be two shopping bags stood up and moved directly in front of the lead tank. As the tank tried to move around him, he repeatedly repositioned himself in front of it. Finally, he climbed up on the tank and engaged the tank commander in a dialogue, basically asking "Why are you here?" Eventually the tanks withdrew and the image of a single man standing up to the massed power of the largest nation in the world became an iconic global image of the strength of a single individual to make a difference. As reported in a *Time* magazine article (Iyer, 1998), "he stood up against the . . . Great Man of History theory" (see also Witty, 2009).

are affecting our current understanding of leadership, leadership researcher Margaret Wheatley (1994) notes that,

> earlier, when we focused on tasks, and people were the annoying inconvenience, we thought about "situational" leadership—how the situation could affect our choice of styles. A different understanding of leadership has emerged recently. Leadership is *always* dependent on the context, but the context is established by the *relationships* we value. (p. 144)

Bringing Out the Best in Others

Two contemporary models of leadership stress the importance of relationship building. *Transformational* (Bass, 1985; Burns, 1978) and *servant* (Greenleaf, 1977) leadership models emphasize that an effective leader is someone who focuses on other group members and provides individualized consideration and appreciation of followers.

Transformational leadership emphasizes the role a leader plays in transforming the outlook and actions of other group members so they move beyond concern for their narrow, individual self-interest to focus on what is either good for the entire organization or for society as a whole. Bass (1985) proposes that transformational leaders try to foster an environment where relationships can be formed by establishing a climate of trust in which visions can be shared.

A transformational leadership approach can be relevant for service-learning projects as this type of leadership can contribute to a range of positive outcomes for society, *depending upon the goals of that particular group*. For example, transformational leadership in the national Get Out the Vote project helped focus members of 14 different organizations into a single campaign that registered more than 500,000 people between the ages of 18 and 30 and contributed to a 24 percent increase in voter turnout for the 2006 U.S. congressional elections (Oshyn & Wang, 2007). Similarly, **servant leadership** seeks to transform others, but this approach emphasizes empowering others and helping them meet their own identified needs. According to Greenleaf (1977), the focus of servant leadership is on others rather than upon self, and therefore the underlying motivation is bringing about greater good for others rather than self-interest. Similar to transformational leaders, servant leaders provide vision for the group, but here the emphasis is on developing capacity among others and helping them flourish and accomplish their goals (McMinn, 2001).

Servant leaders are influential because other group members see them as credible and trustworthy. Servant leadership is particularly relevant for service-learning projects because of its emphasis on empowering others and encouraging them to exercise their own abilities.

For example, since 1999 the Student Leaders in Service Program at Portland State University, built on the servant leader model, has cultivated and supported a yearly cohort of 25 students who make a full academic-year commitment to serve up to 10 hours a week at

---

⁂ Exercise 8.2: You as a Leader

Think about your own experiences as a leader in different areas of your life: home, school, sports, work, volunteering.

- Describe the best leadership experience you ever had.
- What kind of leadership style you were using in this situation? Explain your response.
- What effective strategies did you use in this leadership experience?
- What personal qualities do you think contributed to your success as a leader in this situation? Explain how each quality contributed to your leadership success.
- What effective strategies did you use in this leadership experience?
- How might the effective strategies you used in this situation be used in your current service-learning project?

local organizations where they provide direct service and act as liaisons between the university and the community, connecting institutional resources to university partner organizations to build their capacity to address significant social concerns. In 2011 student leaders facilitated projects that involved more than 1,500 Portland State students, faculty, staff, and community members through days of service that included Alternative Spring Break, New Student Day of Service, Martin Luther King, Jr. Day of Service, and Earth Week (Portland State University, Center for Academic Excellence, 2011).

Leadership in Intercultural Contexts

To influence any given situation, a leader has to take into consideration not just his or her own goals and values, but as highlighted in chapter 5, also the goals, values, and culture of the complex network of people the leader interacts with. What might be an effective leadership style at one service-learning site like a school could be perceived differently in another nonprofit organization like Planned Parenthood. Moreover, interpersonal styles and group dynamics may have subtle but important differences when working with African American communities, Latino neighborhoods, or Russian Ukrainian immigrant outreach programs.

Where do our ideas about what constitutes effective leadership styles come from? They come from our life experiences and the strategies we've used in the past, successfully and unsuccessfully, to achieve different goals as part of our everyday lives. Lipman-Blumen (2000) refers to these strategies as *achieving styles*, sets of actions or implementation scripts individuals use to achieve important goals. As children, we learn how to get things done. For example, you may prefer to work alone because you always have a clear idea of how to proceed, and other people just seem to get in the way; or if you are bigger than other kids, you figure out you can use the threat of force to make them comply with your wishes; or if you are charming and a good communicator, you find out you can persuade others to give you what you want. Because we grow up in different families with different sets of expectations and cultural norms, we don't all learn to emphasize the same sets of behavior. Through process of trial and error, rewards for success and punishments for failure, we discover combinations of strategies that tend to work best for each of us.

Achieving styles are directly linked to effective leadership. Leadership is the result of individual achieving styles used in a group setting. In today's interconnected global society, successful leaders need to be able to draw upon a repertoire of multiple leadership styles or approaches to maximize positive group outcomes (Lipman-Blumen, 2000; Wheatley, 1994). No single approach will always produce optimal results. Instead, what constitutes an *effective* leadership style depends upon what needs to be accomplished in a particular context.

As mentioned earlier, culture plays an important role in determining whether a specific leadership approach is perceived as legitimate. The varying cultural foundations of different groups make identifying what is an appropriate leadership approach in a given situation a complicated issue. For example, some cultures value leaders who are perceived as strong-minded individuals with a clear vision for the group (often referred to as *direct leaders*), while other cultures value leaders who work as quiet facilitators amid the group (often referred to as *indirect* or *relational leaders*). Still other cultures value a blending of these two modes (sometimes known as *persuaders*).

This means that as we engage in service-learning experiences on complex issues in our communities, like promoting literacy or protecting the environment, we will be forced to deal with other groups of stakeholders (e.g., community partner agencies, neighborhood residents) whose ideas about what constitutes appropriate leadership styles may differ greatly from those we are most comfortable with. As a student, you need to become familiar with a wide range of leadership strategies (or tools) that you can apply appropriately to the intercultural situation, since each individual, group, organization, and community are unique.

Metaphorically, you can imagine the categorization of your leadership knowledge and skills as a kind of toolbox or tool kit, as shown in figure 8.1. The *leadership tool kit* contains compartments that contain the best strategy for the issue, problem, or challenge to be addressed. For example, recall in chapter 4, when group cohesion is waning, a variety of leadership approaches could be used with varying success outcomes. Gaining insight into the cultural dynamics of groups and deciding which style of leadership to apply is one of the learning tasks and opportunities of service-learning.

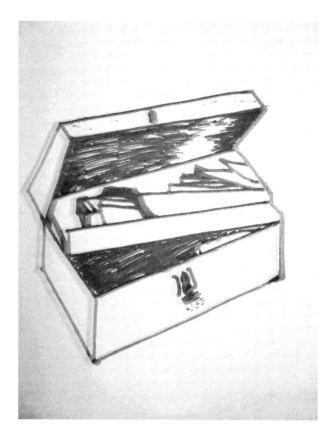

Figure 8.1. Leadership Tool Kit

The Leadership Tool Kit

Jean Lipman-Blumen (2000) identifies three groups of leadership styles: direct, relational, and instrumental, which when used in cultural congruence with the individual, group, or organization she calls ***connective leadership.***

According to Lipman-Blumen (2000), we all have certain leadership preferences. Some of us are more direct, telling others our visions and inspiring them toward those goals. Others are more relational, connecting the strengths of individuals to achieve group solidarity. Still others are more instrumental, linking people, plans, and resources to accomplish outcomes.

So just as a tool kit can have separate sections for screwdrivers, wrenches, and hammers, each compartment in our tool kit corresponds to a particular family of leadership approaches: direct, relational, and instrumental. And just as carpenters, framers, and plumbers each use different tools in getting their work done, it is helpful for students in service-learning classes to be able to use different leadership approaches depending upon what needs to get done. This is the essence of connective leadership, understanding when to be a ***director***, ***connector***, or ***persuader***.

✮ Exercise 8.3: You and Direct Leadership

Central to a direct leadership approach in groups is the idea that the leader's power allows him or her to direct group members on how to proceed with the task in question. This power to direct others may be based on authority (i.e., power acknowledged as legitimate by society or the group, such as a police officer or elected official) or expertise (i.e., recognition that the leader has more knowledge and experience in regard to the group's task). A direct leader typically believes he or she has the best plan for dealing with the group's task. We encounter direct leader situations in multiple areas of our lives: work, the military, sports teams, and especially at school. In this exercise, you are asked to reflect upon your past experiences with direct leadership and to consider when this style of leadership is appropriate for use in service-learning projects.

- Describe a situation where you used a direct leadership approach in a group setting.
- Was this approach successful in accomplishing the group's goals?
- How did the rest of the group respond to your employing this leadership approach?
- How did you feel about your experience using this leadership approach?
- When might a direct leadership approach be appropriate to use in a service-learning project? Explain your response.
- When might a direct leadership approach be inappropriate to use in a service-learning project? Explain your response.

> ### Spotlight on Service: Case Study: Direct Leadership in a Service-Learning Exerperience
>
> The Math in the Park capstone class brought together college, high school, and middle school students as part of a program to increase middle school students' engagement with mathematics through a series of beyond-the-classroom activities. Part of the goal of the program was to help middle school students see that math could be fun by providing them with new and different experiences. In the program, college students worked with high school students to develop activities that supplemented the middle school mathematics curriculum, and then supported the high school students who delivered the activities to middle school students.
>
> The college students were primarily pre-education majors (i.e., on the path to becoming teachers), and the capstone instructor was a member of the mathematics faculty. The pre-community service part of the capstone included helping students' clarify the knowledge they already had about appropriate pedagogy (i.e., how to present learning materials) as well as identifying the elements covered in the middle school mathematics curriculum. By the time they began to work with their high school student partners, the college students were relative experts in both areas.
>
> In the first part of service experience, the college students visited a local high school class. The high school class was divided into teams, with a college student facilitating each team. The college students used brainstorming activities to elicit ideas from the high school group about possible activities that could be used to supplement and illustrate the math lessons (e.g., angles, distances) being learned by local middle schoolers. After a range of possible activities had been identified, the group next selected several possible activities that seemed they would be of interest to middle-schoolers. Then the college student team leaders helped the group refine the activity, especially in making sure the activities were clearly demonstrating the skills they were intended to demonstrate, and that the choice of how to deliver the activities worked.
>
> The high school students then tried out the activities under the supervision of the college students. The activities all involved whole body motion, with students literally moving from one place to another. Example: A team of middle school students would be given a long piece of string and a set of directions ("Start here, lay out 4 feet of string, turn right 90 degrees and go 2 feet, turn left 60 degrees and go 2.5 feet . . ."). After the team followed all the steps in the directions, it ended up with a picture.
>
> The actual delivery of the activities to the middle school students was very successful. The middle schoolers enjoyed having the high school students visit their class. The activities really enhanced the math experiences of the middle school students. They talked about it being more like learning from big brothers or sisters because there was less of an age difference, and they could relate to high schoolers because they all came from the same neighborhood. The high school students were very engaged in the project; they felt respected because they were teaching younger students and because the college students were asking them for ideas. In post-project reflection, they mentioned being really inspired to go to the middle school to teach games to promote math skills. And in their own reflection, the college students emphasized how much they valued the opportunity to use the knowledge and skills they already had in a real-life situation.

Directors specialize in a ***direct leadership approach***. In a group setting, a director uses power/authority to lead by telling others what to do. Many times directors are sure they have the best plan for accomplishing the task. Directors also can be very competitive and may only be satisfied when exceeding the performance of others. Directors may use technology to influence and control other group members. For example, a director with a favored plan who wants to push group members from the planning to the action part of a service-

> ## Spotlight on Service: Case Study: Relational Leadership in a Service-Learning Experience
>
> In a senior-level service-learning course titled Effecting Change, students form their own community partnerships (in which they share 25 hours of time over the course of a 10-week term) collaboratively decide to pursue several group projects that will further the mission of one or more of their community partners. This course helps students identify the synergies between their efforts to make change in the community and learn concrete skills for consensus decision making.
>
> On the day students first brought their brainstormed ideas to class for the initial consensus-building conversation, many ideas were floated for projects: assist a local environmental organization with the cleanup of a vital watershed area, design and build a new kennel and drainage system for an agency that trains assistance dogs, host a family dinner night for students at an alternative school. One student, Maria, suggested that the students in the class could be really helpful to the agency where her aunt works—the county's Department of Human Services. Maria's aunt had mentioned in passing that the rooms where children in foster care have supervised visits with their parents are institutionally dismal and filled with dirty and broken toys. Knowing that Maria was enrolled in a service-learning class, her aunt wondered if there might be any students interested in rehabing the room to make it more inviting for the children who spent their quality time with their parents there.
>
> Immediately Maria's classmates gravitated to her idea, and they wanted more direction on how to proceed. Maria did not have a pre-conceived idea about what an updated room would look like, but she said she would be happy to serve as a liaison with the agency. Through many conversations between the interested students and the agency—conversations brokered by Maria—a proposal was collaboratively written and presented to the agency, which green-lighted the work. With Maria as the hub of the wheel of service learners, the students joining the project requested and received many donations of painting supplies and toys, and they involved friends and loved ones who contributed their time and talents to the project as well.
>
> On the day of the project, Maria showed up bright and early to facilitate the efforts of the students and other volunteers. The first shift of students cleared out the room and cleaned the walls to receive bright coats of kid-friendly blue paint. After this base coat dried, it was time for the Dr. Seuss murals to be painted. Given her artistic skill, Maria agreed to draw the figures onto the walls but refused to take total control of the mural creation, supporting other students—including those who insisted that they were not artists and couldn't possibly paint the features on the Cat in the Hat—to pick up a brush and start coloring in her outline. In all, about a dozen students and volunteers directly contributed to the planning and execution of the project, with all of them making their own mark on the collective whole. As the group was working, agency staff kept sticking their heads in the room to check out the progress. Even more satisfying were the kids who stopped by, gleeful to see the changes wrought by relational leadership and eager to return to play in such a cheerful, happy place.

learning project might set up a doodle scheduling poll with a limited range of choices. While this approach is actually encouraged in many academic settings (e.g., grading on a curve), in a service-learning project it is important to know when using this leadership approach is appropriate and when it might prove counterproductive.

Connectors specialize in the relational leadership approach and tend to be more interdependent. They also prefer to work in groups as a means to attaining goals, but instead of focusing on personal goals like persuaders, connectors prioritize the goals of the group. Connectors value cooperation and helping others reach their goals because the connector can identify with them. Many times connectors serve as *social glue sticks* that facilitate group success by connecting with others and facilitating new connections among other people. Connectors may use technology (e.g., shared Google documents, establishing wikis) to facilitate connections between groups and among group members of their own group. The transformational and servant leadership models, discussed ear-

lier in this chapter, are examples of this approach to leadership.

Persuaders specialize in the instrumental leadership approach. They tend to be social and prefer to operate in group settings. A persuader will try to use every re-

---

✳ Exercise 8.4: Tools for Relational Leadership: Developing Coalitions (Group Exercise)

One characteristic of relational leadership is the ability to achieve group success by connecting with others and facilitating new connections among other people. In this role-playing simulation, students enact the parts of stakeholders associated with particular community issues by initially defining each stakeholder's interest and then seeking out potential allies to build coalitions around each issue in question.

1. As a class, identify one or more important community issues. (Note: You will need one issue for every six to eight students in the class.) Write each issue on a whiteboard or flip chart so everyone can see it.
2. As an entire class, brainstorm which community groups—local, state, or federal agencies or special-interest groups—need to be at the table to resolve one community issue. When the class agrees that a particular stakeholder should be part of the discussion, write the name of each identified stakeholder on the whiteboard or flip chart under the issue. The number of stakeholders that are identified must correspond to the number of students who will be in that group. Write the name of each stakeholder on an index card. Repeat the process for each of the other issues identified in the first step.
3. Divide the class into issue-based groups and distribute the stakeholder index cards to each student in the group face down, making sure no group member knows the identity of another stakeholder. Give each student five minutes to develop his or her stakeholder's initial position on the issue as well as one or more arguments in support of the stakeholder's position.
4. Without students identifying the stakeholders they represent, have them circulate in the group, sharing their stakeholder's position on the issue with other group members while listening to the other students playing their stakeholder roles.
5. Each student then tries to figure out who else in the group might be a likely ally in addressing this issue and who are likely to be opponents. Still without identifying the stakeholders they represent, students should form coalitions based on similarities between their stakeholder's position and the views of other group members.

After each group has completed the coalition formation, have the class come together. For each issue, review the names of relevant stakeholders associated with the issue developed in step 2. Next, allow the students representing each stakeholder to share that stakeholder's position and state which other stakeholders with whom they believe their stakeholder would be allied.

Discussion Questions:

- What was the most interesting thing you learned from this exercise?
- What challenges did you encounter in trying to put together coalitions?
- Who was your most surprising ally in your coalition?
- Who was an unexpected opponent in a competing coalition?
- How might your service-learning project facilitate coalition development on the issue in question?

source at his or her disposal to get other group members to adopt positions or take on tasks that reflect the persuader's goals. Persuaders also try to steer others toward or away from resources (e.g., sending group members links to websites supporting the persuader's chosen position), plans, and logistic details. For a persuader, when it comes to influencing others, everything is fair game, from one's own personal qualities

---

Spotlight on Service: Case Study: Instrumental Leadership in a Service-Learning Experience

The Recycling Awareness Project brought together college, high school, and grade school students in settings where they could learn from each other about recycling, waste stream reduction, and energy conservation issues. One goal was to improve neighborhood recycling, particularly in large federally subsidized housing projects, by targeting elementary school-age children because they were the ones who typically took out the trash and therefore had to decide whether to place certain items in the recycling containers or the garbage. Direct appeals by adult city workers to promote recycling in these target neighborhoods had proven unsuccessful, so project organizers hoped to induce more appropriate message sources—local high school students—to effectively pass along the needed information about how to recycle appropriately.

In the first term of a two-term capstone course at a local university, college students learned about recycling and video production and created a recycling promotion video. They also received instruction on the behind-the-scenes work necessary to produce a successful video project, including how their perceived free choice of video topic, visual sequence, and script had been influenced, facilitated, and redirected (when necessary) by the class instructors. The college students were then shown techniques on how to achieve these same results to keep their high school student groups realistic and on track. In the second term of the capstone course, the college students used their newly acquired recycling expertise and video production experience to teach local high school students in a six-week resource conservation module at three different local high schools. One key element of the course was helping high school students produce their own recycling promotion videos, which were subsequently shown to third, fourth, and fifth graders at local elementary schools. Regardless of their initial level of interest in recycling, all the high school students wanted to make their own videos; as a consequence, they learned about recycling as part of the video production process. The high school students visited local elementary school classrooms to make recycling promotion presentations using their own videos. The high school students who were taught by the college students at one level became the teachers of elementary school students on the next level. The project was successful on both levels, community and individual. An example of a successful community-level outcome was at one large apartment complex where a six-week monitoring program of materials set out for recycling collection at nine garbage/recycling systems identified a clear improvement in the quantity and quality (e.g., uncontaminated) of recycling materials after the high school recycling promotion class activities. On an individual level, high school students demonstrated significant increases in their level of recycling knowledge, greater frequency of enacting positive recycling-related behavior, and a greater level of identification with the prosocial role of recycler post-program compared to a control group. In their course reflection, the college students noted how participating in this project increased their knowledge of waste reduction issues as well as their interest in being involved in recycling promotion activities in their own neighborhood. In this project, the college students' instrumental leadership—their ability to use their recently acquired knowledge of video production—played an important role in convincing high school students to actively participate in the project. As one high school student commented about his college student mentor, "He was a good team leader. He got us moving [with the recycling project] and helped us make a good movie."

⚹ Exercise 8.5: Tools for Instrumental Leadership—Recognizing Your Assets

Note: This exercise can be done individually or as a group activity.

A defining characteristic of instrumental leaders is a willingness to use any resource at their disposal to influence others to help realize the leader's goals. While everyone has something to contribute to your group's effort to make a service-learning project successful, many times students are initially unaware of valuable assets they already possess.

In part one of this exercise, make an asset list of all the things you do well, including your skills (e.g., acting experience, graphic design training, ability to speak a second language), hobbies (e.g., woodworking, baking, gardening), and interests (e.g., listening to music, playing or watching sports, blogging). Be creative in generating your list; do not be afraid to think big in identifying your assets. Use the left-hand column of the Recognizing Your Assets Worksheet (appendix 8.1, p. 135).

For the second part of this exercise, consider how each of your assets might be used in your service-learning project. Interestingly, even after identifying a wider range of personal assets than they initially thought they possessed, many students tend to underestimate the potential value of specific assets to the service-learning project. Assets can be used in a variety of ways, including *building rapport* (e.g., through a common interest in hip-hop music), *facilitating communication* (e.g., using second language skills to share project information with non-English-speaking community members), and *providing services associated with service-learning projects* (e.g., gardening knowledge and skills that could further the development of a community garden). Use the right-hand column of your Recognizing Your Assets Worksheet to describe how each of your assets might be employed in your class project. It is fine to have more than one potential use for any given asset.

If this is being done as a group activity, start part one of this exercise by having each student develop a personal asset list. Then develop a master list of group assets by having each student share one item from her or his personal list, until all students have shared all the assets on their list. For part two of this exercise, have the group consider how each item on the master list of group assets might be used in the current project. Encourage brainstorming among the students on possible ways each asset might be used.

(e.g., attractiveness, charm, charisma) to carefully crafted arguments to convince others that the persuader's approach is right. Persuaders are quick to use technology to try to influence others, from forwarding position-supporting e-mails, to cascading group members with multiple Twitter posts to try to shape the direction of group discussions. Persuaders' goals are to instrumentally link human and material resources for leveraging change.

Service-Learning Leadership for Leveraging Change

Service-learning experiences offer college students opportunities to develop a wider range of leadership styles than they might develop in traditional college courses. One of the important reasons students pursue college degrees is to develop skills, including leadership skills, they can use to achieve their career goals. However, in light of an acknowledged rapidly changing world, students face a very real challenge. How can they develop the wide range of leadership styles needed for successful leaders in today's world within a context—educational institutions—that strongly favor individualism and director leadership styles and particularly a competitive orientation? We need look no further than chapter 4, "Groups Are Fun, Groups Are Not Fun" and the students' comments about disliking group assignments because one's individual grade depends upon other students' efforts to find evidence of students' preference for direct achievement styles and individualism.

An important benefit of participating in service-learning courses as part of your total academic preparation is to add tools to your leadership tool kit. Clearly, to be a leader in today's interdependent world, you will need to be more than a director leader, relying solely on the direct achieving style typically emphasized in traditional higher education. Service-learning experiences provide students with opportunities to try out and develop their own personal persuader and connector leadership approaches.

Sometimes an unusual circumstance forces us to use different achieving styles, and if we enjoy success, we may include these new styles in our leadership repertoire (Lipman-Blumen, 2000). Service-learning experiences intentionally make this happen by getting students out of their comfort zone while providing opportunities for them to try out new leadership styles. This involves the cycle of success: When a student enjoys success through using a new leadership style, his or her confidence increases, which then reinforces the student's perceived value of and comfort with using that style. Service-learning courses particularly provide opportunities for developing relational leadership styles through collaborative projects with community partners aimed at attaining goals identified by the community as most important.

Another benefit for students participating in experiences is getting to compare community partners' approach to specific issues or situations with their own. Effective leaders need to be able to evaluate a situation for cues that indicate which combination of leadership styles would be most appropriate and effective in producing maximum outcomes. Most of us think we are pretty good at reading even subtle situational cues, yet we are surprised to learn that others in the same situation interpret the same signals differently. By participating in a service-learning project, students can tap into the expertise of community partners by learning how they interpret specific situations and decide which achieving styles are most appropriate for that situation. Sensitivity to cultural and organizational cues is a hallmark of effective leaders.

When we use the full repertoire of leadership behaviors available to us, we can select styles more appropriate to the unique demands of the situation. By combining leadership opportunities in community settings with deep reflection on those experiences, service-learning helps students broaden the range of leadership styles in their tool kits.

Recommended Readings

Green, M., Moore, H., & O'Brien, J. (2011). *Asset-based community development: When people care enough to act* (2nd ed.). Toronto, Canada: Inclusion Press.

Greenleaf, R. K. (1977). *Servant leadership: A journey into the nature of legitimate power and greatness.* Mahwah, NJ: Paulist Press.

Johnson, D. W., Maruyama, G., Johnson, R., Nelson, D., & Skon, L. (1981). Effects of cooperative, competitive, and individualistic goal structures on achievement: A meta-analysis. *Psychological Bulletin, 89*(1), 47–62.

Komives, S., Lucas, N., & McMahon, T. (2006). *Exploring leadership: For college students who want to make a difference* (2nd ed.). San Francisco: Jossey-Bass.

Kuh, G. D. (1995). The other curriculum: Out-of-class experiences associated with student learning and personal development. *Journal of Higher Education, 66*(2), 123–155.

Lipman-Blumen, J. (2000). *Connective leadership: Managing in a changing world.* Oxford, UK: Oxford University Press.

Peet, M. R., Walsh, K., Sober, R., & Rawak, C. S. (2010). Generative knowledge interviewing: A method for knowledge transfer and talent management at the University of Michigan. *International Journal of Educational Advancement, 10,* 71–85.

Stone, A. G., Russell, R. F., and Patterson, K. (2004). Transformational versus servant leadership: A difference in leader focus. *Leadership & Organization Development Journal, 25*(4), 349–361.

Tourish, D., & Vatcha, N. (2005). Charismatic leadership and corporate cultism at Enron: The elimination of dissent, the promotion of conformity and organizational collapse. *Leadership, 1*(4), 455–468.

Wheatley, M. J. (2006). *Leadership and the new science: Discovering order in a chaotic world.* San Francisco: Berrett-Koehler.

Key Concepts

connective leadership	instrumental leadership approach	servant leadership culture and leadership
direct leadership approach	leadership tool kit	situational model of leadership achieving styles
director	persuader	
great person theory of leadership	relational leadership approach	transformational leadership

Key Issues

- How are servant and transformational leadership both similar and different?
- How do service-learning experiences provide college students with opportunities to develop a wider range of leadership styles than typical college courses?

ADDITIONAL EXERCISE

✵ Exercise 8.6: You as a Leader Revisited (to be done at end of service project)

Now that you have completed the community service part of your service-learning experience in this class, go back and revisit your responses in exercise 5.2 about your previous leadership experiences. Thinking about your most recent class experiences,

- What were some of the things that went well in your service-learning project?
- What were some of the things you would have done differently, knowing now how the service-learning project turned out?
- What was your leadership role in your class service-learning project? Which of the leadership models best describes your leadership style in this project?
- What were some of the other leadership styles demonstrated in your service learning project? Which styles were most effective? Explain why you think each of these styles was effective in this project.

Appendix 8.1: Recognizing Your Assets Worksheet	
Assets	*Possible Use in Service-Learning Project*
1.	
2.	
3.	
4.	
5.	
6.	
7.	
8.	
9.	
10.	

CHAPTER 9

Failure with the Best of Intentions

When Things Go Wrong

JANELLE DeCARRICO VOEGELE AND DEVORAH LIEBERMAN

Two roads diverged in a yellow wood,
And sorry I could not travel both
And be one traveler, long I stood
And looked down one as far as I could
To where it bent in the undergrowth;

Then took the other, as just as fair,
And having perhaps the better claim,
Because it was grassy and wanted wear;
Though as for that the passing there
Had worn them really about the same,

And both that morning equally lay
In leaves no step had trodden black.
Oh, I kept the first for another day!
Yet knowing how way leads on to way,
I doubted if I should ever come back.

I shall be telling this with a sigh
Somewhere ages and ages hence:
Two roads diverged in a wood, and I—
I took the one less traveled by,
And that has made all the difference.

Robert Frost, "The Road Not Taken"

WE CAN all relate to the experience of looking back over a long-term project that started with enthusiasm and vision but ended with discouragement, anger, resentment, and despair. It happens to everyone from time to time. When you engage in a community-based project and begin to work with various others,

including faculty, students, and community partners, it is not unlike embarking on an unfamiliar road, to which you bring a unique set of skills, strengths, and prior experiences. Some of those prior experiences include situations that went relatively smoothly, some that may have been wildly successful, and others that were not productive. Perhaps some were downright dismal. Consider the following case study in light of previous experiences you may have had with successful (and not so successful) group project work.

Roadblocks and Flat Tires: A Case Study

When entering any collaborative experience, it is necessary (and useful) to spend focused time reviewing what has and has not contributed to *success* and *failure* in previous settings. Even if this is your first learning-through-serving course, you bring a wealth of firsthand experience relating to other human beings in a variety of contexts. When you view those experiences—the great, the good, the bad, and the ugly—with "fresh eyes," your perspective is enhanced and your ability to respond flexibly and creatively expands as well. You may have much more to contribute to the success of this project or course than you ever imagined.

Service-learning is often a journey into uncharted territory. Even with meticulous planning, carefully outlined expectations, and outstanding effort on

Roadblocks and Flat Tires

"Not again," thought Darrell. "Not another problem with this class! When were we supposed to meet with the community partners—10 minutes from now?" And here he was, backed up in traffic behind a construction roadblock. The last meeting had been canceled because one of the partners had a flat tire, and the time before that, a problem at the community organization, and the time before that, midterms, and the time before that. When would they ever get together all in one place? "Without a doubt," thought Darrell, "if this weren't a class involving grades, we'd have all given it up by now."

As traffic slowed to a complete stop, he sighed, leaned back in the driver's seat, and thought back over the sequence of events of the past several weeks. In the beginning, he recalled, everyone had seemed excited about the work they were doing. The subject matter was interesting, there weren't any tests, there was a lot of hands-on experience working in the community and the chance to do something that real people could benefit from. How many times in school did that happen?

Then, practically overnight, it all seemed to go downhill. The first time Darrell knew something was wrong was when things got heated in his project group. That was the day he and Chun got into it over what the community partners needed. What *did* they need? Everyone seemed to have a different idea.

"Why don't you ask the partners these questions?" Dr. Davis, their professor, had responded. A good idea, if they would call back. One week, two weeks passed with no response. Then Chun got nervous and began to work on her idea with two others in the group, which further annoyed Darrell. Why was she so closed-minded? Darrell chose not to involve himself. Why should he? No one asked his opinion.

Finally, someone from the community organization left a message with Darrell that the volunteer coordinators had both resigned and that a new interim person would be assigned to work with them shortly. "Now what?" everyone seemed to be wondering. Dr. Davis had given a good pep talk, Darrell remembered. He reminded them how much they were needed at a time like this. The class remained focused on the course material while they waited for further communication, but it felt like the wind had gone out of their sails. The interim coordinator agreed to meet with the students in class, but she seemed overwhelmed and not sure which direction to take. The next day she called back: "I have a project for you to do," she announced excitedly. By then, Chun's group and one other faction had devoted a lot of time outside of class to other ideas and were less than excited about jumping in a new direction. Darrell recalled that he had tried the role of peacemaker. "Why don't we just give her idea a chance?" he had wondered out loud to several students before class.

Jay, a student in the "Chun Fan Club," as Darrell liked to call them, reacted angrily. "You've just sat around, waiting for something to happen and letting us do all the work! Why should you have the right to tell us what to do now?"

After that, Darrell thought, it went from bad to worse. Dr. Davis had arranged for a lengthy discussion with the new volunteer coordinator, reminding the students that they should begin by listening to her ideas and working from there. The session appeared to go okay; to Darrell, at least, it seemed like everyone had listened and been open to the coordinator's ideas. At the community site, however, there had been conflicts over how to begin the project. Some students thought they should take the lead on the specifics of the project, since they had already volunteered for several weeks whereas the new volunteer coordinator had only just arrived. Not surprisingly, she reacted defensively. "It's the professor's job to teach the class, it's the students' job to volunteer, and it's my job to supervise the volunteers," she responded when two students approached her with concerns about her directions. "You need to do what the community organization wants, not the other way around." So Dr. Davis scheduled another mediation session, which had to be rescheduled, and rescheduled.

Which brought him to the latest roadblock, a real one this time. Yet, it seemed to him that the course had been like that all along—a potentially exciting journey that had somehow turned out all wrong. Roadblocks and flat tires all the way. Could we have foreseen any of them, Darrell wondered? Could any of the problems have been prevented? Well, too late now. Or was it?

everyone's part, things can go wrong. The good news is that we can prepare ourselves for and avoid many of the "roadblocks and flat tires" along the way. This preparation occurs in several steps. First, we encourage you to explore some prior experiences in collaborative contexts while considering how those experiences have been framed and defined in terms of "success" or "failure." Second, we will look at common roadblocks in the service-learning journey. Third, you will have a chance to consider alternative response strategies for negotiating unexpected events and circumstances. Finally, the chapter concludes with a discussion of community-based learning in retrospect, focusing on framing and learning from various experiences at the "end of the road."

Choosing Directions: The Meaning of "Failure" in Service-Learning

Let's be honest—the term "failure" doesn't exactly conjure up the most pleasant mental associations. It may bring to mind visions of a scrawled red "F" on the side of a term paper or exam or the unpleasant group experience you would rather not think about. One of the ways to prepare for these and other potential problems is to understand the dynamics of failure in the context of service-learning. As you read through the following list of typical "failures" in

community service contexts, remember that these dynamics do not by themselves cause failure; instead, the challenge of how you react to them may result in perceptions that some aspect of the course has failed (or failed to meet initial expectations). Therefore, when those involved can focus on the underlying dynamic of those events as well as the perceptions of events, the progression to learning from and responding to those events can become clearer. It is important that you frame your experience as opportunities to "learn from" and "respond to" these situations. The intervening variable or event may be out of your control, but how you respond to it is within your control. You have the power to impact the outcome of the entire learning-through-serving experience, influencing your community partners and your classmates through your choices.

Everything is going really great. I like our professor—she knows so much about this subject. And I like the group I'm working with, which hasn't always been the case in other classes I've taken. Also, the volunteering turned about to be so much fun that I actually look forward to going every week. So it's all okay—thinking about something as depressing as "failure" makes it seem like we're waiting for the luck to run out or something.

✯✯ Exercise 9.1: Roadblocks and Flat Tires Reflection

- What do you imagine will happen next in this situation?
- What factors may have contributed to the difficulties faced by the students and community partners?
- What might have prevented or minimized the difficulties in this situation?

Some common and familiar dynamics of service-learning failures include the following:

- **Difficulty anticipating the unknown (ambiguity).** Typical "unknowns" in service-learning experiences are (1) reactions of community members to your presence in their lives, (2) what exactly you will discover in long-term research projects for community partners, (3) how your work will be received by stakeholders, and (4) how you will learn the skills you need for the community service project. People react differently to ambiguity in their lives, and the same is true for reactions to unknowns in community-based learning. For example, in the case study at the beginning of this chapter, Darrell preferred a "wait-and-see" approach while Chun and Jay responded by developing their own plans for the project.

- **Responsibility to community need (responsibilities).** In chapter 1, the complementary but competing forces of freedom and responsibility were discussed in relation to the development of educated citizens. A feeling of responsibility to those with whom you work as part of your community experience may at times appear to conflict with your own personal beliefs or competing commitments. As you expand your awareness of the complexity of community needs, you may feel overwhelmed or concerned about whether you are truly making a difference or "doing enough."

- **Reliance on others whom you do not know well (trust).** Reliance on others for assistance, expertise, direction, and support takes a great deal of effort and goodwill. Trust is an issue throughout the stages and phases of collaborative group effort.

- **Conflicts with students and/or community (controversy with civility).** Remember the "Visionary Skeptics" and "Mudslingers" from chapter 4? Which group had more conflict? Although the conflict exhibited throughout the Mudslingers' process is no doubt more memorable, the answer is that neither group had more conflict. The type of conflict certainly differed between the two groups, as well as the response strategies used by individual

participants in each group. In this chapter we will extend the discussion on the storming phase of group development to include ideas for positive individual orientation toward conflict, as well as strategies for engaging in constructive, rather than destructive, conflict.

- **Flexibility in the face of rapidly changing conditions (adaptability).** Just as people react in various ways to ambiguity, they may also respond differently to circumstances in which plans have to be cancelled, assumptions are challenged, and goals must be revised. According to Schon (1987), flexibility and acceptance of uncertainty are two key characteristics associated with the ability to think creatively in problematic situations. Even if you generally describe yourself as "laid back" when it comes to last-minute changes, there are other factors in service-learning that can impact creative problem solving. For example, you or your classmates may wonder if your grades will be impacted by changes in the partnership or project goals. You or your classmates—not to mention your professor and the community partner—may experience stress, as multiple constituents with competing commitments and busy lives attempt to "re-group" and invest time and energy responding to unplanned events.

- **Unexamined assumptions about the role of failure and success (redefining success).** When we characterize a situation or event as having been a "success" or "failure," what do we mean? Unless we answer this important question, we may equate our framing of events as "failures" or "successes," closing off the possibility for alternative interpretations of events. Articulating individual and group meanings for the experience of success and failure sets the tone for productive communication and creative problem solving.

In this section, we have explored the underlying dynamics commonly related to perceptions of success and failure in service-learning environments. It is often the case that more than one dynamic operates simultaneously, making the task of responding flexibly and creatively more challenging. Have you ever en-

---

☀ Exercise 9.2: Exploring Success and Failure

Completing this activity will help you see how you have evaluated and "framed" your past experiences. What you learn will help you "re-frame" your current and future learning and serving experiences.

1. Think of an experience in college where everything "came together," when you said to yourself, "This is what I really enjoy about being a student." Now think about a time where there was a problem or an unsuccessful experience. Write a few brief notes about those two experiences. Be as specific as possible. What made these two experiences satisfying or unsatisfying?

2. If possible, discuss your responses with one or two other students. Try to derive at least one general statement that seems to sum up your responses. For example: "Successful experiences made us want to continue; unsuccessful experiences made us stop and reevaluate things."

3. Compare your statement to the following quotes about failure:

   > Sometimes a person has to go a very long distance out of [the] way to come back a short distance correctly. (Albee, 1960)
   > Failure after long perseverance is much grander than never to have a striving good enough to be called a failure. (Eliot, 1986)
   > I have learned that success is to be measured not so much by the position that one has reached in life as by the obstacles which [one] has overcome while trying to succeed. (Washington, 1901)

4. What similarities and differences do you see between your general statements from number 2 and the previous quotes?

5. What does "failure" mean to you? What does "success" mean to you? Make a list of those meanings either on your own or in your group.

6. Very often, multiple and conflicting meanings for failure and success exist side by side. For example, failure may be described as "uncomfortable" and "a possibility for growth" simultaneously. Try to answer the following two questions:

   In what ways does this course allow for success *and* failure? (For example, the community partners understand that we're all learning as we go; the course syllabus does not state "You will be graded down for mistakes," etc.)

   How will you respond to failure? (For example, be open about it, be accepting of others' errors, set aside time to problem-solve, etc.)

---

countered a situation in which it felt as if no mutually agreed-upon solution could be found, as though you were surrounded by "Road Closed—No Detour" signs? Next, we will discuss common roadblocks you may face in service-learning experiences and offer practical suggestions for framing and responding productively to those events that initially seem insurmountable.

Checking the Map: Common Roadblocks

In preparation for our service work at a food bank, our class discussed our expectations and perceptions about the work. It was an awkward moment for me when another student in my group said that she had never met anyone who had to go hungry as a kid.

Although I wanted to, I didn't know how to speak up and say, "Yes, you have. You've met me."

Service: Unfamiliar Territory or Coming Home?
Perceptions of service-learning can be influenced by prior life experiences connected to the focus of service. The previous example was a reflection from a real service-learning course focused on issues of homelessness and food insecurity. The roadblock in this case was not the fact that one student had never experienced hunger while another student had, but that it was a difficult subject to discuss openly and honestly. In fact, as Lee (2004) observes, personal issues connected to socioeconomic status can greatly impact service experiences, and often become most salient when working within communities that are economically different from students' own experiences, or when returning to a social setting that is similar to one's current or previous life experience.

Students may be returning to neighborhoods from which they came, or working in settings that serve individuals facing situations they have experienced. Students may be serving in neighborhoods that are significantly different economically than those with which they are most familiar. There may be subtle but significant differences in the ways that service activities are viewed by students, instructors, and community partners.

As you read in chapter 5, culture is the creation of learned and shared values, beliefs, and behaviors in a community, and is impacted by many factors, including socioeconomic status. This implies that cultural self-awareness includes socioeconomic self-awareness, or the ways that socioeconomic factors have influenced your identity and perceptions of community partners and the work that they do. You may also be aware of social stereotypes that exist about your own or another socioeconomic group. How might those stereotypes impact perceptions of the individuals and groups served by your community partners?

Not only can perceptions of community issues differ between students, but they can also result in conflicting expectations within students (e.g., feelings connected to serving in a context with which one has direct experience). However, many students in these situations have discovered their shared background experiences with community partners to be a great asset (Lee, 2004), providing insight and common ground.

If the diversity of life experience connected to these differences among students, instructors, and community partners can be explored as they impact perceptions and expectations of outreach activities, then the resulting collective insight can be a source of civic responsibility and social change (Lee, 2004). Voicing constructive responses to situations where expectations conflict is the focus of the next section.

> At this point, it might be helpful to revisit **Exercise 5.2: I and We and You and Us and Them**, focusing on the socioeconomic factors that have contributed to your identity and factors that affect the people served by your community partner. What would you add to your earlier observations?

Conflicting Expectations: Faculty, Community Partners, Students
In the previous section, different life experiences connected to socioeconomic status were highlighted. Expectations related to the nature of service may also differ. For example, students may be expecting a direct-service experience or an internship, when a project-based experience is planned, or vice versa. Community partners may assume that students will carry out their work independently, while students expect more input or supervision from the community partner. Faculty and community partners may discover that they have differing ideas about one or more aspects of the service portion of the course. If you have read and completed the exercises found thus far in this book, you have created a strong foundation for clarifying your own and others' expectations. However, as you proceed with the course and your community service, you will find that clarifying expectations and assessing progress toward intended goals is fundamental to success. Repeated clarification of expectations will serve to help your group progress and to deepen your personal understanding and commitment to the group, the project, and the community partner. As long as you are interacting with others, you will always be interpreting layers of meanings, some of which will be closer (or further away) from what others intended. Moreover, you need to be vigilant against social loafing, missing deadlines, and not fulfilling promises.

As Edelman and Crain (1993) remind us, "Everything we see and hear is processed through the filter of our own personal history and our own perceptions of a situation" (p. 63). We often assume that we are understood by others until future actions prove that—surprise!—our message was filtered, often inaccurately, in surprising ways. Given the complex nature of communication, Edelman and Crain suggest that team members accept *misunderstanding*, rather than understanding, as the norm in human interactions. In other words, problems are normal.

When you approach interactions assuming that you're likely to be misunderstood rather than understood, you need not be surprised or embarrassed or waste time trying to get at the truth of "who misunderstood." Blaming or identifying who is in error is not a productive part of this process. Instead, accept misunderstanding as inevitable and focus your energies on clarifying expectations and group communication practices for the future. As an additional bonus, this state of mind leads to a more habitual practice of effective listening strategies.

Changes in the Community Partnership

In the case study at the beginning of this chapter, the students were caught off guard by a change in staffing at the community organization in which they were preparing to work. There are several types of changes that potentially impact the partnership:

Staff change: Many service-learning courses are associated with agencies in which there is great need for assistance. As a result, there may be change in staffing that occurs during any community partnership. As a result of these changes, community organization staff may be reorganized. Though these staff changes are in no way directly related to the student actions or project, students may feel abandoned or somehow personally offended by staff changes. There may be external pressures or other organizational realities of which you are not aware. If you experience a staff change at some point in your course, you can do many things individually or as a team to make the transition go more smoothly for everyone involved.

☝ If you do experience a staff change at some point in your course, **Exercise 9.5: Responding to Staff Changes** on page 149 can help to make the transition go more smoothly for everyone involved.

Infrastructure changes: In addition to staffing changes, infrastructure and administrative changes can impact community-service activities. Examples of these changes include revisions to organizational procedures and policies, job descriptions, and hours available for volunteering, among others. Infrastructure changes are often made for specific reasons but may also have unintended consequences. If unintended consequences impact you, you can address this by communicating honestly, openly, and constructively.

First, immediately discuss the situation with the appropriate person (instructor, students, and/or community partners. Another good source may be your college's community service or volunteer office for some advice on how to handle the situation). Let's say that you are serving at a community organization where a decision has been made to cut back on volunteer hours. You are very upset by this, because you feel that the volunteers were not consulted and that the decision shows very little regard for your (and other volunteers') perspectives. You could ask,

> Why were the hours cut back so much? Do volunteers really matter around here or don't they? Don't you know we have families and jobs outside of this place, in addition to school?

Alternatively, you might say,

> Since volunteer hours have been restricted to Tuesday and Thursday, I'm only able to be here for part of the hours that the clients are actually here, since I have to go to work on Thursday afternoons. I really want to be able to keep supporting the community organization and continue interacting directly with clients. What suggestions do you have in this situation?

The second response is more specific, speaks from the student's perspective, does not assume that the community organization was automatically aware of unintended consequences, shows goodwill, and invites others to collaborate in generating a solution. Most likely, the person in the organization will not feel defensive or attacked. Remember, a result of making the comment should not be, "These volunteers are more hassle than they are worth," but, rather, "I'd like to address these volunteers' issues so that they can continue to contribute to the organization."

Perception of Need or Community Issue

Most service-learning courses are working toward a common goal in collaboration with the community. Ideally, the "common goal" is a result of input from all involved—community, faculty, and students. In our work with community-based courses, we have observed that perceptions of the problem to be solved, issue to be addressed, or "common goal" change over time. Often, as multiple constituencies work together in community-based settings, they learn from one another. As part of this multilayered, complex learning process, it is not surprising that views of issues evolve and change.

Look closely at the picture in figure 9.1. What do you see? Most people initially see a duck, and then, with time, perceive a rabbit. With more time and practice, it is easily possible to perceive both at the same time. Learning in partnership with community is somewhat like this: You are framing, reframing, and defining what you see as you move through the process. Metaphorically, you may begin by seeing mostly "ducks" in the beginning and then move to "rabbits." For example, what all participants perceive as the major goal of your volunteer work may have subtly shifted as the work progressed. What is important to the partnership is that these changes in perceptions are articulated and clarified regularly; otherwise, as the partnership continues, you may be proceeding on assumptions as different as ducks are from rabbits.

Conflict within the Student Team

In chapter 4, you read about the distinct phases of group development: *forming, storming, norming,* and *performing.* This model assumes the inevitability of conflict; in fact, conflict is understood to play a necessary and productive role in the process. It should be noted, however, that "having a difference of opinion" is not the same as "experiencing conflict." Let's take some time to define conflict and address the compo-

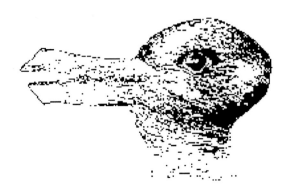

Figure 9.1. What Is It?

nents of conflict. Folger, Poole, and Stutman (1995) define conflict as "the interaction of interdependent people who perceive incompatible goals and interference from each other in achieving those goals" (p. 404). When two individuals working toward the same goal perceive that the other is "the" deterrent to achieving that goal, then conflict arises. The critical element is not the conflict, in and of itself, it is how these two individuals approach and deal with the conflict that is the most important factor.

There are two primary approaches to conflict: *destructive* and *constructive.* The following chart articulates some of the basic behaviors associated with each conflict style.

> ❓ To explore conflict patterns in your own life, see **Exercise 9.6: Identifying Your Conflict Patterns**, on page 150.

Let's focus our attention on approaching conflict civilly and constructively. Since constructive conflict involves focusing on the source of the conflict, identify

Examples of **Destructive** *Conflict*	*Examples of* **Constructive** *Conflict*
• Open hostility: Attacking or undermining others' ideas • Subtle hostility: Lack of cooperation or withdrawal • Imposing and forcing solutions on the other	• Listening to opposing views with the goal of feeling empathy and understanding • Discussing the nature or source of the conflict (a person's position on something rather than the person him or herself) • Welcoming various possible solutions

---

> ### Exercise 9.3: Assessing Your Journey
>
> Completing this activity will help you assess your learning and serving thus far so that you can adjust your framing of roles, responsibilities, timelines, tasks, and objectives, if necessary. This activity can be done on your own (e.g., in a reflective response that may be shared with the course instructor) or can be completed and discussed in class.
>
> This reflection might include answers to the following questions:
>
> - How do my own life experiences differ from the neighborhoods in which I am experiencing my community engagement?
> - How are my life experiences similar to those with whom I am interacting during my community engagement activities?
> - Depending on my perceptions of similarity/difference, how am I bringing my own judgments, stereotypes, opinions to bear on these interactions? How might these be helping or hindering the openness I express to those with whom I am interacting?

the source. In student working groups, differences over goals, priorities, and approaches to the project are common sources of conflict. First, look at the following checklist and identify which of the elements may be acting as roadblocks to constructive conflict either in your own group and/or within the community organization. Then, read the suggestions for working through the conflict constructively.

1. **Identify the root of the conflict.** The following checklists may help:

What's going wrong?

___ We're not listening to each other.
___ We keep repeating the same arguments instead of moving on or agreeing on a solution.
___ We constantly interrupt each other.
___ We allow aggressive members to dominate and quiet members to become more passive and less invested in the project.
___ Some of us don't contribute.
___ We don't compromise or collaborate enough.
___ We don't have clear tasks or objectives for our group or the individual members of our group.
___ We are not clear about what has been decided. (Adapted from Gibbs, 1994)

What seem to be the sources of this conflict?

___ Our individual differences over project goals or priorities
___ Our misunderstandings over each others' intentions
___ Our competition for control
___ Our personality clashes that we don't resolve
___ Our differences over methods to achieve goals
___ Our individual frustrations over roles in the group and the opportunity for all members to make an impact
___ Our perceptions that someone is at fault or undermining
___ Our positions (conclusions individuals have reached)
___ Our interests (reasons for taking one position over another)
___ Our talking behind each others' backs instead of addressing the sources and the continuing conflicts

2. **Listen carefully to others' views on the nature of the conflict.** It is possible that the conflict stems from more than one source.
3. **Work together to focus on the source(s) of the conflict, rather than the people involved.** This may seem difficult. What if a

difference in personality is one of the issues? Rather than focusing on the individuals who clash, explore the nature of the clash. Does one perceive something about the other's intentions that may or may not be accurate? Is the personality difference actually related to differences in approaches to interaction or the roles and responsibilities that have been assigned to the individuals? Can the group, without assigning blame to any one person, be helpful in exploring these differences and generating alternative approaches toward moving forward with the project?

4. **Demonstrate that everyone's views have been understood.** Work for understanding at this stage, not agreement. You can accurately summarize everyone's views on the source of a conflict without necessarily agreeing with those views. Ask questions often to clarify your assumptions about the exact nature of others' views on the root of the conflict. Remember, "understanding" does not necessarily mean that you agree.

5. **Identify any common goals and mutual interests that underlie various participants' views on the conflict.** For example, in the "Roadblocks and Flat Tires" case study, Darrell, Chun, and Jay were all concerned about doing the best job possible for the community partner, but they used different approaches. Darrell assumed that waiting to hear more about the new coordinator's needs would be the best approach, while Chun and Jay wanted to begin on their own. Had they discussed the nature of their conflict, they might have discovered that it involved differences in methods for reacting to staff change, rather than Darrell's laziness (Jay's assumption) or Chun's closed-mindedness (Darrell's assumption).

6. **Generate possible solutions based on common goals and mutual interests, with specific, achievable tasks for all participants.** More than one solution may be appropriate, based on participants' diverse needs. For example, Darrell and Chun might have decided on two solutions: (a) carefully assess needs based on the new volunteer coordinator's perspective,

and (b) begin developing a student proposal. By working on these approaches together, removing incorrect assumptions about intentions, Darrell could function as the initial contact with the new coordinator while Chun took the lead on the student proposal. Eventually the project could merge both efforts.

Conflicts with Community Partners

In addition to conflict within the student team, conflict with community partners may arise. When approaching conflict with community partners, it is crucial to create a climate of support, goodwill, and mutual benefit. For example, students may unintentionally misread community partners' assumptions about their role in the project. The community partner may mistakenly have stereotypes about student commitment, student work ethic, and student intent. These assumptions can easily cloud everyone's perceptions and lead to assumptions about behaviors, creating a defensive climate. Defensive climates prevent listeners from focusing on the message and increase the likelihood that they will focus on defending positions, rather than attempting to understand your views.

The climate that you help to establish will set the tone for all the communication behaviors that ensue. You have the power to create an environment that fosters supportive communication or that breeds defensive communication among interactants. The next section represents a communication process for responding to common challenges in ways that encourage collaboration, empathy, and reciprocal learning.

Reading the Signs: Redirecting around Roadblocks

In the previous discussions, we addressed communication strategies for achieving constructive and productive outcomes and ways to create a more supportive communication climate. The following section addresses a sequential process for moving from "recognizing a roadblock" to "redirecting around a roadblock."

Does the Map Fit the Territory?
Language (whether written or spoken) may be understood as a map (Korzybski, 1921). Imagine a map of

the United States. The map includes all the variables that make up a particular area, and these variables are exhibited in relation to one another. In the case of the roadblocks, we must ensure that "the map fits the territory" rather than making the territory fit the map. This reminds us that our written and spoken language gives us information about the situation which allows us to see the greater picture (map). The more accurately we portray each communication variable (parts of the map), the better we will understand the entire situation (the overall map). In order to achieve this, we must continually assess and reassess, for accuracy, the parts of the map (Russell, 1999). It is always possible to act based on inaccurate maps, especially when we proceed without checking our perceptions of maps given to us by others and misread maps based upon prior assumptions or what we would like to believe about the territory, accurate or not. The following strategy, adapted from Lieberman (1996), offers a concrete process to monitor our assumptions, our listening, our language, and our behavior for continued development in self-knowledge and working with others across differences.

The D-U-E Process

The **_D-U-E Process_** is a framework for understanding social, socioeconomic, cultural, or personality differences that may be roadblocks to effectively listening to or working with another individual or group. _D-U-E_ stands for the following:

- **Describe** what you observe
- **Understand** social, socioeconomic, cultural, or personality differences
- **Encourage** communication

Step 1: Describe. Self-talk loaded with evaluative statements or adjectives ("She is inconsiderate and pushy") is one indicator that you need to apply the D-U-E Process. Think: Is the map I am creating of this person's behavior an accurate representation of events or my inaccurate interpretation of those events? The first step is to pause for a moment and describe to yourself as specifically as possible your reasons for your evaluations (interpretations). For example, a person's behavior may seem "inconsiderate and pushy" to you because (descriptively) she begins speaking before you have completed your sentence

and because she speaks very quickly, without much vocal inflection. The description you would think to yourself would be "This person is speaking before I have finished my sentence." It doesn't evaluate her behavior as "good" or "bad"; it merely describes her behavior.

Step 2: Understand. The second step is a reminder to think about possible social, socioeconomic, cultural, or personality differences that lie below the descriptions you generated in step 1. For example, rules for interruption, rate of speech, and vocal inflection vary from culture to culture _and_ between various groups within cultures. In the example in step 1, let's imagine that the person who interrupts and may seem "inconsiderate and pushy" comes from a part of the United States where the average rate of speech is much faster than the area in which you were raised. How might that influence your perception of her, and, possibly, her perception of your speech?

Step 3: Encourage communication. If you take the second step of the process seriously, you will often arrive quite easily at the third phase of the D-U-E Process, and you can begin to focus on the what, or the content of the message, and focus less on the how, or the manner in which the message is presented. You can also paraphrase the speaker's message, demonstrating your understanding, and save much time that would have been wasted had you allowed cultural or personality "noise" to interfere with your understanding.

It may seem like a great deal of work because it is not something you are normally used to doing. Yet the whole process takes only a few seconds and can dramatically affect your response to others and your ability to comprehend their meaning.

The View from Yesterday: Making Meaning at the End(?) of the Road

Throughout this chapter, we have asked you to consider a variety of meanings for and responses to "failure with the best of intentions." We have explored typical dynamics of failure, common roadblocks to community partnerships, and strategies to see with "fresh eyes"—framing, re-framing, and responding to

---

✦ Exercise 9.4: Redirecting around Roadblocks

Completing this activity will assist you in using the D-U-E Process. Record your responses in writing so that you can easily refer back to them in the future.

Think of a recent situation with another person or persons in which the D-U-E Process might have been helpful (for example, a conflict or misunderstanding).

Describe: What were your interpretations of others' behaviors in this event? How did you respond? Specifically what about their actions (in the form of description) led you to interpret events as you did?

Understand: How might their actions have been interpreted (understood) differently?

Encourage communication: How might you have interacted with this person to encourage ongoing communication?

---

unexpected events. Negative situations can truly allow for tremendous learning. Eyler and Giles (1999) investigated the process of understanding and applying knowledge in service-learning and concluded that students' ability to work well with others led to an increased sense of personal efficacy, leadership capabilities, and self-knowledge. All of these outcomes comprise the knowledge and skills for effective civic engagement and your ability to create positive community change. Chapter 3 recounted a story in which students were able to successfully analyze and respond to initial "failures" to utilize their knowledge and skills to create a renewed commitment to success. In the end, success was defined not only by what was accom-

plished, but also by the ability to remain committed in the face of difficulty that provided a powerful conduit for the development of personally meaningful and connected knowing.

Service-learning is a journey into uncharted territory. We hope that you will make this an ongoing journey, as you continue to build upon what you have learned and increasingly translate that learning into action even after you graduate. The commitment to continued growth, self-awareness, community awareness, and social change may not always be the easiest road, but we, along with Robert Frost, whose poem began this chapter, invite you to take the "road less traveled by," as it truly can make "all the difference."

Key Concepts

constructive conflict	D-U-E Process	success
destructive conflict	failure	

Key Issues

- What are the most common dynamics of service-learning "failures"?
- What does it mean to allow failure as a possibility in community-based settings?
- How would you describe the difference between destructive and constructive conflict? What are some of the characteristics of each?
- How might you turn conflicts with another individual into constructive conversation by using the D-U-E Process?

ADDITIONAL EXERCISES

⚲ Exercise 9.5: Responding to Staff Changes

Completing this activity will give you the tools to respond, should there be unexpected organizational changes in staffing with your community partner.

First, review the "Roadblocks and Flat Tires" case study. Then write down or discuss in class your answers to the following questions:

- In "Roadblocks and Flat Tires," the volunteer coordinator resigned unexpectedly. What do you notice about the reactions of the students? The faculty?
- What led up to the eventual conflict at the community organization? How might this have been handled differently?
- Generally, what do you think a student can do to achieve a smooth transition during and after a staff change with the community partner?

℗ Exercise 9.6: Identifying Your Conflict Patterns

Completing this activity will assist you in identifying conflict patterns that you may have established in your own life. Set some time aside and write down your responses to the following questions. It may be helpful to share insights from your responses with your student team, if possible. Together your group (or class) can give one another feedback on developing constructive conflict patterns.

- Think of a conflict that you have had with another individual.
- What do you think was the overarching goal that you were both trying to achieve?
- What was your recommendation for achieving that goal?
- What was the other person's recommendation for achieving that goal?
- How did you respond to the other person's recommendation? For example, did you just disagree and say that the person was wrong? Did you listen to the other person and talk through his/her perspective? Looking at the behaviors in the chart on page 144, specifically identify which of the behaviors you exhibited.
- How do you think your behavior exacerbated or resolved the conflict?
- Do you think your behaviors were primarily destructive or constructive?
- If your behaviors were primarily destructive, how might they have been more constructive?
- Think of one or two other conflict-based situations that involved you. Go through the same process as you just did with the first situation. Are you beginning to see a pattern in how you approach and resolve conflict? If these patterns tend to be more destructive than constructive, identify patterns you would like to change and patterns you would like to adopt.

℗ Exercise 9.7: Roadblocks and Flat Tires Reconsidered

In contrast to the outcome described in the case study "Roadblocks and Flat Tires," which opened this chapter, create an alternative case study, one in which Darrell, Jay, and Chun are able to respond to conflict constructively, creating a supportive climate for listening and communication.

CHAPTER 10

Expanding Horizons

New Views of Course Concepts

CHRISTINE M. CRESS AND JUDY PATTON

It's 8 p.m. on a Friday. I would certainly rather be out with my friends tonight. Instead, I'm stuck inside a warehouse counting cans of soup for the food bank. What a boring service project.

I never thought that paying tuition meant I would have to measure manure piles. It's gross. What do I care if a cow poops two feet or two miles away from the creek?

I have blisters on my hands from pulling ivy away from the library building. Shouldn't I be inside reading to kids or something? Wouldn't that be a lot more valuable?

SOMETIMES IT'S HARD to see the connections between our service-learning tasks and larger social and political issues. If we are dealing with cans, animals, or buildings, it might be difficult to understand how these relate to hunger, water rights, or urban renewal. Yet, most community concerns are multifaceted as well as interdependent.

Consider this example: A state in the Midwest had to cut custodial services to all public facilities, including libraries. The laid-off janitors and groundskeepers made use of local food banks for their families while they were seeking new employment. Unfortunately, milk and milk products such as cheese were in short supply in the wake of a court battle over watershed contamination. The case had pitted farmers against environmentalists and resulted in a farmer protest in the state capital, where hundreds of gallons of milk were poured into the streets. This led to a public outcry against senators and legislators, who were blamed for inept budgeting processes. The representatives, in turn, pointed the finger at voters for rejecting a recent initiative to raise property taxes in order to enhance the state revenue.

Given the previous scenario, you may ask what you, your class, or your school could ever do to make a difference. As the anthropologist Margaret Mead (1971) is quoted as saying, however, "Never doubt for a moment that a small group of individuals can change the world. Indeed, it's the only thing that ever has." By stocking shelves in the food bank and discussing family needs and sources of donated support, you may gain greater insight into hunger issues and state economic policies. By interacting with farmers and hydrologists, you might learn of the complexities of sustaining family-owned farms and the preservation of drinkable water downstream. By working with architects, historians, and urban planners in the preservation of an old library, you may come to view differently the relationship between libraries, literacy, and juvenile crime.

So, are we saying that serving soup to the homeless is not enough? Yes. Is picking up litter on a beach just the first step? Yes. Is tutoring a third grader to read a good thing in and of itself? Yes. To go a step further, we are challenged by colleges and universities to do more than just single acts of kindness. The whole idea behind service-learning is to *learn*. We must try to use our service-learning experiences to expand our understanding of the underlying issues that create community problems and to find the solutions individually and collectively.

Transformational Learning

In chapter 9, you read about service-learning as a journey, one that is sometimes fraught with disappointment and frustration. So, too, every journey provides us with new vistas. When we journey into new experiences, we may notice that things don't look the same as they did a week ago, yesterday, or even an hour ago. Many educators have referred to this phenomenon as a shift in *consciousness*. Indeed, Mezirow (2002) calls the process *transformational learning*.

Transformational learning involves far more than memorizing facts or reciting information. It is deep learning where new knowledge becomes personally meaningful and connected to community. In other words, our experiences give us new insights and new skills that allow us to interact differently with our world. In chapter 5, we learned that being interculturally competent involves a mindset, a heartset, and

a skillset. Similarly, transformational learning uses these competencies to ask critical questions, to engage in reflection, and to identify strategies for leveraging change. It means living conscientiously, knowing that everyone's individual actions in some way affect the lives of others. Thus, the essence of transformational learning is using your talents and skills (including your academic knowledge) to make your community and your world a better place in which to live, work, and play.

Ways of Knowing

Engaging in transformational learning involves knowing your own preferred styles of taking in and processing information. This is called **ways of knowing** (Belenky, Clinchy, Goldberger, & Tarule, 1986), which are closely related to learning styles (Kolb, 1984; see chapter 6). For example, some students are especially skilled at doing research and writing papers. Others are best at interviewing community members or providing counseling assistance. There are those who excel at organizing tasks and developing project timelines, while others are artistically and visually creative.

You might think these are just differences in personality, and that is true to some extent. How we act and interact, however, is intricately connected to how we learn. Some of us would rather research and analyze the latest crime statistics, while others would prefer to talk with prison inmates about their own experiences. Some of us are more concerned with

---

✵ Exercise 10.1: The Menial and the Meaningful

1. Whether you are working alone or in a group, make a written list of five to seven menial tasks that you have performed as a part of your community-based experience (e.g., making copies, setting up appointments).
2. Connect these tasks to the larger goals of the project. How are these rather simple tasks helping to meet the intended outcomes of the project?
3. Connect the project goals to larger societal or political issues (e.g., does removing graffiti assist a neighborhood in community-building?).
4. Identify the specific capacities needed to create positive community change. How does addressing these issues require a mindset, a heartset, and a skillset? How does transformational learning result from the application of these capacities to the issues at hand? How might your community work and class learning facilitate a renewed sense of meaning for and with your community partners?

> ### Exercise 10.2: Art for Art's Sake
>
> After reading the following newspaper headline—"Local School District to End Extracurricular Activities"—concerned college students in a community-based learning course decided to work with a local high school to raise money to keep its arts, drama, and music programs alive for one more year. The college students planned to get donations from community businesses for a silent auction that would take place during a talent show performed by the high-school students themselves. Assume that you are one of these students and that this is your service-learning project:
>
> 💡 Optional exercises:
>
> • Identify a list of roles and tasks that need to be completed to carry out the project.
> • Which of these roles and tasks would you like to perform?
> • How might these interests connect to your preferred styles of learning and knowing?
> • How could you use your styles to facilitate the learning, knowing, and doing of others?
>
> ✸ Exploring the underlying issues:
>
> • Was this type of project necessary? Why or why not?
> • How does it help meet community needs?
> • How might the project be avoiding larger community, political, and societal issues?
> • What project could the class do instead to address these larger issues?
> • What information, ideas, theories, and/or conceptual models from your academic major might provide insight into these community challenges and offer possible solutions?

how our community project affects the people involved (regardless of what gets accomplished), while others of us want to make sure the project is efficient and effective (maybe even at the expense of some people's feelings).

What is the right answer or approach? All of the above. The more we can understand our own ways of knowing, the better we will be able to contribute to community problem solving. In turn, this may give us more patience and empathy for those with whom we are working who may be different from ourselves. Ultimately, that is one of the most distinguishable characteristics of transformational learning.

Complete exercise 10.2. Notice that the last set of questions requires us to think beyond the logistical details necessary for completing a successful project. Indeed, at the end of the evening, the students were very successful in raising over $6,000 for the high school programs. In terms of long-term impact in the community, were the students successful? Was community change created, or was this merely a "BAND-AID" approach to a bigger problem?

Critical Inquiry

Transformational learning means using our ways of knowing to deal with issues directly in front of us (for example, money needed for new band uniforms) and to ask challenging questions as a part of **critical inquiry** into the economic, societal, and political sources of community problems.

Critical inquiry is comparable in many ways to critical thinking and active reflection. When you are engaged in critical inquiry, you ask yourself and others questions like the following: What are the internal and external influences keeping an organization in crisis? With whom and where does the power for change reside? Are there issues of privilege, oppression, or discrimination involved? What specific strategies (or **leverage points**) could create opportunities to make a positive difference? What values and beliefs are important to the organization? What does the individual need? What does the group need? What does the community need?

As opposed to simply being cynical, negative, or snide, critical inquiry is less about making judgments than being a means for understanding underlying and connected issues. In the case in exercise 10.2, lacking art or theatrical supplies is merely a symptom of larger administrative and economic problems. Critical inquiry asks *why*: Why is there no money for supplies? Critical inquiry asks *who*: Who is empowered to make decisions about how funding is distributed? Who is responsible for managing the money? Is this an individual management problem? Is this a problem of the funding stream from the state? Both? Critical inquiry asks *when, how,* and *where*: Did these issues first arise at the school district level, or have federal priorities shifted funding from providing holistic education to meeting standardized test requirements? Critical inquiry asks, *Is there a relationship* between spending money on computers and learning outcomes? How does this compare with the learning outcomes realized by spending money on a field trip to the local history museum or the production of a play at the school?

In some educational realms, this inquiry approach is referred to as ***deconstruction***. For example, a community problem such as teenage vandalism could be deconstructed by critically examining answers to a myriad of questions, such as the following: Is teenage vandalism simply caused by a few misdirected youth? Is teenage vandalism a consequence of poor parenting? Is teenage vandalism a failure of schools and educational efforts? Is teenage vandalism a result of hard economic times? What are the roots of teenage vandalism? How might we find solutions to the problem?

The intent in deconstructing social issues is to identify and scrutinize layer by layer the elements that support the problem. Once these factors can be identified, then community problem solving can begin.

Academic Disciplines as Critical Inquiry

In collective problem solving, a valuable tool that works in tandem with ways of knowing and critical inquiry is the lens of the academic discipline. Indeed, business and community members have told leaders in higher education that one of the most important skills needed in its graduates is the ability to communicate across disciplines. If you plan to be an engineer, you may need to be able to talk with environmentalists. If you want to be a botanist, you might work collaboratively with public health specialists. If your desire is to become a lawyer, you may find yourself asking for advice from mental health counselors in assisting your clients.

At some point in your academic career, you will focus on a major area of study. In colleges and universities, disciplines fall into four major categories: science, social science, humanities, and professional schools. We might say that academic disciplines are particular frames of critical inquiry. They are ways of considering issues through specific theoretical frameworks or sets of questions to ask. In science, the scientific method is central to understanding and being able to do science. In English, literary theory is the way English majors think about and look at written text. Bringing multiple disciplinary perspectives to a community issue or need often provides the means for thinking differently and broadly enough to find a strategy or solution (leverage point) that is perfect for that moment and one that an individual working alone would never have discovered. Disciplinary lenses and frameworks can also inform each other. The most groundbreaking work in research is done at the fringes of disciplines, where they meet and mingle with one another. Consider biotechnology,

---

⚹⚹ Exercise 10.3: Who's to Blame?

- Brainstorm a written list of everyone and everything to blame for the issues addressed by your community partner. Make sure to consider local, county, city, state, national, and even global sources.
- Next, examine this list in terms of categories or patterns. Are there sources that can be linked together, such as economic, political, societal, environmental, geographic, and so on?
- Now, ask some critical inquiry questions about what you see, using the list of critical inquiry questions as a guide.
- Finally, what can you identify as strategic or key areas (leverage points) for creating change? If possible, discuss your ideas with others working on your project.

medical anthropology, or the genome project. All of these advances demand an understanding and expertise in more than one discipline, in more than one way of knowing and thinking critically.

A significantly challenging aspect of service-learning is discovering how to use and apply the knowledge from your academic discipline in the community. As the learner who is serving, it is very easy to focus directly on the client or project (through tasks that can take great amounts of time and effort), forgetting to apply—reflectively and effectively—your academic learning.

In working with a community health organization, a student who was an English major could not easily identify a strategy for contributing to his class's project. Then the community partner described the need for information that explained its services to its clients. This student knew how to target written materials to particular audiences and how to write effectively. Because of his suggestions and abilities, the project developed brochures and other media pieces on specific health issues for homeless youth. Moreover, all the students in the course worked collaboratively to create both a computerized tracking system for donated medicines and a business plan for the agency. Pre-med majors, English majors, business majors, and graphic design majors contributed their unique skills and talents to meet the community partner's objectives and have a positive impact on the health needs of youth at risk for compromised health.

Consider this community situation and think about what you would do: A city transportation authority contacted the engineering department of a local college. Administrators were concerned about the safety of passengers in wheelchairs after a recent accident indicated that their chairs were not being strapped in properly. Engineering students teamed with physics majors and mathematics majors to examine the harnessing systems. In the lab, the operability of the equipment seemed more than adequate. So what was the problem? And how would they solve it?

The students decided they needed information from real-life examples. They asked anthropology students—whose disciplinary background and skills emphasized the value of data collection in real-world settings—to take the bus to school over a period of two weeks and observe how the harnessing systems were used by riders in wheelchairs. The anthropology students noticed that, for bus drivers to assist with the strapping mechanism, they had to hug and touch the passenger from behind. Given social norms against physical contact between strangers, the harnessing could not be connected properly. What seemed to be a mechanical issue was actually a human interaction issue. Still, the entire apparatus had to be redesigned and then tested by employing the insights of psychology, communication, anthropology, and sociology students.

You will be challenged to apply your academic knowledge and skills in unexpected ways. In the case of one service-learning project, faculty and students from a university business school intended to create a marketing plan for a start-up technology company. When the class arrived at the community partner's site, however, it became clear that the company

---

💡 Exercise 10.4: The Disciplinary Lens

Make a list of the skills or critical inquiry perspectives for your major or academic discipline. Next, compare this list with the kinds of activities that your community partner or project needs. Start with the easiest connections and then tackle the more challenging ones. (Try to think differently about the typical activities in a major. If you are a graphic design major, how could you contribute to a cancer survivor research project? If you are a history major, what skills could you bring to a senior activist interview project?) Finally, write a short reflection on how your academic lens will contribute to your service-learning work now and in the future.

If you are working in a group, you might complete this exercise on your own and then compare your responses to others. This will be especially revealing if there are a wide variety of academic majors in your class. You might also replicate the exercise using your skills and knowledge from your academic minor.

needed basic reorganization before any kind of plan was even possible. The students and faculty were faced with the politically sensitive issue of how to work with managers who were not strong leaders and employees who lacked commitment to the organization. Their first step was to develop a corporate vision and philosophy that engaged both the workers and the directors.

Similarly, graphic design students who were invited to design informational signs for a community recreation site found there was great controversy about the signs and whether there was a need for them at all. While students were under the impression that their work was to create a simple design product, what they learned, instead, was that their skills in listening to and negotiating with neighbors were the critical elements of the project.

Getting experience thinking on your feet, reacting in the moment, and managing conflicting values and priorities are part of living and working in the world. Unlike most classes where the "right" answers are filled in on the "test," the service-learning project will test you to consider multiple approaches.

Community Partners as Sources of Expertise

A key feature of service-learning is the opportunity for students to use their skills and learning in actual situations. Moreover, critical inquiry and conceptual knowledge are very important, and seeing those ideas and concepts in action is crucial for lasting and deep learning to take place. However, a prime source of learning is the community agency itself. Community professionals have a variety of knowledge and skills drawn from their experiences that are uniquely distinct from what can be provided in a college classroom (no matter how knowledgeable the instructor might be). Community partners look to students and faculty to share their academic *expertise* to address community issues; students and faculty learn through serving the community (with its own expertise) as they turn theory into practice. This symbiotic relationship exemplifies *reciprocity*. Service-learning establishes a *reciprocal learning* process between the college and the community.

For instance, education students who agreed to tutor immigrants and refugees at a local support center assumed that their expertise in teaching skills would help participants learn English. What quickly became apparent, however, was that the participants would not always agree to talk with one another to practice their language skills. Frustrated, the education students complained to the community partner that the participants were uncooperative and unwilling to learn. The community partner then provided the education students with a workshop on the cultural, religious, political, and historical backgrounds of the immigrants and refugees. The education students came to understand that it is *not* just a "small world after all" as they discovered that national, social, and political factors can inhibit engagement across differences.

At times, students may find the expertise of the community partner difficult to accept. Architecture students who were assisting Habitat for Humanity got a lesson in budgeting and urban planning when the project coordinator dismissed all twelve designs for low-income homes because they were impossible to build on the selected site and within financial constraints. A marketing class that developed a slick brochure for a local YMCA's services was literally sent back to the drawing board by the agency director for using college-level language when the average reading level of their clients was seventh grade.

Such lessons from the community may not feel like the type of reciprocal learning you hoped to gain. Thus, reciprocity (to and from the community) requires openness to new views and a willingness to consider issues from the community perspective.

> To further understand community perspectives, complete **Exercise 10.6: Both Sides of the Table**, on page 160.

As a service-learner, ask yourself these questions: Have you been intentional about listening to community professionals' viewpoints? Have you included community partners in planning sessions and meetings about the project? Have you made explicit the goals and objectives of the project while concurrently attending to the values and motivations of the community partner? In sum, reciprocity involves not just the project's product, but also the process you used to complete it. Reciprocity is the impact you had on the community and the community had on you.

Being fully aware of the process as well as the hoped-for outcomes may give you additional insights. As with internships or practicum experience, service-learning projects may allow you to explore the professional standards of various career fields. For example, in a project to design a marketing logo for a new construction company, students learned about the culture of the firm, including expectations about work behavior, dress, communication, decision making, and acceptance of critique and feedback.

In another case, students created a CD to help cancer survivors. The project gave the student team exposure to medical terminology and community health needs, as well as experience in software development. Most importantly, students were challenged by their own ethnocentric perspectives. Originally planning to have all information in English, the students realized, in working with a diversity of cancer patients, that they had to identify and include website links with health information in multiple languages. In addition, during meetings with physicians and nurses, the students were privy to discussions about healthcare coverage and differences in prevention and treatment options depending on clients' socioeconomic status. It is this type of service-learning that will be forever memorable, providing you with richer insights and learning about the real world of healthcare than could ever be addressed inside a classroom.

Thus, when academic theory meets actual community issues, a different level of understanding and actions frequently results. The community partner generally has knowledge and expertise that can be integrated into the project and utilized to gain broader insights into community concerns. Working side by side with community professionals, you will learn that social problems are complex and that solutions require thoughtful and intentional involvement and intervention.

Finally, reciprocal learning is frequently gained from working directly with the community clients. Even though our good intentions are to help others, we often receive more than we give. A sociology major reflected in her journal:

I'm so impressed with the perseverance of some of these women [at the domestic violence shelter]. It's incredible what they go through. Many of them have kids, so they push the courts to act faster, they

deal with school administrators, they negotiate bill payments even when they can't return to their homes safely. Their organization and tenacity is amazing. They've taught me to not take anything for granted.

Similarly, an English major who was tutoring non-native English-language learners noted the following from his experience:

Yes, I'm teaching them grammar and sentence construction. They're teaching me about Vietnamese culture, Buddhism, and a whole different way of being in the world. I'm teaching them about language elements. They're teaching me about life elements.

Conscious Living

In a service-learning project called "Equalizing Access to Justice," students at a community college worked with juvenile justice services and marginalized youth. At the end of the course, a history major noted in his journal how he had understood inequities theoretically before the class, but, after witnessing the issues for himself, he now had a more realistic sense of historical racial and ethnic stereotypes inherent in the system.

I always believed that one of the strengths of the American judicial system was to treat everyone equally. That illusion has been totally demystified. My client was a 15-year-old Latino who worked hard the last three months with our class. In court, the probation officer hadn't filed his behavior report, and his attorney met him just five minutes before the proceedings. Just because he had one minor curfew violation, the judge sent him back to detention. I felt so powerless. I knew this was a good kid, but the system saw him as a troublemaker. I'm left wondering if a white kid in the same situation would have been let off.

The understanding of this college student's experience gave him a transformed view and new consciousness about the reality of those without power and how they have to deal with the policies and procedures of the justice system. For him, history came alive.

Shifting our worldview is an implicit goal of most service-learning courses. Unless we come to see how political, economic, and judicial systems tend to favor one group over another, we will be forever prevented from truly assisting those in need. In a service-learning class working with recent refugees from South America, the students were initially naive about the geography of the region. One student admitted in her journal, "Since the weather is much warmer in Latin America, it's not so hard to live on less. Being homeless is easier there than it is in the United States."

Students' perspectives began to change as they worked with families who had fled to the United States because of political unrest and the lack of citizen rights in their country. The students researched historical and current political events, worked with the community agency to learn about cultural life issues, and held dialogues with their refugee partners. To their surprise, students learned that, to protect corporate interests, the United States had funded a military coup that led to civil war. Now, as they examined the issues through the lives of their refugee partners, students felt a different sense of connectedness and responsibility:

We tried to see what it was like through their eyes, even though we were from such different places. We learned a lot, but more than that, I think I'm a better person. I've got a sense of understanding and being part of a much bigger issue. My government helped create their situation—so, in some ways, I did too. I see now that I need to be more aware and politically involved.

As part of a summer school project, an industrial technology student participated in a camp for severely disabled children. In working with the campers, the student changed her career direction by taking additional courses in physical therapy so that she could develop equipment to support these children's ability

---

✶ Exercise 10.5: Expanding Critical Consciousness and Career Skills

Recall a situation at your service site when your view of the people or place suddenly shifted. Perhaps you thought more positively about the service because a client was especially appreciative or passed a crucial academic exam because of your help. Alternatively, perhaps you thought more negatively about the service because a client didn't show up for a tutoring appointment or maybe the community partner forgot to organize critical details for your project. Try to remember a critical moment or incident that sparked your emotions and your thoughts in new ways. Then, read each set of questions and either share your responses with a classmate or write them down in a reflection journal.

- How did you react to the situation? Did you feel happy or mad? To what or whom did you attribute the cause? Did you blame the individual (such as he's lazy or she's flaky)? Did your thinking move beyond initial responses to larger social, political, or organizational root causes of issues?
- What facilitated your consideration of other factors that led to the situation? Did you write a reflective journal or essay? Did you talk with a classmate or instructor? Did you do additional reading or research? Did you consider academic concepts from your own major or other disciplines? What helped change your view from critique to critical consciousness?
- How did/does a heightened sense of critical inquiry and consciousness inform your actions? How did/do you act or behave differently at the service site?
- As a result, describe how your perspectives and sense of self have been transformed?
- How will these transformed perspectives and ways of being assist you in your future career? In your role as an engaged community member and citizen? How might you use your new knowledge and skills to leverage change professionally and personally?

challenges. She told her faculty member that she had finally found her "true calling."

It is these personal transformations and a conscious shift in how we view ourselves and our place in the world that service-learning can effect. For many, the feeling that we do not count and cannot really do anything to change things is very different after an experience in the community. The point of these examples is to ask you to think about yourself and how you understand your goals, aspirations, and values. Right now, you may just be thinking about finishing this course. If you're a senior, you may be dreaming about graduation. For graduate students, the main issue may be finding the right advisor or thesis topic. However, at some point you will be finished with your education and continuing your life beyond college. What kind of life do you want to create for yourself? How do you plan to live consciously? For what do you want to be known?

Summary

Service-learning courses give you practice using theory (academic concepts) in a real setting (experiential learning) to achieve both a heightened sense of consciousness and transformational learning. In this chapter, we have examined the relationships between course content and community issues in order to connect your experiences with the larger world of ideas and issues outside the college campus. Ultimately, service-learning courses should help you learn how to create change actively and intentionally. In our final illustration, a group of students at Portland State University planned and opened an organic restaurant after a service-learning project on sustainable ecology and the food-service industry. The restaurant currently provides a place where students can find healthful vegetarian meals. The students also influ-enced the competing food service company on campus to offer alternative food choices and organic fruits and vegetables.

We hope that you consider the social, economic, environmental, and political aspects of your project, using questions like these as a guide:

- What have you learned through your community service project that you would not have learned in a traditional classroom?
- What insights have you gained about your community, your state, and your world as a result of the project?
- How are these issues simultaneously interconnected and interdependent?
- Have you discovered cultural stereotypes and assumptions that influence community interactions and individual lives?
- What new skills, knowledge, and insights can you apply to improving current systems and practices for addressing issues in the future?

The result of your service-learning experience is a broadened understanding of the complexities of community interactions and an informed sense of how to translate your beliefs and values into action. These newly acquired skills and knowledge, which have been reinforced and extended by your academic discipline lens, can then be utilized in your community in countless ways. Further, you know how change is created (that is, the internal and external influences and leverage points). As you are more fully cognizant of issues of power and privilege, you are better positioned to facilitate equity and social justice. In the end, we hope you believe that continuing such connections with community organizations will make your life richer and more meaningful by contributing to a greater sense of the common good.

Key Concepts

consciousness	expertise	reciprocity
critical inquiry	leverage points	transformational learning
deconstruction	reciprocal learning	ways of knowing

Key Issues

- What relationships do you see between course content and community issues?
- How can you use your academic discipline to better understand community problems?
- How do abstract concepts and experiential learning inform each other?
- What are the relationships between social and political issues at your community partner site?
- How is your community a source of knowledge and expertise?
- How has this experience expanded your understanding of yourself?
- How has this experience expanded your understanding of organizations?

ADDITIONAL EXERCISES

 Exercise 10.6: Both Sides of the Table

If you are working in a group, break into two smaller groups. One of these will be the "college group," and the other will be the "community group." Members of the "college group" will work together to make a list of all the assumptions and plans that you and your faculty had at the beginning of the project. You may consult your notes and reflections from the beginning of the service-learning experience. The "community group" will list all the changes and new perspectives that the community partner brought to the project. When you are finished, compare notes and discuss the evolution of your partnership through the reciprocal learning process.

 Exercise 10.7: In Retrospect

Imagine that a biographer is coming to interview you about your life and work 30 years from now. Because you want to be prepared, you jot down some notes. What have you been doing in terms of career, family, community, and political involvement? What do you think is most noteworthy? Has your life been fulfilling? What has made it so, or not?

If possible, meet with another person (or as a group) and share elements from your reflection. What type of communities will you create if you bring to fruition what you have imagined here?

PART FOUR

Assessing the Engagement Effort

The goal of part four (chapters 11–14) is to assist you with evaluating the results of your community-based engagement. Did your efforts with the community actually make a difference to that community and its stakeholders? As for yourself, what skills, knowledge, and values did you gain in the process of connecting with the community? How might you leverage this learning in future efforts to make positive change in your community?

KEY SYMBOLS

 Exercises of utmost importance to complete (working either on your own or in a group)

 Optional exercises (strategies for gaining deeper insights into the issues)

 Exercises that provide further resources and information in your quest for understanding community problem solving and change

CHAPTER 11

Beyond a Grade

Are We Making a Difference?: The Benefits and Challenges of Evaluating Learning and Serving

SHERRIL B. GELMON, SUSAN AGRE-KIPPENHAN, AND CHRISTINE M. CRESS

I had no idea that less than a mile from our university children were going hungry. If we improve the life of even one kid I'll feel like I did something good.

IN THE PREVIOUS QUOTE, the student contemplates children going hungry and the importance of helping them. While no one would argue with the need to do "something good," it is important to put our work into context. In assisting others, is it sufficient to provide a single meal, or do we need to work toward finding a long-term solution to hunger?

At this point in your project, you have probably discussed many of these types of issues. For example, you may have researched how many children are in a similar situation in your community. You may have decided during what period of time you could provide assistance (for example, the Thanksgiving holiday). You may have evaluated, individually or as a group, whether it is most valuable to feed a child, hold a food drive, or write a grant to connect families and communities with existing service providers. Moreover, you may have tried to use the theoretical and academic models of your disciplinary major to address these issues.

As you bring your service-learning experience to a close, ask yourself, your classmates, and your commu-

nity partner about the impact of your efforts and work: Did you do something good? Did your project make a difference? On the surface, these are deceptively simple questions. In all likelihood, you did help. You did do something good. As we've learned, however, in previous chapters, service-learning is a complex, integrated approach to learning. As such, it is imperative for you to engage in a strategic and methodical evaluation to determine what effects you have had on the community, as well as to identify how these interactions have affected you. In so doing, you may find yourself reevaluating some of the premises and assumptions that you and your classmates initially brought to learning and serving in the community. In chapter 9, we asked you to investigate your assumptions about "failure" in order to contextualize your progress on the service-learning journey. Similarly, in this chapter, we will help you explore and broaden your definitions of "success" by increasing your knowledge of and ability to use assessment techniques. Specifically, we offer strategies for better understanding the impact of your project by introducing a tripartite framework (*concepts, indicators, evidence*) for examining and evaluating your experiences. We will also build upon the earlier ALPS work you have completed to make explicit the importance of assessment at the beginning, middle, and conclusion of your service-learning experience.

Did We Make a Difference?

The question "Did we make a difference?" can yield multiple responses. The "difference" may depend upon the perspective of the respondent (student, instructor, community partner, or client). It may also depend upon who or what you are evaluating: a person, a group, an organization, a population, or a pressing societal issue like hunger or homelessness. When we can state that we have had successful experiences working with the community and provide documentation, data, stories, case studies, and other evidence that support this assessment, we not only demonstrate impact, but we position the community organization for even more positive change.

For example, at a high school in a poor neighborhood, the student drop-out rate had risen from 11 percent to 19 percent in just three years. Concerned, the school principal approached an English professor and a math professor at a local community college, and the three teamed up to create an interdisciplinary service-learning project focused on basic academic skill acquisition and student retention. At its most fundamental level, the community college students provided tutoring for the high school students. More importantly, as the high school students improved their skills, they were trained to tutor one another. Within two years, the drop-out rate decreased to 7 percent, and the overall number of students who enrolled in college after high school graduation increased by 18 percent. Impressed by these numbers, a philanthropic foundation gave the school district and the community college a $450,000 grant to continue and expand the program.

While the impact of some projects may not be immediately apparent or the scope of impact may be more limited than you, your classmates, or your professor had originally anticipated, it is still essential to evaluate your accomplishments carefully. Indeed, there are a myriad of outcomes you can examine:

- **Creating and strengthening community partnerships**: In an ideal service-learning experience, the community partner becomes a true collaborator. Our ability to identify what we contributed, as well as what we received, makes real the concept of *reciprocity*.
- **Measuring personal growth**: Community experiences provide opportunities for us to reflect on our values, to develop skills and expertise, and to consider our personal career plans. Insights about our newly gained knowledge expands our capacity to be effective workers, family members, and citizens.
- **Examining the teaching and learning process**: Service-learning courses have explicit goals for connecting community experience to the academic experience. Evaluation can strengthen courses, contribute to faculty learning, and have a long-range impact on student experiences and program development.

What Do We Mean By "Evaluation"?

Evaluation provides a structured opportunity to reflect upon what has been accomplished (or not) and the value of such accomplishments. It involves participating in a thoughtful iterative process in which multiple aspects of an experience are considered and constructive feedback is provided. Frequently, the terms *evaluation* and *assessment* are used interchangeably. Regardless of what term you use, the goal of evaluation is to help us articulate and share our learning with others in an effort to make improvements. In this sense, evaluation can be imagined as a loop or learning cycle (figure 11.1). You evaluate (*assess*) an experience, draw insights (*analyze*), try something new (*implement*) based on those insights, and *evaluate* the experience again. This evaluation cycle is fundamentally about learning and putting those new insights directly back into practice.

In introducing the concept of *reflection* in chapter 6 (page 95), we discussed what are essentially three levels of evaluation for the service-learning experience: (1) *pre-service reflection* (project identification and planning), (2) *reflection during service* (meaning, observations, analysis, and adaptation), and (3) *post-service reflection* (new understandings and application). Thus, in completing those exercises, you have already been actively participating in the Evaluation Learning Cycle.

Now that you are reaching the *post-service reflection* component, a critical element for determining new understandings and applications that can be shared with others is to demonstrate how you successfully achieved your **outcomes**. Outcomes are the goals you accomplished. Imagine that your project goal was to rebuild

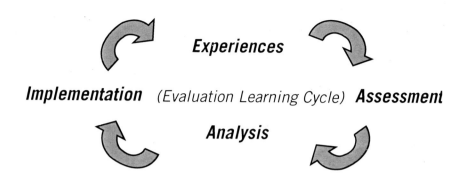

Figure 11.1. Evaluation Learning Cycle

the playground equipment in a local park, and you successfully accomplished this task, thus turning the refurbished equipment from being a shared goal to a realized achievement or outcome. How did you reach this goal? What *evidence* supports your assertion of this achievement? Suppose, for a moment, that you finished with more donated lumber than you needed for the playground equipment, so you redonated these materials to Habitat for Humanity. Evidence of your success certainly starts with the rebuilt park equipment, and it also includes the amount (board feet) of lumber you gave to the nonprofit organization. Other evidence of the outcomes of your success might be the amount of time you took to accomplish the project (you completed it faster than expected), the number of people participating (fourteen neighbors volunteered to help), the amount of money spent (you were under budget by $465), and even comments and quotations you wrote down from happy parents and children at the park.

In evaluating an entire service-learning course (as opposed to a single community experience), students, faculty, and community members may take a critical look at the goals and objectives of the course, the activities that supported those objectives, and the resulting outcomes. Depending on the course and the nature of the project, the outcomes or evidence can vary from the number of children served in an after-school recreational program to the production of a public television announcement on how to become a mentor. You might count the number of homes participating in a new recycling program. You might have created a book of narratives from interviews with women who worked in factories during World War II. In other words, you might gather ***quantitative data*** (things you can count) and/or ***qualitative data*** (written descriptions of observations and experiences). Indeed, many researchers use

multiple methods of evaluation (quantitative and qualitative) in order to best uncover strengths and weaknesses of a project, to prove or disprove assumptions and assertions, and to allow for creative forms of communicating and disseminating the information depending on the nature of the report and the audience (such as charts, photographs, quotations, short stories, etc.)

Evaluation of service-learning courses can also be conducted from other perspectives. Your faculty member may want to identify which reflective exercises and activities best helped you learn. Institutional administrators may want to know the impact of your service-learning course on community-university urban renewal efforts. The community agency may want to do a time-cost analysis of resources the organization expended and benefits the organization received from your work and involvement.

Thus, good evaluation flows logically from course and community partner goals and thoughtfully utilizes both quantitative (numbers) and qualitative (interviews, observations) methods. These results can then be summarized in graphs and data tables, and/or in rich stories and descriptions based upon personal experiences. When evaluation is done in this way, subsequent course design and planning are based on actual data rather than hunches and drive continuous improvement in response to the needs and performance of you, your classmates, faculty, and community.

Challenges to Evaluation

Consider the various perceptions stated in the following examples. Clearly, each person has a particular perspective and set of expectations about service-learning. Many reasons may compel us to "make a difference"

✦ Exercise 11.1: Conquering the ALPS

In chapter 2, you articulated your understanding of the goals, roles, and responsibilities for the service experience. From this you developed a document (**Exercise 2.7: Action Learning Plan for Serving**, on page 31) that specified action items, the person(s) responsible, and a timeframe. In chapter 4, you refined your ALPS to delineate tasks within your team and a timeline for accomplishing them.

For this exercise, start by reviewing those documents, and then write down your responses to the following questions:

1. List three to five achievements you personally accomplished through the service experience.
2. If applicable, list three to five achievements your group accomplished through the service experience.
3. For each of the items listed in numbers 1 and 2, indicate how you can "prove" these accomplishments; in other words, what evidence of outcomes can you show to others?
4. Make a list of questions you have or additional evidence you want to gather.

If you are working with a group, discuss your responses with others.

---

through service-learning experiences, including community issues, academic considerations, and issues of personal growth. While all of these are valid, they may not be equally *valuable* to each of the participants in the service-learning experience. This is a crucial consideration in assessing the project and determining overall impact.

I don't know if we really did anything important at the community center. We spent most of our time just talking to the kids. I didn't understand why the professor never spent time in class discussing how the work at the community center related to our readings in the class.

Student

Working with children at the community center provides opportunities for students to recognize and apply the developmental theories they have been learning in class while offering a meaningful resource for the community.

Faculty

It was so valuable to have college students there to interact informally with the kids at the center. Many of them had never met anyone who had gone to college.

It changed their ideas about the future. The kids want us to organize a trip to campus to see what it is really like there.

Community Partner

We made an institutional commitment to service-learning. Our long-term community partnerships have caused us to reevaluate our resource allocations and organizational support.

University Service-Learning Director

The priority for the community organization may be keeping kids safe. Faculty may be split between addressing community needs and course-specific learning objectives. Students, including yourself, may care about the community and academics, but within the context of your own career plans. From an institutional perspective, the university or college may be balancing the resource efficiency of courses with an institutional commitment to community relationships. This range of priorities results in a related range of values placed on outcomes. (It may be helpful to refer to chapter 9, "Failure with the Best of Intentions," to review the discussion on the potential for conflicting expectations among the faculty, community partner, and students. Fortunately, the strategies developed in chapter 9 can be applied to thinking about conflicting priorities in terms of evaluation as well.)

Other challenges to evaluation may be timelines, resources, resistant participants, fear of findings, shelved reports, and/or lack of expertise. The good news is that strategies do exist for overcoming these challenges.

A Strategy for Evaluating Service-Learning

Just like the actions and behaviors needed for conducting your service-learning project, evaluation and assessment take thoughtful action and coordinated effort. A comprehensive model for doing this was developed at Portland State University and then modified and enhanced through application in several other institutional contexts (Gelmon, Holland, Driscoll, Spring, & Kerrigan, 2001). The model allows evaluation to focus on areas such as individual student learning in terms of achievement of personal and course goals, as well as satisfaction with the learning experience. The model also provides strategies to assess faculty involvement in, and commitment to, service-learning, as well as institutional support for service-learning. Finally, the model addresses evaluation of the impact on the community agency, as well as on community-university partnerships.

As noted previously, evaluation is part of an ongoing learning cycle that should be woven from front to back within the tapestry of any service-learning project. By assessing your actions, you can recognize strengths (individual and programmatic), identify opportunities for improvement, and make evident academic and community connections on both real and theoretical terms.

To begin, ask yourself (or discuss with your classmates and/or community partner) the following questions in considering how to assess your service-learning project:

- What is the aim of the assessment? What do I need to know?
- Who might want or need the assessment information? What do others (students, faculty members, community partners, clients, colleges) need to know?
- What resources are needed and available to support assessment?
- How might I conduct the assessment?

- How can I ensure that the results will be used proactively?

At first, these questions may seem a bit daunting. Most of us have had little experience with formal assessment practices. But the process can be divided easily into a useful framework of three components: *concepts*, *indicators*, and *evidence*. The framework terms are defined:

- ***Concepts***: What do we want to know?
- ***Indicators***: How will we measure it?
- ***Evidence***: What can we gather, show, or demonstrate?

Let's say, for example, that you want to identify what your classmates learned about their community as a result of their service experience at the local homeless shelter. The *concept* that you are evaluating is students' community awareness about homelessness. An *indicator* of this concept might be student knowledge about underlying issues that contribute to homelessness. The *evidence* you might gather could include data from a survey you create and distribute to your classmates (quantitative data) and/or examples of essay questions (with student and faculty permission) that your faculty member asked on an exam about the connections between course readings on low-income housing and clients who use shelter services (qualitative data).

- ***Concept***: Student awareness about homelessness
- ***Indicator***: Knowledge of factors contributing to homelessness
- ***Evidence***: Results from surveys (quantitative data) and/or students' essays citing research on homelessness (qualitative data)

Now suppose that you want to assess the impact of your service-learning course on the homeless shelter itself. Here, the *concept* is the impact of the service-learning course. An *indicator* of this concept might be placement of homeless clients in free and low-income housing units. The *evidence* you might gather could be the actual number of clients placed (quantitative data) and/or interviews with the shelter staff about how your class assisted their efforts (qualitative data).

- *Concept*: Impact of student service at the homeless shelter
- *Indicator*: Placement of clients in low-income housing
- *Evidence*: Number of clients served/placed (quantitative data) and/or quotes from interviews with shelter staff about how students assisted their efforts (qualitative data)

In determining your assessment methodology (strategy/design), other issues are important to consider as well: client satisfaction, cost, time, level of collaboration with other social service agencies, travel issues, and so on. What is most important is that you (and your group) determine a reasonable scope for the extent of your evaluation and a plan for how you will gather, disseminate, and communicate your findings for community benefit.

The *CIE model* (concepts, indicators, evidence) is particularly useful in evaluating the overall service experience (exercise 11.2). The next section discusses other techniques for helping you evaluate your individual student growth, the teaching-learning environment, and contributions to community organizations and their constituents.

Understanding Your Own Experiences

In **Exercise 11.1: Conquering the ALPS**, you began to evaluate your contributions and achievements in this service-learning experience. Your ability to identify and articulate your skills and knowledge with respect to the service-learning activities may depend on how many previous service-learning experiences you have had in other settings. Remember, while you or other students may have had no formal service-learning prior to this experience, you may have had other relevant experiences or bring skills that have made substantial contributions to your own learning as well as that of your classmates.

In the past, students have observed that the personal impact of service-learning is cumulative over time. As such, individual "success" or "failure" in a service-learning activity is complicated to determine, and evaluation cannot be approached from a "one-size-fits-all" strategy. Thus, the learning impact must be placed in the context of your own prior experiences, as well as the present project activity.

To do this, let's look at the *Self-Assessment Matrix*, which enables you to determine strengths by recognizing your own individual levels of experience with various dimensions of the service-learning activity. The matrix is an adaptation of a skill acquisition model originally applied to professional experience (Benner, Tanner, & Chesla, 1995; Dreyfus & Dreyfus, 1996), and further refined for use in faculty development within service-learning courses and research (Gelmon & Agre-Kippenhan, 2002).

The Self-Assessment Matrix (figure 11.2) shows how experience and learning evolve along a continuum. At each stage, skill levels are categorized as roles

---

✯ Exercise 11.2: Utilizing the CIE Model

Create an assessment plan utilizing the following matrix. Ideally, you want to link *concepts*, *indicators*, and *evidence* with your original goals from your ALPs (see exercise 2.7 on page 31). Later, you will identify tasks and timelines for this assessment plan, just as you did as part of your action planning. Be sure there is a clear connection between your initial goals and your process for evaluating the success of the service experience.

Goal	Concept	Indicator	Evidence
1.	1.		
	2.		
2.	1.		
	2.		

Self-Assessment Matrix (SAM)				
Activity Component	◄——————— Skill Level ———————►			
	Explorer	*Novice*	*Engaged*	*Expert*
Experience	None or Limited	Initial	Some	Extensive
Learning	Exposure	Observation	Participation	Leader
Personal Development	Self-focused	Self-aware	Connected to others	Big picture
Reflection	None or limited	General insights	Connected	Rich and integrated
Connection to Community	Individual benefit	Recognizes community needs/assets	Connected locally with community	Facilitates community linkages
Intercultural Competence	Personal focus	Aware of others	Respectful and appreciative of others	Seeks out and adapts to others
Civic Engagement	Unaware	Participates in activities	Organizes	Initiates social justice action
Capacity to Work in Communities	Unknown	Limited and directed	Responds to requests	Imaginative, self-directed leadership

Figure 11.2. Self-Assessment Matrix (SAM)

(e.g., "engaged") and illustrated as descriptors (e.g., "participation") that you might demonstrate for each element of the service-learning experience. A brief definition of each skill level and type of service activity follows. See appendix 11.1 for descriptors. Review the matrix and the descriptions that follow, and then proceed to **Exercise 11.3: Using the Self-Assessment Matrix.** (A comprehensive explanation of each category can be found on in the following sections.)

Skill Levels in the Self-Assessment Matrix

- An *Explorer* student asks: What is this service-learning experience all about?
- A *Novice* student asks: What are the things that can help me get started in this service-learning experience?
- An *Engaged* student asks: What am I able to do and contribute through service-learning, what else do I need to learn, and what other skills should I develop?

- An *Expert* student asks: How can I help others learn what I have learned through service-learning and other experiences?

Activity Components of the Self-Assessment Matrix

- **Experience**: Exposure to service-learning, prior involvement in related activities
- **Learning**: Nature of involvement in creating knowledge for self and others
- **Personal development**: Integration of learning with personal skill development and career/life decisions
- **Reflection**: Deliberate process of thoughtful review and analysis of the service-learning experience with the express purpose of identifying key areas of learning and connecting the service-learning experience with the academic content of the course
- **Connection to community**: View of self as related to community

---

✦ Exercise 11.3: Using the Self-Assessment Matrix

Review the matrix and each of the descriptors carefully. Using a highlighter, mark the one descriptor for each component that best described you at the beginning of this service-learning experience. Consider specific examples, if possible, that illustrate these components. (Most people have answers in different columns for the various components.)

Next, take a different-colored highlighter and mark the descriptor for each component that best describes you now, at the end of this service-learning experience.

- What comes to light for you? How have you changed?
- What facilitated your change(s), and how did those factors cause that change?
- Remembering the CIE model, frame these changes in terms of *concepts*, *indicators*, and *evidence*.
- What could you do to further evaluate your own learning experience and your contributions to the community?

- *Intercultural competence*: Recognition of similarities and differences among different population groups and ability to interact between and among different groups
- *Civic engagement*: Scope of personal involvement in activities (both academic and nonacademic) that support community development and participation
- *Capacity to work in communities*: Individual recognition and awareness of potential for present and future involvement in work in relevant communities

Methods for Evaluating Learning Environments

As you well know, service-learning courses are significantly different from traditional courses. Rather than spending all your time in the classroom, you are out in the community. Rather than listening to an instructor lecture to you each day, you are involved in workgroup discussions. Rather than taking tests, you decide on the timeframes to get the project completed. Granted, not all service-learning takes place within an actual course. Some of you may be doing community service as a part of cocurricular activities on campus. Others of you may be involved in federal work/study programs where you chose to perform your project in the community. However you came to be involved in service-learning, we hope that all of you are engaged in some

kind of active reflection and are not just "doing" your service. Indeed, that is the whole idea behind service-learning: that we serve and learn.

I found myself thinking about our class all the time. It affected my own decisions.

After taking one service-learning class I felt more confident taking on and even leading community projects.

Stop for a moment and evaluate what has *supported* your learning. Did you complete readings on community issues that gave you insights into your clients? Did the instructor or administrator with whom you are working provide clear goals and information about the project? Did you attend an orientation or training session with the community partner to familiarize yourself with their needs and interests?

Now assess for a moment what has *inhibited* your learning. Was the amount of time you actually performed the service too short? Did the instructor or administrator give you too much freedom and responsibility? Did the community partner fail to keep promises about information and support?

Assuming that you are completing this service experience as a part of a course, you may be able to assess the environment for learning by using a set of teaching and learning continua that describe the classroom context. These continua offer a lens through which one can evaluate a service-learning course, examine the learning process itself, and illustrate a range of interactions among and between students and instructors (Gelmon, et al., 2001). The five elements in the continua can be defined as follows:

- **Commitment to others**: In a traditional class, the focus is on students' (academic) needs, while in an ideal service-learning classroom the focus is both on students' and the community's needs. Questions asked to assess the learning community include the following: Do students and faculty seem to be interested in other people's needs and interests? Do they express a commitment to discovering these needs and interests, both for the community and for their peers?
- **Student role**: In a traditional class, students are relatively passive learners. In this service-learning class, are the students actively involved in the teaching and learning processes? Do they make decisions about course content, process, and activities? Do the students transition from a role as a learner to a role as a learner *and* teacher as they take on responsibility for their own learning and contribute to their learning of their peers?
- **Faculty role**: In traditional classes, the faculty is directive in managing, ordering, and instructing. Is this the role of the faculty in this service-learning class, or does the faculty facilitate collaboration and offer support? Does the faculty share the authority in the class with the students? Is the faculty member open to learning as well as teaching?
- **Learning orientation**: In traditional classes, the focus is on individual learning, where many service-learning classes are concerned with collective learning. Is the learning environment a collective one in which students and faculty work together? Or is it one in which each individual focuses solely on his or her own individual learning?
- **Pedagogy** (teaching strategies): In traditional classes, faculty may demonstrate a "banking" approach where they "deposit" information into students' minds; students are then expected to regurgitate information for periodic "withdrawals" such as exams or presentations. At the other extreme, the faculty creates a "constructive" environment where they facilitate experiences and students construct their own meanings and learning. In the service-learning environment, is knowledge created that both finds answers and generates questions? Is there an emphasis on combining theory and experience to construct knowledge?

Regardless of the type of service-learning in which you are engaged, your thoughtful reflection on commitment to others, student roles, instructor roles, the learning orientation, and teaching strategies (pedagogy) can be useful in providing feedback to others about your experience (exercise 11.4). After all, evaluation itself is a learning process. As noted earlier, you assess your experiences, develop insights through analysis, and offer ideas for implementation. Moreover, you identify evidence for the outcomes of the experience. Say, for instance, that a roommate asks you, "What did you like about the service experience?" Your response might be, "Everyone made an explicit commitment to the group process even though we had really different personalities. This made the group both fun and interesting, and amazingly each person made every meeting that was scheduled."

Staying with this example, let's imagine that your roommate next asks, "So what does your teacher do?" You might state, "He acts as a facilitator rather than an instructor. He helps us brainstorm and problem-solve, but he's made us ultimately accountable to the community partner."

Measuring Benefits to Community

By now, you have identified how the service experience has made a difference to you and to the class (possibly even the instructor). Did it also make a difference to the community? Working on your own and/or in a group, you have probably already gathered some evidence (quantitative and qualitative information) of your success, especially as you reviewed personal and group achievements in the first activity. Look back at the list of questions you made in **Exercise 11.1: Conquering the ALPS** (page 166). What else do you need to know in

---

💡 Exercise 11.4: Evaluating the Classroom Learning Environment

What does it feel like to be a student in a service-learning course? Are the methods used by the instructor the same or different from those in traditional courses? Look at the following five elements of teaching and learning, and for each mark an "X" that best indicates how you would describe the teaching/learning context of this class.

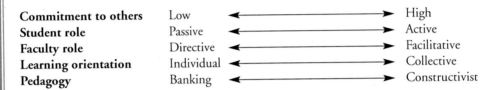

Commitment to others	Low	⟷	High
Student role	Passive	⟷	Active
Faculty role	Directive	⟷	Facilitative
Learning orientation	Individual	⟷	Collective
Pedagogy	Banking	⟷	Constructivist

What evidence can you identify for your positions? If possible, discuss your insights with another classmate or in a group, and generate a list of suggestions or recommendations you would offer for future service-learning courses.

---

order to determine your effectiveness? What else do you need to gather to demonstrate this effectiveness?

Your service-learning work can have a significant effect in addressing real community issues and in providing additional resources to support community activities. Your involvement (and that of your classmates) may have enabled the community partner to provide new or additional services and programs that would otherwise not be available without this contribution. Developing a thoughtfully planned assessment with a defined scope, clear roles and tasks, and strategies for dissemination of findings provides leverage for guiding future actions and community impact. (Complete exercise 11.5.)

Understanding benefits to the community can be directly achieved by asking the community representatives themselves about the work of the students and their shared experiences. One strategy for doing this is to hold a guided conversation (much like a focus group) with students and community representatives (including clients, if possible). An outline for such a conversation is presented on page 175 (**Exercise 11.6: Community Evaluation of Service-Learning**).

Other Important Issues in Evaluation

Other considerations can affect service-learning evaluation. These range from very specific areas such as economic impact and benefits, to issues that are more difficult to measure, such as cross-cultural challenges and humanitarian considerations. We must also con-

---

✬ Exercise 11.5: Measuring Success: A Planned Approach

Building from **Exercises 11.1: Conquering the ALPS** and **11.2: Utilizing the CIE Model** (and any other worksheets you find relevant), create a planned approach for your assessment effort.

1. Note your *concepts* or *indicators*.
2. Next, identify the type of evidence (quantitative and qualitative information) you will seek.
3. Now identify who will gather the evidence (collect data) and from whom (other students, the instructor, clients, the community partner) and in what form (surveys, reports)?
4. Identify the timeline when this will occur.
5. Finally, be specific about how the data will be analyzed and synthesized into a report or a presentation that includes a set of recommendations for implementation.

sider evaluation against a backdrop of service decisions made by the community organization and career decisions made by both students and faculty. The relevance of these issues will be determined by the context of the specific course or service experience.

- **Economic impact and benefits**: Service activities are sometimes measured in terms of what they would cost if the agency provided the service itself. For example, if each of twenty students provides four hours a week of tutoring for the duration of a 10-week course, then the class has provided a total of 800 hours of tutoring. A monetary value can be attached to these services using comparative market values. Community partners and institutions can then use these measures to help communicate the kinds of resources that students provide. While not a complete expression of value, this is one example of a measure that is understandable to a wide audience. In addition, community partners may need to report to funding organizations, and economic measures can be helpful. However, economic measures do not give the entire picture of the service-learning experience; they may not be completely accurate, as students are learning as they work in the community, and their efficiency may not be at its maximum.
- **Cross-cultural challenges**: As we've already discussed, there are often competing expectations and priorities at work that affect evaluation. In chapter 5, we looked at intercultural competencies and attendant issues. Bringing together diverse groups of people from different cultures and institutional backgrounds poses issues that affect evaluation. There may be language barriers that impact the ability to discuss goals. There may be cultural preferences that affect the ways that students and communities interact. These differences may create roadblocks to meeting outcomes. Redirecting around these roadblocks can be a crucial step to evaluating specific service-learning courses. Cross-cultural challenges can also affect how various evaluation methods are designed and implemented. (For more on cross-cultural service experiences see also chapter 12, "Global and Immersive Service-Learning").

- **Humanitarian considerations**: There may be significant humanitarian concerns that affect service-learning courses. Faculty at an institution may choose to work with a specific community on a number of projects. Alternatively, an institution may select several key issues to address. There may be some community issues that cannot be ignored. These considerations may give priority to certain projects and may determine students' placements where they are perceived to be most important as service providers rather than where they can best be academically designed or evaluated.
- **Service decisions**: Given choices, students may gravitate to service experiences for any number of reasons that can affect evaluation. They may be limited by schedules that are packed with classes and family concerns and therefore select courses that fit into their schedules but are not of great interest to them. Other students may choose a service opportunity that connects with their experiences in school or in their private lives and be able to bring a great deal of expertise to the work. A range of interest levels and skills may make for uneven accomplishments and increase the difficulty of evaluation.
- **Career decisions**: Future employment opportunities may be a critical consideration in selecting a service experience. Students may place importance on the success of a course that they feel helps prepare them for their careers. They may also feel a disproportionate responsibility for anything that does not go smoothly. It may be impossible to evaluate such experiences without accounting for the career implications, and findings must be interpreted accordingly.

As an evaluator, you can meet these specific challenges by anticipating how these factors will affect the service-learning experience and by addressing them in your evaluation strategy. Use the evaluation expertise of your faculty member, community member, and/or college institutional research office to ensure that all evaluation methods are ethical and meet college or university safety guidelines.

A final step in evaluation is reporting the results. Once you have collected your data, be timely and responsible in your analysis of it, and report your findings to the various parties involved (other students, faculty, community, institution) to improve future processes and outcomes. A fairly typical approach is to write an assessment report that describes goals, activities, methods of measurement/observation, results, and recommendations (Gelmon, Foucek, & Waterbury, 2005). It is also common for the results to form the basis for presentations (in class or to the community agency), for publications (student newspapers or journals), or for displays (local malls). Care must be taken to ensure that no confidential information is disclosed and that the community organization has given permission for its evaluation findings to be released. Some of the most convenient ways for sharing information include posting results on a website, preparing a poster for display at the community organization, integrating results into an annual report or some other form of report to the community, or incorporating them into an informational brochure for the community partner.

Once careful assessment of your achievements has been completed, it may still feel like there is much left undone. Children are still hungry, families are still homeless, and communities are still unsafe. There is almost always more to be accomplished in a community than we are able to do during a single service-learning experience. We hope that your thoughtful evaluation of your efforts will provide you and others with inspiration and commitment to keep engaging in and working on community issues since you were, in fact, able to demonstrate that you *can* "make a difference" in the lives of others. We encourage you to remember that your focused community engagement and kindness can have lasting impact even after your experience and contribution is long over.

In our graphic design class we created an identity system for a nonprofit that provides mentors for kids starting in the second grade and continuing through their high school graduation. The organization was thrilled with our work. They were invited to the White House, where they handed out a brochure we designed. The most rewarding thing for me was that a few months after the class ended I was at a Saturday football game and a van pulled up with our logo on it. Out poured a whole football team of middle-school kids wearing shirts with our logo. It was amazing to see!

Key Concepts

analyze	engaged	learning
assess	evaluate	outcome
capacity to work in community	evidence	Novice
	experience	personal development
CIE model	Expert	qualitative data
civic engagement	Explorer	quantitative data
concepts	implement	reflection
connection to community	indicators	Self-Assessment Matrix
	intercultural competence	

Key Issues

- How might you identify the best method for evaluating your service-learning experience?
- What are some ways to observe and measure the outcomes to a service experience?
- How might evaluation be integrated into ongoing course activities?
- What are some of the challenges to evaluation, and how might you overcome them?
- How might the evaluation findings best be disseminated?

ADDITIONAL EXERCISE

Exercise 11.6: Community Evaluation of Service-Learning

In order to get feedback from community representatives on the service-learning experience, select community representatives (and/or clients) and invite them to participate in a guided discussion with yourself, other students, and your faculty member. Assign a facilitator to guide and monitor the conversation. (You may even want to identify and invite an independent facilitator, not the faculty or anyone else directly involved with the class). Encourage everyone to participate, making sure that no one person dominates the conversation; the goal here is inclusion, not consensus or agreement.

Here are some sample questions that you can adapt to fit your own service experience:

1. Please introduce yourself and indicate your role in this service-learning course.
2. What went well during this experience? What factors contributed to successful outcomes? What evidence do you have of this success?
3. What obstacles or barriers did you encounter during this experience? Please describe how these could have been avoided.
4. Did you accomplish your own personal goals for this experience?
5. What would you do differently next time? What is one thing you would change?
6. What might the college do differently in preparing students or community representatives for the service-learning activity?
7. What might the community organization do differently in preparing students or faculty for the service-learning activity?
8. How would you describe this experience to another student or community representative? What would you emphasize?

After the conversation, debrief the experience and discuss what you will do with all the information that was shared. Who should have access to it? In what format?

Appendix 11.1: Self-Assessment Matrix Descriptions

Learning is an incremental process, with skills and expertise building as you progress. A detailed explanation of each component of the Self-Assessment Matrix follows. As you read this, consider how it applies to you personally based upon past experiences.

- **Learning**: At the *Explorer* level, students have no prior experience with service-learning and learn through their initial exposure to the pedagogy, to community involvement, and to the idea of working in a collaborative setting. *Novices* learn through specifically observing the processes and interactions and through the ways in which their faculty model collaboration. Students who are *Engaged* learn through active participation in the experience. At the *Expert* level, students learn by leading others through the activities that contribute to a service-learning course.

- **Personal development**: *Explorers* are generally self-focused on their personal concerns, without considering integration of learning skills and decision making. The *Novice* student is developing self-awareness and the ability to employ a more integrated approach to learning and personal decision making. *Engaged* students view their learning and decision making as connected to, and influenced by, others. *Expert* students construct the "big picture," integrating their learning and skills with long-term career and personal decisions.

- **Reflection**: At the *Explorer* level students do not actively employ reflection as a learning strategy. As a *Novice*, reflection is deliberate (and often assigned!) but not integrated into learning. Reflection typically is presented in journal entries as a "weather report"—a self-conscious listing of activities that does not connect to concepts, readings, or other course activities. At the *Engaged* level, students begin to make connections among the various aspects of the service-learning experience. The *Expert* demonstrates reflection that is rich and integrated. Students thoughtfully examine the associations among readings, course goals, community experiences, and their own personal development.

- **Connection to community**: As *Explorers*, students view themselves individually and without connection to community. As *Novice*, students start to recognize community needs as well as community assets and begin to see their own connections to the community. At the *Engaged* level, students begin to forge relationships with the local community and define themselves in the context of their community. At the *Expert* level, students recognize interconnected needs and facilitate community linkages.

- **Intercultural competence**: As *Explorer*, students view the world through their own set of values. As *Novice*, they develop an awareness of the similarities and differences of diverse groups. *Engaged* students are cognizant of differences and respectful of others' viewpoints, values, and priorities. Students at the *Expert* level recognize the importance of seeking diverse input to community issues. They appreciate differences and see them as a vital component in service-learning.

- **Civic engagement**: *Explorers* are unaware of the construct of civic engagement. At the *Novice* level, they participate in various activities without knowingly viewing them as contributing to community development. At the *Engaged* level, students understand the concept of "civic engagement" and have the capacity to organize activities that contribute to its development. As *Expert*, students have developed a comprehensive understanding of civic engagement, can initiate activity, and have developed an understanding of social justice that they then can apply to community problems.

- **Capacity to work in community**: With no prior experience, the capacity of the *Explorer* is not known. For the student at the *Novice* level, interaction with community is limited and directed, so they follow the course assignments and participate as requested. At the *Engaged* level, students develop a more independent ability to respond to requests without the specific direction needed by the *Novice*. At the *Expert* level, students work with the community in imaginative ways that recognize and respond to need; they are self-directed and able to provide leadership to others.

CHAPTER 12

Global and Immersive Service-Learning

What You Need to Know as You Go

CHRISTINE M. CRESS, STEPHANIE T. STOKAMER, THOMAS J. VAN CLEAVE, AND CHITHRA EDWIN

THE PURPOSE of this chapter is to assist you with the preparation and processing of service-learning for those of you who will be participating in intensive live-in experiences that take you away from your home country to another place on the globe or take you to new places in your country for an extended period of time (immersive) for one week up to a couple of months.

Certainly any type of service in a new area of the city or unfamiliar neighborhood means thoughtful preparation and processing of the experience. A White college student going to a primarily Latino section of his or her town will have to learn cultural and interpersonal expectations for effectively interacting with this community. Similarly, an African American college student who grew up in a middle-class family may find that providing tutoring services to at-risk Black youth in a lower-income school district means learning new catch phrases and culturally based languages to gain the trust of the youth.

However, if these two college students are living in these settings, perhaps with a host family, as part of an alternative spring break (such as to Juárez or Philadelphia) or have traveled to another country to work with these populations (such as Brazil or Kenya), then the logistics of service and the demands of learning increase exponentially.

This chapter is divided into three primary categories:

- Preparation—what you may need to do and know before you go, pre-departure

- Praxis—how to make sense of learning through serving while you are there
- Performance—how you know if you made a difference or experienced change

Preparation: Pre-Departure

While study abroad and education abroad courses and programs may include volunteer or service elements, the tips and strategies here are primarily directed toward alternative spring breaks or courses where faculty and students travel together to live and serve in a new location for a few days or weeks. For example, students and faculty from Occidental College in California travel to New Orleans during spring break to assist with post–Hurricane Katrina recovery efforts: painting schools and planting community gardens. Pacific University students and faculty in Oregon are hosted during winter term (the short academic term between fall and spring semesters) by the Navajo nation in Arizona. Service there focuses on assisting elders with home projects (e.g., chopping wood, tilling gardens) and tutoring children at the tribal school. Graduate students at Portland State University travel to India each February for three weeks where they assist orphaned children, abused women, and HIV-positive sex workers.

Clearly, where you are going, what you will be doing, and with whom you will be performing the service is the context for each of the following preparation categories.

Logistics: How Do I Get There? What Should I Bring? Where Do I Sleep?

In many programs and courses students have to apply to be selected to participate in an immersive or global service-learning experience. In fact, it might be a competitive process in which you have to complete an application, solicit letters of recommendation, submit academic transcripts, and participate in an interview. If you do, pay close attention to the application materials or other information provided by the trip coordinator. Otherwise, examine carefully the course syllabus provided by the instructor. Ask yourself these questions:

- Where and for how long is the trip? Can I complete other school assignments during this time? How might I handle work or family obligations?
- Will this count for my academic major? Could the knowledge and skills assist my career aspirations? Will my adviser be supportive?
- Whom does the project serve? Why might I like (or not) to work with these populations? What might I like (or not) about the service activities?
- What are my real motivations for going? To get away from my parents? To party? To proselytize? To meet a new boyfriend or girlfriend? To see a new place? To serve and learn?

You may also have other special circumstances that require advance discussion with your trip leader or faculty. For instance, if you have a physical disability you may need to inquire about access or accommodation challenges on the trip. If possible, have an honest and frank discussion about the kinds of supports you may need. While not every situation can be anticipated, don't leave your physical safety and comfort to chance.

Similarly, don't assume that your physical limitation should prevent you from participating. Linda, a student without sight in one eye, thought she couldn't participate in a service trip to Nepal because she has depth-perception issues that make it difficult to judge her steps when hiking in rough terrain. In conversation with the faculty, it turned out the group would be taking jeeps to the mountainous villages and only light

walking was required of participants. The trip was life changing for Linda, who worked on nutritional issues with village mothers. She returned and changed her major from psychology to community health with an emphasis on international health education.

Prior to global and immersive service-learning trips, most programs and courses will have pre-departure meetings, orientations, or classes. Make sure to attend since the instructor or facilitator will usually cover in detail the myriad of logistical details necessary for traveling and living at the service site. You should ask the following questions if they are not covered:

- How will travel be handled? Should I make my own plane reservations? Will we drive together in a van?
- What travel documents do I need? Passport? Country entry visa? Travel insurance?
- Are immunizations or vaccinations recommended?
- What clothing and other items are needed? (Remember to pack prescriptions.)
- What kind of housing is provided? Will rooms be shared?
- What about food and my dietary restrictions (if you have any)?
- Are cell phone service and other technologies available?

While these may seem to be common-sense questions, the fact that individuals need to have their basic food and housing needs met first before they can connect with others to serve and learn should not be underestimated. Based on work by Maslow (1954) and known as the ***hierarchy of needs***, this model contends that before common bonds of affiliation and community can be made one's primal survival needs (nutrition and shelter) must be managed (see figure 12.1).

Assuming these foundational life needs are met, and community is formed, one can then engage in reflection, which leads to insight and learning (or self-actualization). Indeed, if hungry, cold, or scared of others, one is not likely to have the resources to engage in higher-order learning. Instead, the person will be focused on surviving. As a case in point, many schools provide breakfast for low-income kids so they can focus on reading and writing.

Why might this pyramid of priorities be important to keep in mind? Quite simply, most of us don't eat

Figure 12.1. Hierarchy of Needs and Learning Based on Work by Maslow (1954)

of needs to their concerns about the street kids. However, what they did not understand was the myriad of cultural issues intertwined with their complaints. Many of these kids were controlled by adult gang leaders who expected the children to bring them money and stolen items each day. Nice clothing was stripped from these kids to sell for profit by the adults. Given the immensity of issues, the best thing that could be done for these children was to provide them with a sense of care and love through learning.

Understanding Individuals, Community, and Culture
Your instructor or program coordinator will probably provide you with readings and websites to help you understand the history, religion, politics, and culture of the individuals and populations you will be living with and serving. Most people are not in need because of their own choosing or doing. Rather, things like war, prejudice, and poverty (to name a few) can create ripple effects that last for generations. As an outsider, you will never fully understand the political, economic, environmental, religious, social, and historical antecedents of their plight. But it is imperative that you try so the best of your intentions can be accepted rather than rejected.

and sleep well in new environments, and we may lose patience with our companions. If that happens, then it is quite difficult to stay engaged in learning.

As an illustration, American service-learning students in Mexico City became quite frustrated with the nonprofit organization they were assisting by tutoring street kids in math. The college students felt the organization should focus on clothing and housing for the children rather than education. Intuitively, the service-learning students were applying the hierarchy

Individually and collectively, we may make mistakes or commit cultural offenses. But the more we learn and prepare ahead of time the less likely we are to do so (see also chapter 5 for more ideas on intercultural preparation). Search out websites and YouTube videos of customs, non-verbal communication, and

---

Spotlight on Service: A Poopy Story

Students from an engineering college in the Midwest came to the state of New Mexico to install solar composting toilets for families of a tribal nation in a rural area that was off the electrical grid. The students worked with a local community college math class that provided the community connection and helped with design and building. By the fifth installation, some of the engineering students noticed that young children of the families often ran around partially naked, their bottoms without diapers. The engineering students generously pooled their money to purchase packages of cloth diapers that were presented to the tribal elders at a closing thank-you ceremony. Rather than appreciating the gift, the elders gently scolded the students for their insult and ignorance. Rural families in the desert did not have enough water to wash cloth diapers, and children were potty trained at an earlier age than urban children because Native adults paid close attention to their children's bodily needs. While they needed solar toilets, they did not need diapers.

spoken language in the country or area where you will be working. Just being able to say please and thank you in the local dialect can be highly meaningful.

Moreover, find out in advance about common courtesies, especially concerning your dress (Are shorts inappropriate?), introductions and meetings (Is it okay for men and women to shake hands or sit next to one another?), and gifts (Is chocolate a universal favorite?).

Take the initiative individually or as a class to start a wiki or web page where everyone can share resources, videos, or blogs. See if you can access these sites and add to them once you arrive at your service site (technology depending, of course).

Some of you may be returning to your communities of origin to serve. Without placing all the responsibility on yourself for being a cultural representative or expert, see if you can share with your classmates a few of the cultural values and priorities that can facilitate helpful interactions. You may have music or videos to give fun insight into traditions and celebrations. Also, consider (like Maria in chapter 8, p. 129) whether you have personal, professional, or family connections that could help to best direct the service and projects.

As well, if you are returning to your community be prepared that your experience could be different from what you remembered, and others in your community may now see your positionality differently (for more on positionality and standpoint theory see chapter 5). This happened to some African American college students in a lower socioeconomic sector of Chicago. Rather than being welcomed by the teenagers they were tutoring, the high school students called them "Oreo cookies"; meaning they were Black on the outside but White on the inside. Such rejection from your own community can be discouraging and disorienting. If this happens to you, find a trusted confident you can share your feelings with.

Service and Project Preparation
Your service sites and activities may be prearranged by your coordinator or instructor. Alternatively, while the general location might have been established, the specific sites and tasks may not be determined until after your arrival. Or, what was agreed upon in advance may change, and a new project may now take priority.

To the best of your ability, find out what you may be doing and with whom. If you will be working with children, do you need to prepare tutoring materials or come with a host of interactive games? How might these translate or be translated into another language? If you are working with adults, are there cross-gender considerations such as men not being able to work with women or female children? If you are working in health care, will there be medical equipment and medicines? What about materials for building, painting, and planting? Are there computers or printers or phones?

As you get ready for departure, perhaps the emotional and psychological preparations are more significant than the physical ones. Consider your reactions to these challenging questions:

- How will you feel holding an orphaned infant whose toes were chewed by rats as she lay abandoned in a garbage heap? Will you manage for the rest of the day if she wets on you?
- Can you sit for an hour next to a weeping woman describing domestic violence and listen with your heart since you can't understand her language?
- Can you look into the face of a male sex worker and hear with compassion as he tells of being sold by his father at age 7 to child traffickers?
- Can you hold the hand of a drooling mentally challenged person without apprehension to convey that you care through the language of love?

Of course these are rather extreme situations, but depending on your location and type of service, you may encounter even worse. What you see, what you hear, and what you smell may come close to overwhelming your senses (see also "Spotlight on Service: Blemished and Beautiful in India and America," p. 105). Yet you will be called upon to put aside your visceral responses for the sake of patient and gracious service. You may have to serve and learn despite your feelings.

This can be especially disconcerting for an intellectually well-prepared student. Unlike most college experiences where we think out answers and smart responses, in these service situations there are no easy answers or solutions. Rather, our compassion must precede our intelligence. Only by understanding through compassion can we then begin to identify larger systemic and organizational solutions through application of our academic and disciplinary knowledge.

This is the main theme of the next section, Praxis—trying to make sense of the experience with your heart and head once you are in your service location.

✰✰ Exercise 12.1: Negotiables and Non-Negotiables: Anticipating Your Boundaries

Read each of the following scenarios, and find one that might happen as you anticipate your own upcoming service-learning journey. While the case study may not represent you, how would you react if this were one of your classmates? Write your response in a pre-departure journal that you will take with you on the service experience. If possible, find a classmate who will be joining you on the trip, and compare reactions and thoughts.

Case study 1. Emily is a devout Christian from a religious college in Nebraska. While she read about Hinduism before going to India, she didn't realize that the service-learning trip would involve entering temples where Hindu priests would bless them with incense and place a red dot on her forehead. After praying about it, Emily has decided that she can no longer condone or participate in the worship of idols. This is a personal issue of faith that cannot be crossed. From now on she will wait outside any temples.

Case study 2. Josh was invited to family dinner by his student mentee, D'Sean, at Ballou STAY High School. Josh is studying electrical engineering at the City College of New York but went to Washington, DC, for alternative spring break where he is assisting general educational development (GED) completion students with computer skills. D'Sean's grandmother had tears in her eyes and expressed sincere appreciation for Josh's help as she served him pork sliders. Josh is of Jewish descent and had been a vegetarian for the last four years. He felt completely conflicted about what to do.

Case study 3. Henry was a graduate student in education from Seattle. He went with his class to assist with building schools in Sudan that had been destroyed during the civil war. As an African American, Henry was thrilled to be on his ancestral home continent and felt a connection to the Sudanese teachers and students that he couldn't fully explain to his White classmates. Some of the schoolteachers asked Henry if he was on Facebook and if they could friend him to stay in touch. Images from his Facebook page flashed through Henry's mind. These included his civil union ceremony to his male partner, Steve. Sudan is one of 54 African countries that ban homosexuality, and in Sudan it is a crime punishable with the death penalty. Henry pondered what to say.

Case study 4. Mindy had been adopted from Vietnam by a White family. Among other projects, her service-learning course instructor had made arrangements for the class to work with the orphanage Mindy had been adopted from. Some of the nurses at the orphanage had been there during the time that Mindy was an infant. While they didn't remember her specifically, they felt certain they had helped care for her. Late one afternoon, a nurse approached Mindy in the courtyard where she was playing alone with a toddler. The nurse quietly pleaded with Mindy for money because the nurse's mother needed surgery. The nurse added under her breath, "You are Vietnamese. It is your obligation to help."

Case study 5. Jacob held the three-year-old Sri Lankan girl, Dayani, in his arms and made funny faces. She laughed at him, and for the next 30 minutes they played together; sticking out their tongues, rolling their eyes, and giggling all the while. Jacob found great joy in the interaction, which reminded him of time spent with his four young nieces. When it was time to leave, the girl cried loudly and clung to Jacob, not wanting to let go. Jacob tried to console her and promised that he would be back the next day. But as Jacob boarded the van to leave he was informed by the site director that single men would not be allowed to work at the orphanage for their ongoing service. They could only work making bricks for a new school at a different location. The director passed around a clipboard to gather names of married men. Jacob had lived with his girlfriend the past two years, and they planned to get officially engaged upon his return. Tears filled his eyes as he thought of Dayani and stared at the clipboard in his hands.

Praxis: Learning through Serving

The word *praxis* simply means applying ideas to real-life situations, or, to state in a more academic way, the application of theoretical research and conceptual models in problem-solving lived scenarios and community conditions. After all, that is the purpose of learning through serving, doing short-term good while gaining insight into issues to which you can apply your knowledge and skills toward longer-term solutions.

When you first arrive at your service location, your ability to immediately engage in praxis will be limited. Rather, your immersion into the new sights and sounds and getting settled into housing will take precedence (recall Maslow's hierarchy of needs on p. 179). As well, you may be exhausted from a long trip (e.g., jet lag or days of driving).

The following praxis strategies are intended to help you make the transition from initial adaptation shock to fully immersed server and learner. Obviously, read this section prior to embarking, but also consider taking a copy with you on your journey.

Adjusting to Site and Community

Stabilizing your basic physiological (e.g., food, water) and safety needs will likely take significant amounts of your energy at the beginning. As we noted earlier, where you eat and sleep matters, and your level of comfort will determine how much you emotionally and psychologically struggle in adapting to your new surroundings. But until you do feel comfortable it will be hard to engage in higher cognitive processing (Maslow, 1948).

Realize that culture shock is a normal response to unfamiliar people and places. And while there will be moments (perhaps even minutes, hours, or days) when you feel that you must flee back to the safety of your familiar life, recognizing these emotions is the first step to behaving and acting in interculturally sensitive ways.

In fact, Goleman (1995) refers to this recognition as higher forms of *emotional intelligence*, when how we feel does not dictate how we act. Instead, we can choose to act respectfully and responsively despite our fears and negative culturally biased responses. Such awareness combined with our actions can help us to develop *intercultural sensitivity* (Bennett & Bennett,

---

✯ Exercise 12.2: How Do I Really Feel?

Take out your personal journal, or if you have electronic options, create a new file. This should not be an exercise you do in a class reflection journal to give to your instructor or to put on Facebook for all your family, friends, and colleagues to see. This is a place for you to be fully honest and authentic. You can edit it later for others to read if you choose.

1. What person, place, or thing is upsetting you? Are there sights, sounds, or smells that overwhelm or horrify you? *Describe* what you have experienced or are experiencing.
2. How does this make you feel? Write down as many *feeling words* that come to you. While you write, notice your multiple feelings of sadness, anger, guilt, disgust, confusion, fear, powerlessness, passion, and so on.
3. If you need to cry for a while or punch a pillow, do so. The truth is that feelings are not soft; they are hard sometimes.
4. Now sit quietly and breathe deeply for 60 full seconds. Don't read or write or think or feel. Just breathe.
5. Look back at your journal entry and pick just one feeling from your list of many feeling words. Draw a line to create two columns. On the left side, write: Why I am Fully Justified in my Feelings. On the right side, write: What Cultural Factors May Be Influencing My Feelings. Make lists of words and phrases for each side.
6. Start a new entry following these columns. Write: Given that I cannot control circumstances but I can control my responses to my feelings, this is what I will do (act, behave). Be explicit and describe when, where, and how you can feel your feelings while acting in interculturally sensitive ways.
7. If you need to repeat the exercise for another feeling do so. Otherwise, make a commitment to yourself to enact your behavior in the next 24 hours.

Spotlight on Service: Attributing My Feelings to Others

Tired and jet lagged, a group of college students from America were invited to a traditional wedding on the second day of their stay in a small town in southern India. The ceremony was quite long, and by 2 p.m. the group had not yet been called to lunch. Along with her classmates, Sarah waited in 97 degree heat surrounded by hundreds of well wishers with high-pitched music blasting in her ears. She focused her gaze on the beautiful bride receiving gifts in the reception line. Sarah knew that as with most weddings in India the groom had been chosen for the bride by her family; this was an arranged marriage. As Sarah watched the bride, she couldn't imagine being forced to marry someone she didn't love. She contemplated the wedding night and felt sick to her stomach. Sarah got angrier and angrier and thought to herself, "How can all these people be celebrating a situation likened to slavery!" She was outraged and wanted to scream. Instead, she took a breath, became conscious of her internal fury, smiled, and acted as if she were happy for the couple too.

Later that evening, Sarah learned that the couple had known one another for years because their fathers were good friends and they often spent holidays together. They were not in fact strangers but may have even had a budding romance all along. Sarah was glad she hadn't freaked out. She realized that things are not always as they seem and that perhaps love can bloom in ways she had never imagined.

2004), where our experience of difference moves from being reactive to adaptive (see also chapter 5), and our perspectives shift from ethnocentric to ethnorelative. Essentially, we become less judgmental and more accepting.

The intent of recognizing our feelings is not so we can wallow in our emotions or lash out at others. In complex situations, we may not be aware of how our feelings are affecting our actions. We must come to recognize that our feelings, while true for us, may not be true for others; their perspectives and reactions to what we are feeling may be different. As such, we may have to act, literally *act*, as if we were portraying a character in a play who does and says the right things in spite of our immediate emotions.

Similarly, recall in chapter 4 that we discuss the concept of **attribution theory**. With attribution theory different emotions are associated with different attributions in explaining the words and actions of others. Misattribution, when someone makes an incorrect attribution in accounting for another's actions, can have serious consequences in service-learning experiences.

For example, those of us from individualist cultures (like the United States) share an **independent** view of the self in that individuals are seen as self-contained and autonomous and their behavior is primarily determined by internal attributes (e.g., motives, values, and traits). On the other hand, collectivist cultures (like Japan) favor a more interdependent view of self in that the self is seen as more dependent on relationships with others and social groups. As a result, individual actions are more likely to be influenced by social obligations. These differences in self-conceptions have an impact on the attribution process, especially in intercultural interactions.

It is important to honor how we feel while responsibly examining the triggers, associations, and cultural perspectives that can artificially inflate our reactions and potentially reinforce stereotypes. As we learned in chapters 5 and 6, while some cultural generalizations can be made and may even prove useful to our learning and serving (e.g., Vietnamese people like to eat rice), when these "hardening of the categories" become imposed on individuals, they lead to misunderstanding and prejudice (e.g., all Asians are good at math).

Read the the following Spotlight on Service: Sick and Tired of Stereotypes, and respond to the questions with another classmate or as part of a small group.

> ### Spotlight on Service: Sick and Tired of Stereotypes
>
> A student looking out the window of the van on day four of her alternate spring break trip to Tijuana and seeing men sleeping on sidewalks commented with a snicker to her seatmate, "Now I know why they call them lazy Latinos." No one laughed or made a comment. Most students in the van felt drained from the heat, some were recovering from dysentery, and all were exhausted from the intense service experience of walking poverty-filled streets with local community organizers handing out free vitamins and health education pamphlets. That night in their reflection group, the instructor raised the issue of the comment. Apparently, not all the students had heard it because some were napping in the van—taking their own siesta. Jennifer, highly embarrassed, immediately apologized for her rude remark. However, Juan, a Latino college student on the trip responded in anger, "So typical, I can't even come to Mexico and get away from racist statements. I'm sick and tired of it!"

- What may have immediately motivated Jennifer's comment in the van?
- If you were to speculate about Jennifer's background and cultural experiences, what may have led to this kind of comment?
- If you were to speculate about Juan's background, what may have led to his reaction?
- What should the instructor have done differently?
- What are the possible outcomes this can have on the trip? For the class community? For interactions with the community partners? For interactions with the local community?
- Can this become a learning moment for everyone involved, or is the damage from hard feelings too great to overcome?

Engaged Reflection
Recall from earlier chapters in this book the work of educator John Dewey (1966). Dewey believed that learning only fully occurs when ideas and activities are reflected upon to assess mutual fit, relationship, and application. In other words, simply reading about concepts or doing service are not enough. **Engaged reflection** is the glue that connects learning through serving.

Chapter 6 contains a wide variety of activities, including pre-service reflection, reflection during service (see the DEAL model), and post-service reflection. If your instructor or trip coordinator uses a model that is different from DEAL, you can still revisit the DEAL activities on your own or do them with a classmate or small group to enhance your learning.

Certainly, a common and preferred way for individual reflection is to keep a written journal. As noted in exercise 12.2, you may want to keep a personal paper or electronic journal separate from a class journal. It may be that the hard stuff you are processing needs to be kept private until you are ready to share aspects or portions of it with faculty or friends.

One strategy is to record observations or insights from other perspectives. For instance, you could imagine you are a reporter following this group of service-learners. From an objective perspective, how do you describe what they are doing? What might they be feeling? What is behind their motivations and actions? Do you need to interview your subjects—that is, the other students? What about their clients, mentees, or those they are serving?

Alternatively, as a second strategy you could pretend you are the community partner. As the representative who is creating connections with the community, what are your perspectives on the students and of their service to your clients? What do you think about the instructor or trip coordinator? Are your objectives being reached? Are the students accomplishing what you hoped they would?

Re-Evaluating Service Roles and Perspectives
One of the things reflection helps us accomplish is to gain new insights into situations. As seen earlier, if the circumstances are highly foreign to our previous experiences it might be difficult to engage in the service experience. Most of us who do service do so because we want

to help, we want to make a difference. But as we discuss in chapter 1, our concepts about *what is service* and *what is helpful* are highly context and cultural specific.

For example, students from a community college in Hawaii traveled to Oaxaca, Mexico, to assist with civil rights issues of indigenous populations. The students were asked to make copies, file papers, and serve coffee in these nonprofit, free legal aid offices, and rarely, if ever, received a *gracias* for their efforts. By the third day, students expressed indignation and outrage to their instructor. They had traveled thousands of miles at their own expense. This was not the kind of noble service or important contribution they expected to make.

The professor apologized and acknowledged he should have done a better job during pre-departure to help them understand their roles and responsibilities. He went on to explain that in Mexican culture, service is an ordinary, everyday event. High school students must document 500 hours of service, and colleges require one year of service. Mexican service organizations do not praise students for their service because it is a nationally valued responsibility. The professor further explained that many cultures don't overexpress their gratitude because the underlying importance is inherently understood (Renner, Axlund, Topete, & Fleming, 2011).

In this case, while seemingly menial work, the service activities allowed the professional legal staff to focus their time and energy on writing legal briefs, meeting with clients, and advocating for change with local politicians. Indeed, the instrumental and practical importance of the service was significant, even though it was not initially perceived that way by the college students.

Take a moment to consider your own service activities and respond to the following questions in writing or in discussion with a classmate:

- How is what you are doing for service the same or different from what you expected? What do you like or not like?
- How is service perceived in the culture? What are the expectations for members of the culture? How might service by outsiders like yourself be perceived?
- What are some of the underlying social and political issues that have led to this community need? Are these issues, **antecedents** (causes),

and needs similar to or different from those in your own culture or background?

Analyzing Issues through Academic Disciplines

Even if you are primarily performing service during an alternative spring break rather than for a course, what you have been studying as a college student can inform your understanding of the issues and people you are serving. Similarly, not only knowledge but skills can serve your community partner as well as your own learning.

For instance, students in a freshman English 101 course spent their spring break on the south side of Chicago tutoring sophomores in high school. Their mentees (see more on mentoring in chapter 7) asked them questions about different writing formats (such as compare and contrast) and grammar. Because the college students had to answer accurately, their own knowledge of writing increased. In addition, they got permission from the students to electronically share the best examples of paragraphs and other writing samples through Google Docs and wiki sites. The high school students were able to see different ways to structure written arguments and perspectives. The result of the service was improved skills for college and high school students alike.

The breadth and array of knowledge and skills you can gain through service is endless. For instance, geography students enhanced their math and statistics skills when they traveled to Seattle to assist with asset mapping in low-income neighborhoods as part of a city-wide economic reinvestment plan for small businesses. Biology students from Omaha traveled to the Florida coast to perform water analyses of petroleum levels in coastal wetlands following an oil platform explosion. They not only learned field science skills but became aware of the policy issues involved in federal and state environmental regulations, government intervention during disasters, and global responsibility of multinational businesses.

Remember that the purpose of praxis is to learn in deeper ways how academic ideas can be applied (or not) to real-life community situations. In your service-learning experience, you might be learning disciplinary (e.g., history, urban studies, Asian studies) or professional (e.g., nursing, audiology, law) content. Other students may be learning new skills associated with their major or career, such as disability technology,

---

✦✦ **Exercise 12.3: Antecedents, Analysis, and Action: Making Academic Sense of Service**

If you haven't yet selected your academic major, pick a class you are in or may have taken recently. If you have selected your major, try to connect key concepts from your field to the following questions. You can answer these questions as part of a reflection journal or share them in a small group. Or maybe you want to design a PowerPoint presentation or Prezi that you can present to the class or post on Facebook or your course website. Be creative in your responses, but also thoughtful in what you share (are photos of disfigured or malnourished children appropriate?).

- What are the academic or disciplinary goals for this service experience or project? Has your instructor or trip coordinator specified them? Are they on the syllabus? Did you create some individually or as a group in class?
- Pick one academic goal (or create one now). What have you read, researched, done, seen, or learned that helps you make academic sense of the service activities and issues? Are there conceptual models or research statistics that support (or contradict) your experience, those of your classmates, and those of the community you are serving? What fits and doesn't fit your situation?
- From a purely academic standpoint, what have you learned that you need to remember to put in your final paper or project? Or, what can you incorporate into other academic activities or assignments you need to complete?
- So, what? So what can you apply from your college learning to the community? How can these insights lead to new actions or problem solving?
- What should happen next? What needs to be done? What academic actions can be taken?

---

computer software, mechanical tools, or graphic design. Still other service-learning experiences may have as their primary emphasis intercultural competence or larger universal issues, such as poverty awareness, hunger, or HIV/AIDS prevention.

Just make sure that if you have traveled hundreds of miles to new places to serve and learn about new people, let the experience be educative and not just exotic.

Performance: Making a Difference and Becoming Different

Even before the service experience is over, you will begin to note changes in yourself, your classmates, the clients you serve, and perhaps even in your professor. These may spring from individual and shared reflections, or they may suddenly strike you as epiphanies—the ah-ha moment, the "Oh, I get it now" insight, and the "How could I have not seen that before?" awakening.

Obviously the reason colleges have students engage in these kinds of service-learning activities is in the hope they will be transformed by them; meaning that how they see, feel, and think about the world will be radically different (Mezirow, 2002). That is the purpose of higher education, to help you develop critical consciousness that leads to new ways of living and being (Bowen, 1977; Cress, 2004).

So, how do you begin to assess whether through this service-learning experience you have been transformed, changed, or left untouched? And how do you assess whether your efforts made a difference to the clients, mentees, elders, or community? While chapter 11 contains a number of activities to help you evaluate outcomes, the following are some additional strategies to help you discern if anything is different.

Assessing Community Impact

Determining the type and importance of your service on the community is very difficult to judge, especially if the context and culture are unfamiliar to you. Project-based service is usually somewhat easier to see regarding impact because there may be a tangible product (a new website for the community partner) or object (a new house for a family). Having a real reference point such as "I built that brick wall," "I dug that water well," or "I painted that giraffe at the children's home" helps many of us feel secure in knowing that our creative contributions are durable.

In contrast, tasks that seem menial, "I washed diapers at the orphanage," "Our efforts are not well received," or "The kids I tried to tutor in math didn't seem at all interested" can leave us feeling as if our time and energy didn't matter. In fact, our labors may seem a waste of time.

But Mother Teresa said, "What we are doing may feel like a drop in the ocean. But the ocean would be less without that drop." Just like a single vote amid a sea of millions of votes, your individual vote is important and could make all the difference in the ultimate outcome. So don't discount your own metaphorical service droplet, and try to deepen your understanding of its connection to the larger whole. In other words, your service of love matters even if it seems unmeasurable.

Therefore, begin to assess community impact while you are still performing service. Indeed, this may be critical to changing directions or making alterations to your service if it is in fact not working (for more on failure, see chapter 9).

Coordinate with your instructor, trip leader, or classmates to gather community impact data or evidence by answering the following:

- Can you count the number of clients served or hours of assistance provided?
- Can you talk to or interview community members about their experiences?
- How does the community partner feel about your service—what is working (or worked) and what should be changed now or in the future?
- If collecting narratives or stories is not possible because of language, gender, or organizational barriers, how about taking a short survey adapted to the people and area you are serving?

Certainly, be extremely thoughtful about your assessment techniques, and check with a college authority (teacher or adviser) regarding issues of confidentiality and whether you need to obtain formal human subjects protection permission before collecting data. If in doubt, ask.

Your community partner may also have ideas for assessing impact. The partner may have tracked program and service activities for years to which you can link your data to examine short- and long-term trends. You may then be able to disseminate these data to policy makers when offering recommendations for change. For an example, see the following Spotlight on Service: Helping the Homeless.

Spotlight on Service: Helping the Homeless

Sociology students from a community college in San Jose, California, collected data on the number of homeless people who ride all-night buses for shelter. The city had received complaints from citizens (and bus drivers concurred) that homeless riding had increased. Students confirmed the increase by comparing their data with earlier records. But they also spoke with the homeless to find out why they were riding the buses. Apparently, six months earlier city police had begun to enforce the law about no sleeping in parks. The homeless had no place to go. Students presented their findings to the city council. The council members requested a temporary reprieve on prohibiting park-bench sleeping by the police, and they established a social service task force of the police, bus system employees, and nonprofit housing service providers to develop a long-term plan.

You might rightly ask is collecting data like these really a service-learning experience or just research? As they spoke with the homeless individuals, the students also gave them information on homeless shelters, food banks, and free medical care clinics. The students did provide direct client service in addition to assessing their clients' needs.

In collecting and analyzing data, be careful of interpreting data through your own cultural lens. If possible, seek out a cultural expert from the community who can support or counter your own perspectives on the findings and offer potential recommendations or solutions. As we have learned from this chapter, what you think the community might want may not be what it really needs.

Assessing the Impact on You

The various reflection activities provided in this book will give you ongoing insight into your service, your learning, your classmates, and your sense of self. In particular, your reflective journal may give you deeper discernment, weeks, months, and years from now.

Often, students don't start to experience change until they return to their home or campus from the service trip. For students who traveled to Morocco, having easy access to drinking fountains in their science building became a daily reminder of the contrasts between their own lives and the camel caravan people they had interacted with. The fountains became a symbolic motivator for studying international water quality and water access issues.

For other students, re-entry can be challenging. When asked by his housemate, "How was Bangladesh?" Max stood silent recalling the incredible stench of the raw sewage channels in Dhaka and the colorful sights and joyful sounds of the Pôhela Boishakh New Year's festival. Max continued to pause wondering how he could adequately describe his amazing service-learning trip. All he could stammer was, "Uh, great." Ironically, this seemed to satisfy his roommate's curiosity, who left for the fitness center. Max retreated to his room and stared at the wall. He felt as if he had been transported back and forth through a time portal where the two worlds on opposite sides of the space continuum had no conception of the other. And Max's mind and body were stretched across both.

Hopefully, your instructor or coordinator will have post-trip reflection sessions, which should normally be scheduled within two weeks of return when the stark contrasts between your life and those you served are most salient. Even if you didn't become good friends with your classmates or couldn't wait to get away from them, you all have in common a shared set of encounters that will never be fully understood by your truest confidant or loving partner. Processing together during re-entry will unveil additional perspectives and viewpoints you may have never considered during the experience.

At the very least, complete **Exercise 12.4: Individual Impact and Identity**, and then find a tripmate to discuss responses over traditional foods associated with your service site. If you can't find a restaurant that serves such food, get an online recipe and then shop, cook, and eat together as you recall vivid memories and share new personal truths about the experience.

✵ Exercise 12.4: Individual Impact and Identity

Write responses to the following questions over the next few days. Answer some now, but then re-read them and expand your answers the next day and the day after that. Allow yourself to be honest about your thoughts and feelings, seeing what simply emerges. But also hold the questions in your heart and mind as you move through your daily activities of school, work, and life.

- How are you different as an outcome of the trip? Do you think differently? Feel differently? Act differently?
- What lasting memories hold the most meaning for you? (These could be pleasant or happy memories but also hard or difficult ones.) Why are you holding on to them?
- What did you learn about yourself? Your classmates? Your instructor(s)?
- What did you learn about your major or career choice?
- What did you learn about the local community? The new part of your nation or the new country?
- How will you be different now and in the future? What lasting impact will this have on your life, how you view yourself, and how you interact with others?

Iterative Learning and Teaching
This may not have been your first service experience, and in all likelihood it will not be your last. Most of us find that we are called to engage in service frequently throughout our lives, and many continue to seek out service opportunities near and far. For certain, one of the tremendous outcomes of contributing our service multiple times is not just the impact on others but the impact on ourselves as we compare and contrast experiences and further hone a variety of our knowledge and skills in novel situations and contexts.

This is the idea behind ***iterative learning and teaching***; with each new service opportunity we apply what we learned from previous experiences to the current one, and along the way we help educate others about the most effective ways to assist and empower our communities. It is a cyclical process of experiences, assessment, analysis, and implementation (for more on this and a visual representation of the model see chapter 11). In this way, we are critically conscious of our service performance and whether it made a difference on others or on us. Such intentional examination allows us to identify opportunities for larger systemic changes that we investigate in chapter 13.

Key Concepts

antecedents of issues	hierarchy of needs	iterative learning and
emotional intelligence	intercultural	teaching
engaged reflection	sensitivity	praxis

Key Issues

- Why travel a long distance to perform service-learning? Aren't there ample opportunities to serve and learn locally?
- How have you culturally prepared yourself for such an experience?
- Because of the logistics involved, global and immersive service-learning may be service and learning "light." How will or did you ensure that your service matters and that your learning is substantial?

CHAPTER 13

Start Anywhere, Follow It Everywhere

Agents of Change

VICKI L. REITENAUER

IN THEIR BOOK *Walk Out Walk On*, authors Margaret Wheatley and Deborah Frieze (2011) take readers on a "learning journey" (p. xv) to communities in seven different countries where individuals come together in new forms of relationships and with new ideas about how to live and work to solve seemingly intractable problems in our world. One stop on the reader's journey is Joubert Park in Johannesburg, South Africa. The park was once a Whites-only recreational place in the heart of the city during the days of apartheid. Then on April 27, 1994, the park was the site of long lines of voters waiting to elect Nelson Mandela to South Africa's presidency "four years after [he] was released from prison, ten thousand days after he entered" (p. 81). By the late 1990s it had become a hopeless and broken place. Following the end of apartheid, Johannesburg was flooded with migrants and immigrants after decades of prohibition and segregation, which until then had reserved jobs and other opportunities in the city for Whites only. Joubert Park, "the first port of entry for new arrivals" (Wheatley & Frieze, 2011) in Johannesburg, saw a dramatic rise in crime, homelessness, and desperation, as the resources available to absorb the impact of these new arrivals quickly ran out.

Despite the perils in Joubert Park—and in some ways *because* of them—a group of photographers decided to take a stand to change this place. These photographers had made their living taking photos of people visiting the park for recreation, and the deteri-

oration of the park had caused their business to decline sharply. The photographers organized into a neighborhood crime watch, catching muggers and taking pictures of other crimes to turn over to the police. Soon other self-organizing initiatives took root: a group of mothers started the Lapeng ("at home") Family and Childhood Center, which now occupies a corner of the park, and that led to the development of a family support center to teach the unemployed parents of the children reading, math, and science. An initiative to invite inner-city youth struggling with gang violence and drug abuse to express themselves in creative ways also took root.

Into this swirling momentum of individual and collective efforts came Mathibedi Nthite, an art school graduate who had arrived at Joubert Park as a volunteer to organize the Ziyabuya Festival, a celebration of art and culture intended to help build self-esteem and connection to culture for the park's youth. Nthite quickly became immersed in other facets of the burgeoning spirit of the park, and as she did, she noticed that many of the parents of the children at Lapeng day care had come from rural areas where they had been able to grow their own food. The gardening expertise these people had developed throughout their lives was now going to waste while they struggled to find jobs in a bleak employment market and had difficulty feeding their families.

Out of this abundance of passion and skills among the people of Joubert Park, the GreenHouse Project was born in 2002. This initiative occupies the northwest corner of the park and represents one of the most progressive and successful green projects in all of Africa, with sustainable practices built into every aspect of the project. Wheatley and Frieze (2011) quote Dorah Lebelo, the director of the GreenHouse Project, about the heart of the project and the orientation of its community: "We start from a place of abundance—knowing that we've got what we need—and we operate from that. We're not looking to other people to solve our problems; we work to maximize our own potential" (p. 88).

While there are still tensions in Joubert Park, it is a much different place from the one the photographers vowed to change in the seemingly small way that they could. "Start anywhere, and follow it everywhere" (p. 85) is the mantra Wheatley and Frieze use to describe the activities in the park. The authors tell us that if we choose to learn from Joubert Park, we should prepare "to be surprised, for the starting place was simply the moment when a few people stepped forward to act, to create a better future" (p. 84). The photographers started with the things they had at hand: an interest in cleaning up the park so visitors would once again come and have their pictures taken, and the cameras that would help the police identify and remove those who were making the park unsafe. They couldn't do every-

thing that needed to be done to transform Joubert Park, but they didn't have to; there were other people in their community who could follow their lead.

Certainly, the change agency that transformed Joubert Park reminds us of the community described by Marge Piercy in the poem "The Low Road" (see p. 37 in chapter 3). As a community, with everything they needed at hand, the people of Johannesburg reclaimed their park—one photo, one child, one dream at a time.

Start Anywhere

Perhaps this is the first time you have explicitly and intentionally become involved with serving your community and the challenges it faces. Or perhaps you came into this experience with a résumé filled with prior volunteer and community-based experiences. In either case, *starting anywhere* begins with you—with who you are and what you deeply care about, and how you can apply both of those things to your work.

Two quotes help frame what it might mean for you to deepen your reflection on how *you* might *start anywhere and follow it everywhere:* "Don't ask yourself what the world needs. Ask yourself what makes you come alive and then go do that. Because what the world needs is people who have come alive. (Bailie,

---

> 💡 **Exercise 13.1: Walk Out Walk On**
>
> In the book *Walk Out Walk On*, authors Margaret Wheatley and Deborah Frieze (2011) take readers to seven different communities around the world where people are acting as agents of positive change in collaborative and mutually beneficial ways. Visit the book's website at www.walkoutwalkon.net/ to read more about each of these communities and to see videos of various initiatives taking place there. After spending some time immersing yourself in these worlds Wheatley and Frieze open to us, reflect on the following questions:
>
> - What resonates most powerfully for you about these communities? What emerges as especially important to pay attention to as you read the vignettes and view the videos?
> - What, if anything, is provocative, challenging, even disturbing, about what you encountered in visiting these communities? What perspectives did you encounter that confirm your own views, and what perspectives challenge what you have come to believe is true?
> - What connections are there between the communities featured in *Walk Out Walk On* and the community work you have been doing? What disconnects do you see between your service and the communities of *Walk Out Walk On*?
> - What approaches did you encounter on the website that you might consider adapting for your service-learning environment? What might those adaptations look like, and how might you bring them into your service-learning experience?

✦✦ Exercise 13.2: What Makes Me Come Alive to Get Started?

Spend some time reflecting on the story of Joubert Park and the preceding quotes. Then respond to the following:

- Where, in this service-learning experience, have you felt most alive? What about this experience resonates most deeply in you? What does that resonance say to you?
- What connections do you see between the ways you feel most alive and the needs you see in your community and in the world? What is the meeting point of those places for you? How does this service-learning experience connect to that meeting point, and in what ways, if any, does it fail to connect?
- In this context, what does it mean to you to *start anywhere and follow it everywhere*? Have you made a start already? If so, how do you name it? Where do you follow it from here? If this isn't yet your true start, how might you come to understand where and how you might begin?

1996, p. xv). The other is: "[Vocation] is where your deep gladness and the world's deep hunger meet" (Buechner, 1993, p. 95).

Casey Chase, a Portland State University student who has performed community-based course work in a number of classes (including Women, Activism, and Social Change and Girlpower), has thought a lot about what it means to name and pursue what makes her come alive in ways that address the world's deep needs. In the class Writing as Activism, Casey cofacilitated a workshop with a classmate in which she asked participants to develop their personal mission statements. For Casey, claiming a personal mission is a way of practicing **intentionality**. Casey describes an **intention** this way:

"To intend" means to mentally have in mind something to be brought into reality. Setting intentions in our daily lives gives us an opportunity to imagine ourselves acting in a way that reflects a goal we wish to accomplish. For example, yoga teachers ask their students to set an intention at the beginning of each class. This is done so that the students have an opportunity for their brain to communicate to their body exactly what they would like to accomplish during the class session. Setting intentions helps us act in a way that reflects our goals. As students, mentors, and teachers we might think about what we intend to create within our ideal learning community. As volunteers, employees, and community members, we might imagine what our ideal workspaces, organizations and communities might look like. (Chase, 2012)

Take a moment to think about your responses to exercise 13.2 and Casey's words about intention. As a service-learner, what would you say your intentions are in your work? What are you trying to bring into reality when you are engaged in service with your community partner? Beyond the scope of your service experience, what are your larger intentions as a student and a human being? What connections—or disconnects—do you see between your intentions as a student, a human being, and a service-learner right here and right now?

In the next exercise—the one Casey offered to her classmates—you will build on your reflection from exercise 13.2 and the preceding questions as you construct a **personal mission statement**.

And Follow It Everywhere

In chapter 8, we met Maria, a student who used her relational leadership skills to transform a foster care visiting room from an institutional wasteland into a warm, inviting, and child-friendly gathering place. Two other students from a similar course, Terry and Melissa, show us what it looks like to start anywhere and follow it everywhere. Their stories are told in "Spotlight on Service: Starting Anywhere and Spotlight on Service: Following It Everywhere."

⁂ **Exercise 13.3: My Mission Statement**

Now that you have set an intention, it is equally important to claim a mission statement to turn your intention into action. Writing a mission statement provides a tangible way of measuring how you are or how you are not living up to your intention. You can use your mission statement to measure your personal achievements for a day or for an entire lifetime. Either way, you may gain clarity about what you are doing or what you need to do to live your life in a way that reflects your ideal self. We suggest that you regularly view your actions through the lens of your mission statement, to hold yourself accountable to what you have said you want to be about in the world.

Answering the following three questions will help you write your own personal mission statement:

1. What is my life about?
2. What do I stand for?
3. What action am I taking to live what my life is about and what I stand for?

Before you write your mission statement, review the mission statement for your community partner (which was part of exercise 2.5 on p. 26). You might also read the mission statements of other organizations to get a sense of the varieties of ways these statements can be expressed.

Now write *your* mission statement. The following are some tips from Chase (2012) to help ensure that your mission statement is beneficial to you:

- Remember that your mission statement should be revisited regularly. Make adjustments to your words in order for it to make sense and hold value to you.
- Try and make your mission statement a suitable length for you to memorize it.
- Post your mission statement somewhere that you can see daily.
- Make sure your mission statement includes specific and tangible outcomes.

Making Change

So far in this chapter we've explored what it can look like to *start anywhere and follow it everywhere*. For many of us, the start we make involves one person or a group of people; perhaps it's the young child from the Sudan whom you're tutoring in English or a group of refugees you are assisting with résumé writing. Maybe you are writing grant proposals for a museum to increase accessibility for people with disabilities in your community or conducting research for your local transit authority on how to sustainably expand bus service into economically marginalized areas of town. As service-learners, many of us get our start here, in one-on-one or small-group interactions intended to address community needs and make life better for individuals in our communities. As the story of Joubert Park and service-learners Terry and Melissa show us—and, we hope, as your own experiences in service-learning are teaching you too—we each have the power to act, and we can choose to act in our world in ways that not only link us to our own interests but that create positive change in the collective sphere as well.

One way we can follow it everywhere is to think more deeply about this second part of that equation: choosing to act to create positive change in larger and larger ways in the world. One provocative essay that challenges us to think about our change efforts is Paul Kivel's (2000) *Social Service, or Social Change?* in which he implores us to consider the impacts of our actions in the societal and political realms. In particular, Kivel unpacks the ways our work may unwittingly feed the unjust institutions, structures, and systems that create the problems our service is intended to address.

At the start of his essay, Kivel (2000) says this:

My first answer to the question posed in the title is that we need both, of course. We need to pro-

---

Spotlight on Service: Starting Anywhere

Terry, a history major, experiences life with diminishing sight. As an adult, Terry began noticing a vision impairment that has developed into a profound loss of vision. For a long time, Terry coped as best he could. He is a husband and a father, and he worked in the computer industry until his vision deteriorated to the point where he couldn't work in his field anymore.

A history major, Terry determined not to allow his visual disability to prevent him from finishing his undergraduate degree and finding a new career path—law or perhaps public policy. On his way to earning his degree, Terry enrolled in a senior-level service-learning class in which he was required to choose his own community partner. It was an easy choice for Terry: the Oregon Historical Society (OHS). Terry had already communicated his idea to the OHS staff of transforming at least some of the museum's exhibits to be accessible to the blind and visually impaired.

Terry's lifelong love of history made him a regular visitor at museums, particularly those dedicated to preserving and showcasing the historical developments of a place. Many of the artifacts that historical museums feature, however, are delicate and must be shown in low light, which makes it even more difficult for the visually impaired to see. Terry's idea? To work with museum staff to modify exhibits so that facsimiles might be safely handled by visually impaired patrons, to seek grant funding for lighted magnifying goggles for enhanced exhibit viewing, and to create Braille descriptions for exhibits.

In collaborative efforts between museum staff and the staff at his university's disability resource center, Terry spearheaded the process to make these changes. He also wrote and sent a press release to media outlets alerting the public to the changes at the museum. Other museums have taken notice, as well, and are consulting with OHS about how to make their exhibits also accessible to the visually impaired.

And Terry? He's now volunteering as a docent at the museum and sharing his expertise with the public, while he considers how he will put his confirmed belief in the power of community-based action into practice after he has earned his degree. While he isn't yet sure where his path will lead him next, he does know that it will involve working as an advocate to increase accessibility and justice for all people in our communities.

---

vide services to those most in need, for those trying to survive, for those barely making it. We need to work for social change so that we create a society in which our institutions and organizations are equitable and just and all people are safe, adequately fed, adequately housed, well educated, able to work at safe, decent jobs, and able to participate in the decisions that affect their lives.

Although the title of this article may be misleading in contrasting social service provision and social change work, the two do not necessarily go together easily and in many instances do not go together at all. There are some groups working for social change that are providing so-

cial service; there are many more groups providing social services that are not working for social change. In fact, many social service agencies may be intentionally or inadvertently working to maintain the status quo. (p. 1)

Similar to what we read in chapter 1 about the differences between **solidarity** and **charity**, Kivel (2000) continues his essay by describing the present economic and political systems in the United States and identifies how the inequities in these systems are preserved when we focus on fixing individuals without also working to address the inequities in the system that contribute to creating the problems in our communities in the first place. A longtime advocate in the

---

Spotlight on Service: Following It Everywhere

Melissa, a political science major, signed up for her interdisciplinary service-learning class with a bit of trepidation: What could she get from this kind of course that she wouldn't from another upper-division course in her major? An accomplished student, Melissa knew she could be counted on to give her all to the course, but she wasn't sure she needed a service-learning class—despite the fact that her university required it.

In the course she eventually selected, Melissa, like her classmates, was able to choose her own community partner, and she elected to work with Mercy Corps, an organization based in Portland, Oregon, that focuses on disaster response, sustainable economic development, health services, and emergency and natural disaster relief. As part of their course work, Melissa and her classmates engaged in a consensus decision-making process to codetermine several collaborative projects to pursue throughout the term. Melissa found herself drawn to a project proposed by her classmate Therese, a political refugee from the Democratic Republic of Congo, who wanted to work on updating a resource guide for African refugees and immigrants in the greater Portland area.

There was something about the way Therese talked about her experiences of coming to Portland as a refugee that spoke to Melissa and became the focus of her starting anywhere. Soon Melissa was absorbed in finding out all she could about a community that by her admission she had known quite little about, despite the community's presence in the greater Portland area for many years. How is it possible, Melissa wondered, that she could live among people about whom she knew so little? How could she have failed to notice these people and their needs despite all her course work in political science?

After completing her service-learning course, Melissa continued to work on Therese's project, and she augmented the data collection and organizational work she was completing with interviews with professionals who serve the African diaspora community in Portland. Melissa isn't completely sure where her newly ignited interest will take her next—teaching is a possibility, as is public policy and advocacy work—but, at the very least, Melissa understands that she can't un-see those people whose lives are now real and visible to her, and she is actively wondering about the societal forces that create the material conditions that have affected and continue to affect the African diaspora in her community. As a parent, student, citizen, voter, Melissa has been changed by the start she made in service-learning, and she knows she can't help but follow it.

---

movement to end domestic violence, Kivel analyzes how our efforts easily get directed at changing *people* rather than changing *systems*. While interpersonal violence in the United States disproportionately affects people who occupy target status relative to sex and gender—namely, those who are female-bodied, intersex people, women, and trans women and trans men—we acknowledge that violence can also be present and expressed toward those with agent status (e.g., straight men) as well.

To wit, Kivel (2000) notes that

if we see battered women as victims, we will naturally try to protect them from further violence, provide them with services, and try to help them "get ahead." . . . We would measure our success by how many battered women we served, and our success stories would be about how individual women were able to escape the violence of abusive families and get on with their lives. (p. 11)

This sort of approach—one that looks at domestic violence from the level of the individual—moves our attention away from the systemic realities in which battered women find themselves and offers solutions for the problems faced by victims solely on an individual level.

If we widen our frame, however, we might

understand that battered women are caught in cycles that are the result of systemic exploitation, disempowerment, and isolation of women in our society, kept in battering relationships by community tolerance for male violence, lack of well-paying jobs, lack of decent childcare and affordable housing, and most of all by their isolation from each other and from the information and resources they need to come together to effect change. (Kivel, 2000, p. 12)

Notice the subtle but powerful difference in understanding domestic violence at a systems level instead of simply at the level of the individual. "The personal is political," a rallying cry of the feminist social change movement of the late 1960s and the 1970s, expresses exactly this shift Kivel (2000) encourages us to make, as it helps us to link seemingly private suffering with the institutional and systemic forces that bring about that suffering in the first place.

"If this were our analysis of domestic violence," says Kivel (2000), "we would be providing organizational and structural support for battered women to come together to act on their own behalf. We would not be working *for* battered women, we would be working *with* them" (p. 12).

Sound familiar? This approach to thinking about structural inequality and coming together to address it mirrors the change agency by the community members at Joubert Park, who recognized it was in their power and interest to take back their space for themselves. The Joubert Park community stepped into its own power to create community from the foundation laid by its own assets—members' relationships with each other, their expertise and pride as growers of food (and sustainable food systems), and their desire to see their children live productive healthy lives.

Kivel further asserts in his essay that each of us must practice **accountability** in the community-based work we do. Essentially meaning *responsibility*, being *accountable* for our actions requires us to consider the ramifications of our choices on those we are serving and on the change efforts we hope to be a part of.

Think back to exercise 13.3 in which you wrote your own personal mission statement. To be accountable to yourself with regard to that mission requires you to critically assess the ways your mission aligns with your actions as experienced through the lens of those you are committed to serving. In other words, if you are serving women at a domestic violence shelter,

---

✿ Exercise 13.4: Who Benefits from My Work?

Start by reading Paul Kivel's (2000) article *Social Service, or Social Change?* The article is full of rich, provocative, and challenging reflection questions, and we encourage you to sit with and respond to those questions that most resonate for you either in writing or by discussing them with a classmate or classmates. Alternatively, you might consider the following questions after completing your reading:

- What are you experiencing in your body as you reflect on the article?
- What links do you see between this article and your experience as a service-learner with your community partner? In what ways are you providing a social service through your partnership? In what ways are you contributing to a genuine effort for social change?
- How might you orient yourself to your work or shift the ways you think about and perform your work in order to be more effective on the level of change? What could it look like to continue to engage as a service-learner in a way that deepens your impact as a **change agent**? Who would benefit from your making that shift and how? What costs are there in making that shift—to you, and to others?
- How might you take these reflections, born from this experience, into future settings? What might it look like for you to commit to becoming an intentional change agent in the ways that are most important for you? What change could you make right now to bring that commitment into being?

> ### 💡 Exercise 13.5: Provisions for the Journey
>
> If you feel moved to commit yourself to acting on your mission to continue making positive change in the world, we salute you. And, as companions on that journey, we know that we *all* need provisions to do the ongoing work of bringing "our deep gladness" (Buechner, 1993, p. 95) to the needs of the world. One rich source for those provisions is Paul Kivel's website (http://paulkivel.com), where he has posted numerous articles and exercises to help us develop our critical consciousness and gain useful tools for the work at hand. See what resources he's collected for you, including links for further exploration. Then reflect on the following:
>
> - When you think about the journey ahead of you—the journey in which you continue to bring your deep gladness to the world's "deep hunger" (http://paulkivel.com)—what provisions do you need? What kinds of support? What additional knowledge? What sorts of relationships and connections with others?
> - How do you already have access to these provisions? What's already packed for you and ready to be shouldered as you continue on your journey?
> - How will you get those provisions you still need? In what ways will you intentionally build the foundation for your journeying as a change agent in the world?

to use Kivel's (2000) example, how are your actions reinforcing the individual-level understanding of domestic violence, and how are your actions challenging the systems-level view of domestic violence? To what extent are your actions actually helping people come together to confront the structural realities in which we operate and transform those realities, and to what extent are your actions simply reinforcing the idea that domestic violence is a personal issue that can only be addressed by personal solutions?

To be sure, Kivel (2000) is *not* suggesting we step away from our responsibilities to each other as members of communities to do what we can to make life better for others—but he *is* arguing that we often reinforce systems of domination and power in our communities if we do not follow our impulse for change beyond the personal and interpersonal into an analysis of the societal and political forces at play in maintaining injustice. Following our analysis into the wider world allows us to work with others for organizational-, institutional-, and systems-level change in ways that address the root causes of the challenges facing our communities instead of simply offering surface-level temporary solutions aimed solely at the individual.

There are no easy answers to these questions—and actually no easy configuration of the questions either.

But if you are interested in creating genuine change in the communities, institutions, and systems that perpetuate inequity and inequality on the societal and political levels, we invite you to do the seriously heavy lifting of engaging your critical consciousness (as described in chapter 10) in your analysis of your intentions, your actions, and the results of those actions in the world.

And Each Day You Mean One More

At the beginning of this chapter, we refer to the Marge Piercy (1980) poem "The Low Road" that opened chapter 3. At the start of your service-learning experience, we hope you would consider the ways that human relationship is essential to successful change efforts in the world, and that in fact only through concerted communal effort can positive change happen in our communities. Movements for social justice worldwide offer a testament to this, and in this chapter we focus on one expression of that movement in South Africa with the transformation of Joubert Park in Johannesburg. As Piercy reminds us in her poem,

It goes on one at a time,
it starts when you care

to act, it starts when you do
it again after they said no,
it starts when you say We
and know who you mean, and each
day you mean one more.

Start anywhere. Follow it everywhere. And prepare to be surprised by the empowerment that can emerge from collective hope.

Key Concepts

accountability	intention/	personal mission
change agent	intentionality	statement
charity		solidarity

Key Issues

- What responsibility does each of us have in working for change?
- How might we reasonably commit ourselves to making positive change in the world? What is required of us to do so?
- How can we best choose when and how to work for change? What tools can we employ to help us focus our change efforts?
- How can we know if our efforts are addressing systemic problems or simply reinforcing the dynamics that contribute to societal-level problems?

CHAPTER 14

Looking Back, Looking Forward

Where Do You Go from Here?

PETER J. COLLIER AND VICKI L. REITENAUER

A COLLEAGUE of ours at Portland State University begins each of her service-learning courses by asking her students to consider the following: What they are about to engage in as learners-through-serving will ultimately compose only about a third of the totality of their experience. The first third, she says, they've already lived through, in the days and weeks and months and years leading up to this particular moment in their personal and academic lives. The middle third is the collaboration they are embarking on right now. The final third lives in the future, when this group of individuals takes the learning they have gained in the past and in this current moment and applies it to future actions. Remembering that we have had a whole host of experiences that has shaped the persons we are, that we currently are living a new set of experiences that inform our being, and that we make decisions, whether intentionally or not, about who we are becoming, reminds us of the power we have as individuals to choose how to live our lives within communities of others. (Complete exercise 14.1.)

Becoming an engaged citizen is an ongoing journey that requires hard work, critical thinking, clear communication skills, the ability to collaborate with others, and problem-solving expertise. Service-learning and community-based learning courses, like the one you are completing, are evidence of your college's commitment to providing you with opportunities to acquire valuable citizenship-related skills.

We hope that you have been able to use this book as a tool to help you develop a personal understanding of

yourself as a civically engaged individual and to broaden your insights about community issues and the role your academic knowledge might serve in addressing them. Through the activities and exercises, we have tried to foster the realization in each of you that, as engaged citizens, you bring your own unique strengths and skills to collective efforts to promote social justice and the greater good of your communities.

In chapter 1, "What are *Service-Learning* and *Civic Engagement?*" we examined the nature of "service" as it is enacted in service-learning courses and connected this description to a larger conversation about democracy, citizenship, and civic responsibility. The fundamental concept behind learning through serving is the idea that as citizens it is our obligation to contribute to the improvement of our nation and the world. We are accountable for ourselves and for the welfare of others. In this chapter we also explored what role colleges and universities should play in facilitating the development of students' civic capacities. As we discovered, the development of civic mindedness is more than just what you *know*, it is what you *do* with what you know. In essence, community-based educational experiences increase your capacity to apply your knowledge and skills to civic issues.

Chapter 2, "Building and Maintaining Community Partnerships," explored the student–community partner relationship, with particular emphasis on the respective benefits and rights of both yourself as a student and your community partners as part of the reciprocal learning environment. In this chapter, we introduced

---

✦ Exercise 14.1: Reflecting in Thirds

As you prepare to leave this learning-through-serving experience, reflect for a moment on how you got here, what happened for you in this experience, and how those experiences have shaped possibilities for your future choices. You might choose to read through any or all of the exercises you have completed so far, particularly those that have asked you to think about past experiences and reflect rigorously on current ones. After spending sufficient time reflecting, do a 10- to 20-minute freewrite in response to these questions:

- What life experiences (of any sort) prepared you for this learning-through-serving experience? When you remember back to important events and moments leading up to this community service endeavor, what stands out as being especially important to your preparation for this work? How did you enter this experience?
- What happened to you and for you while you were here? When you review important events and moments in this community service endeavor, what stands out as being especially important and meaningful? How were you in this experience?
- How are you poised to leave this experience? When you imagine the places your experiences are leading you, what stands out as being especially compelling for you to experience next as a person, a community member, a learner? How will you move forward from here in your academic, professional, and personal lives?

Adapted from the work of Carol Gabrielli (2003).

---

the ALPS (Action Learning Plan for Serving) which you used to clarify your service project and identify your individual learning and serving goals.

At the end of chapter 2, we highlighted a writer who offers us clues about how to live authentic, engaged lives. Angeles Arrien, in the book *The Four-Fold Way: Walking the Paths of the Warrior, Teacher, Healer, and Visionary,* encourages us to *show up, pay attention, tell the truth,* and *be open to the outcome.* We suggested then that these words might be especially appropriate to service-learning courses, and case studies and quotes in subsequent chapters often illustrated this point. Before we continue our review of the preceding chapters, take a moment to reflect on Arrien's ideas and their connection to this experience that you are concluding (exercise 14.2).

In chapter 3, "Becoming Community: Moving from *I* to *We*," we invited you to bring who you are and what you know into both the classroom and the wall-less classroom (the world beyond your campus) and put it into practice to create change. In forming community with other students, the instructor, and the individuals comprising your community partner, you increased the possibilities for creating change, as you experienced the principle of the whole being more than the sum of its parts. We also examined the Seven Cs of leadership

development as a framework for considering the three levels of involvement in this service-learning course: the individual, the group, and the community. As we learned, each of these levels informs the other: That is, individual students impact the group dynamic and process, and that dynamic and process affects each individual; the group works in concert to effect positive change in the community, which then in turn affects the group; and each individual connects with the service activity in the community and is then shaped by that direct experience as well.

Most service-learning courses seem to involve some level of group work. In chapter 4, "Groups Are Fun, Groups Are Not Fun: Teamwork for the Common Good," we examined several aspects of group dynamics as they relate to "getting the work done" in service-learning courses. For example, the Phase Model of Group Development offered a conceptual framework for understanding how groups develop through a series of identifiable stages. In this chapter, we introduced exercises to broaden your learning and serving goals to include the others with whom you have been collaborating.

Chapter 4 also highlighted some of the challenges in bringing your work as a class team into collabora-

> ### ✿ Exercise 14.2: Walking the Four-Fold Path
>
> Take some time to reflect thoroughly on the following questions. After reflecting, complete a 10- to 20-minute freewrite on the elements of these questions that seem most relevant for you to address.
>
> - When you think about this service-learning experience and your own way of *showing up* in it, what comes to mind? How did you manifest your own particular ways of being and doing in this collaborative endeavor? How were you able to be authentically who you are? What challenges did you experience in regard to showing up? How did you address those challenges?
> - How were you able to *pay attention* during this experience? How well did you listen to others and strive to understand their perspectives and needs? What kinds of things were present but went unsaid in this experience, and how did you pay attention to that? What challenges did you experience in regard to paying attention? How did you address those challenges?
> - How were you able to *tell the truth* as you experienced it during your learning-through-serving? In what ways were your truths similar to others', and in what ways were they different? What meaning do you take from those similarities and differences? What challenges did you experience in regard to truth-telling? How did you address those challenges?
> - In what ways were you able to remain *open to the outcome* of your shared efforts? How was the outcome different than you imagined it would be at the start of your experience? What meaning do you take from the differences between your expectations of the outcome and the outcome itself? What challenges did you experience in being open to the outcome? How did you address those challenges?

tion with a community partner. We introduced the concepts of *task, maintenance,* and *organizational roles,* as well as exercises and activities to help you identify how group members assumed particular roles within your group. Finally, we emphasized the importance of clear communication and active listening among group members and between group members and community partners as a useful strategy for addressing the challenges of working together on a community-based service project.

Chapter 5, "Creating Cultural Connections: Navigating Difference, Investigating Power, Unpacking Privilege," provided you with resources to frame your service-learning experience in ways that expand your capacities for working effectively with those who are different from you and to recognize how to act on shared desires for creating positive change in the world. We asserted that our different perspectives are actually keys to maximizing the innovative problem-solving capacities that exist in any community setting. We explored the ways that our notions of "service" are culturally based and sought out a common language

for serving and learning with respect and integrity. Moreover, to be interculturally competent, we proposed that you need to cultivate a mindset, a skillset, and a heartset. A useful conceptual tool, Bennett and Bennett's Developmental Model of Intercultural Sensitivity, was introduced as a framework to explain the development of increasing sophistication in our experience and navigation of differences. Finally, chapter 5 challenged each of us to explore the ways in which privilege attaches to membership in certain groups in order to better understand the cultural dynamics at play in our community partnerships and to continue to develop our intercultural competence.

In chapter 6, "Reflection in Action: The Learning–Doing Relationship," we turned our attention to the process of reflection and the central role that it plays in service-learning classes. We reviewed the work of Dewey and Kolb and introduced the idea of deep reflection that is composed of three elements: observation, personal relevance, and connection. To practice deep reflection, we offered ideas for different modes of reflection—telling, activities, multimedia, and writing—

that may be helpful as you search for ways to best articulate the insights and meaning that are part of your community-based experience.

Chapters 7 and 8 built upon material introduced in chapters 3 and 4 on forming communities and working collaboratively in groups, and focused on two additional interpersonal aspects of service-learning experiences—mentoring and leadership.

In chapter 7, "Mentoring: Relationship Building for Empowerment," we explored how peer-to-peer mentoring relationships can lead to empowerment and capacity building for mentees. We introduced the dual-function model of mentoring and illustrated how peer mentoring can provide both psychosocial support and role-modeling that can contribute to mentee success within higher education or in the community. As part of a discussion on the relative benefits of in-person and online/e-mentoring, we discussed the concept of "credibility" and explained why it is important for effective mentor-mentee relationships. Finally, we shared a tool for mentors—the New Johari Window—to use to increase their credibility with mentees. This tool can help mentees recognize that they already possess problem-solving approaches.

In chapter 8, "Leadership and Service-Learning: Leveraging Change," we began by reviewing several models of leadership—great person, situational, transformational and servant. However leadership in the twenty-first century tends to be much more complex than how it is explained in earlier models because we tend to operate in varying and intercultural contexts. We explained how a leadership approach that is effective in one service-learning site like a community garden may not be viewed as appropriate in another site such as an elementary school, and an approach that works when working with inner-city residents may prove ineffective when working with migrant workers. We explored Lipman-Blumen's idea of multiple leadership styles and introduced the leadership toolkit as a helpful way to move from idea to action. Finally, through a series of vignettes, we illustrated how success in different service contexts required different leadership approaches and made the case that participation in service-learning classes provides students with opportunities to "develop their toolkits."

In chapters 9 and 10, we highlighted multiple approaches for understanding the community-based experience—when things are going well and when things are not going well. Specifically, these chapters explored how you can bridge the disconnect between learning and doing through reflection, what can be done if the community interaction is a disappointment or is "failing," and how the context and the content of the service-learning course itself provide direction and meaning.

Even with meticulous planning, carefully outlined expectations, and outstanding effort on everyone's part, things can go off-course in service-learning courses. Chapter 9, "Failure with the Best of Intentions: When Things Go Wrong," looked at how to approach breakdowns and conflict constructively. We "walked" you through a three-step program to prepare you to minimize destructive conflict and avoid a range of what we called "roadblocks and flat tires."

First, we encouraged you to explore some prior experiences in collaborative contexts while considering how those experiences have been framed and defined in terms of "success" or "failure." Second, we discussed some of the more common roadblocks in the service-learning journey. Finally, chapter activities and exercises—like the D-U-E Process for understanding cultural or personality differences—provided you with opportunities to consider and "try on" some alternative response strategies for negotiating unexpected events and circumstances.

In chapter 10, "Expanding Horizons: New Views of Course Concepts," we examined how to apply academic discipline-based knowledge in community settings. Unlike most classes where the "right" answers are filled in on the "test," your service-learning project tested you to consider multiple approaches in determining what is right for the community. This is transformational learning—deep learning where new knowledge becomes personally meaningful and connected to community. We examined the relationships between course content and community challenges in order to connect your experiences with the larger world of ideas and issues outside the college campus.

In chapter 11, "Beyond a Grade: Are We Making a Difference?: The Benefits and Challenges of Evaluating Learning and Serving," we examined the conceptual underpinnings of evaluation in service-learning courses and provided you with tools such as the CIE model to help you evaluate the results of your community-based engagement. The Self-Assessment Matrix also enabled you to identify strengths you have gained during the project by recognizing your own individual levels of experience with various dimensions of service-learning. We also asked you to revisit your Action Learning Plan for Serving to examine how the different outcomes of your service project provide evidence for whether you met (or did not meet) specific partner, learning, and service goals.

In chapter 12, "Global and Immersive Service-Learning: What You Need to Know as You Go," we explored some of the additional issues faced by students whose service-learning experiences involve moving to another country or to another part of their home country for weeks or months. In the section on preparation, we discussed issues associated with logistics, project preparation, and cultural sensitivity. We emphasized the importance of engaged reflection as a way to gain insight into cross-cultural/immersive service-learning experiences. We introduced the concept of *praxis* as an intellectual tool for deeper learning of how ideas from your academic disciplines can or can't be applied to real-life community situations.

Finally, in chapter 13, "Start Anywhere, Follow It Everywhere: Agents of Change," we applied the material in the earlier chapters to examine how the community around Joubert Park in Johannesberg, South Africa, came together to transform a place of drug abuse and gang violence into a sustainable garden of celebration and art. We emphasize that on the road to promoting social change *starting anywhere* begins with you—with who you are, what you care about most deeply, and how you can bring both of those things into the world. We encourage you to develop your own personal mission statement and use that as a "blueprint" to put your values into meaningful action, keeping in mind that as service-learning practitioners we need to be accountable to both ourselves and the communities we work with.

As we noted in the beginning of this chapter, the journey toward becoming an engaged community member and citizen requires, among other things, skills, commitment, a willingness to be open to new ideas, and effort. It does not begin and end with a single service-learning course at your college or university. This journey is an ongoing, lifelong one. Still, you have traveled quite a distance on this particular service project road, so let's take one final look back as you begin to prepare for future journeys (exercise 14.3).

We hope that you have evolved from understanding yourself solely as an individual student in a class of other individual students, motivated only by rewards like grades and course credit, to feeling like part of an interconnected community of other students, faculty, and community partners who are all working together to make a difference in our shared world. So where do you go from here? In a famous quote, Mahatma Ghandi challenges each of us to live the values that underlie service-learning: "You must be the change you wish to see in the world." As you have discovered in your service-learning experience, doing so requires skill, insight, patience, courage, compassion, fortitude, commitment, and a host of other ways of being. In our final activity, we encourage you to look forward, into your future as an engaged participant in the life of our communities (exercise 14.4).

On behalf of the persons with whom you have learned through serving over these past many weeks, we thank you for the efforts you have made in and for our shared communities. We all benefit from the work each of us chooses to do. The future is in all of our hands. The next step of your journey is up to you.

✦ Exercise 14.3: The Other Side of the Mountain

You may be familiar with the children's song "The Bear Went over the Mountain." The punchline of the song is that, when the bear crossed over the mountain, what the bear saw was *the other side of the mountain* . . . and then *another* mountain, and another . . .

Working on your own or in a group, you have completed a service-learning project this term. You have "crossed over the mountain" with this project and addressed specific community needs while also realizing personal learning and service goals. As the song promises, there are many more mountains and community needs that are waiting just ahead.

Consider the following questions to identify the new skills, knowledge, and insights you will take with you on the next step of your journey.

- What did you learn about *yourself* in this learning-through-serving experience?
- What did you learn about your *community*?
- What new knowledge related to your *academic discipline* can you utilize in addressing community needs?
- How has the service-learning experience contributed to your sense of being an engaged community member and *citizen*?

✦ Exercise 14.4: Being the Change

Again, take plenty of time as you consider the following questions. In fact, you might return to them again and again as you choose how to bring your personal energy and expertise to the communities of which you are a part.

- When you survey the world (in the form of your family, your neighborhood, your community, your city, your state, your country, or the global community), how would you describe the change you'd like to see in its simplest terms? What change do you wish to see in the world?
- How would this change benefit you and those closest to you? How would it benefit others, and thus contribute to the common good?
- What would it cost you and those closest to you to act in ways that might bring about this change? What would the cost be to others not close to you?
- How might you seek to balance the benefits to your work to bring about this change with the costs to yourself and others?
- How has this service-learning experience prepared you to work for this change? What skills and capacities have you developed that will assist you in your work as a change agent? What skills and capacities would you like to develop further?
- What could you do right now to contribute to this change happening? How might you create shifts in your life such that you might *be the change you wish to see in the world* in an ongoing, committed way?

References

Albee, E. (1960). *The zoo story: The death of Bessie Smith: The sandbox: Three plays*. New York: Coward-McCann.

Altman, I. (1996). Higher education and psychology in the millennium. *American Psychologist, 51*, 371–378.

American College Testing. (2010). *What works in student retention: Public four-year colleges and universities.* Retrieved from http://www.act.org/research/policy makers/reports/retain.html

Arrien, A. (1993). *The four-fold way: Walking the paths of the warrior, teacher, healer, and visionary*. San Francisco: HarperSanFrancisco.

Ash, S. L., & Clayton, P. H. (2009). Generating, deepening, and documenting learning: The power of critical reflection in applied learning. *Journal of Applied Learning in Higher Education, 1*, 25–48.

Astin, A. W. (1977). *Four critical years: Effects of college on beliefs, attitudes, and knowledge*. San Francisco: Jossey-Bass.

Astin, A. W. (1984). Student involvement: A developmental theory for higher education. *Journal of College Student Personnel, 25*, 287–300.

Astin, A. W. (1984/1999). Student involvement: A developmental theory for higher education. *Journal of College Student Personnel, 40*(5), 287–300.

Astin, A., & Astin, H., et. al. (1996). *A social change model of leadership development*. Los Angeles: Higher Education Research Institute.

Bailie, G. (1996). *Violence unveiled: Humanity at the crossroads*. New York: Crossroad.

Bales, R. G. (1950). *Interaction process analysis: A method for the study of small groups*. Chicago: The University of Chicago Press.

Barber, B. (1992). *An aristocracy of everyone*. New York: Oxford Press.

Bass, B. M. (1985). *Leadership and performance beyond expectations*. New York: Free Press.

Battistoni, R. (2002). *Civic engagement across the curriculum: A resource book for service-learning faculty in all disciplines*. Providence, RI: Campus Compact.

Belenky, M. F., Clinchy, B. M., Goldberger, N. R., & Tarule, J. M. (1986). *Women's ways of knowing: The development of self, voice, and mind*. New York: Basic Books.

Benner, P., Tanner, C. A., & Chesla, C. A. (1995). *Expertise in nursing practice: Caring, clinical judgment and ethics*. New York: Springer.

Bennett, J. M. (1993). Cultural marginality: Identity issues in intercultural training. In R. M. Paige (Ed.), *Education for the intercultural experience* (pp. 109–135). Yarmouth, ME: Intercultural Press.

Bennett, J. M., & Bennett, M. J. (2004). Developing intercultural sensitivity: An integrative approach to global and domestic diversity. In D. Landis, J. M. Bennett, & M. J. Bennett (Eds.), *Handbook of intercultural training* (3rd ed., pp. 147–166.) Thousand Oaks, CA: Sage.

Bennett, M. J. (1979). Overcoming the golden rule: Sympathy and empathy. In D. Nimmo (Ed.), *Communication yearbook* (Vol. 3, pp. 407–22). New Brunswick, NJ: International Communication Association.

Bennett, M. J. (1993). Towards ethnorelativism: A developmental model of intercultural sensitivity. In R. M. Paige (Ed.), *Education for the intercultural experience* (pp. 21–71). Yarmouth, ME: Intercultural Press.

Betancourt, H., & Weiner, B. (1982). Attribution for achievement-related events, expectancy, and sentiments: A study of success and failure in Chile and the U.S. *Journal of Cross-cultural Psychology, 13*(3), 362–374.

Bierema, L., & Merriam, S. (2002). E-mentoring: Using computer mediated communication to enhance the mentoring process. *Innovative Higher Education, 26*, 211–227.

Bloom, B. S., Engelhart, M. D., Furst, E. J., Hill, W. H., & Krathwohl, D. R. (1956). *Taxonomy of educational objectives. Handbook I: Domain*. New York, NY: Longmans, Green.

Bourdieu, P. (1977). Cultural reproduction and social reproduction. In J. Karable & A. H. Halsey (Eds.), *Power and ideology in education* (pp. 487–511). New York: Oxford University Press.

Bowen, H. R. (1977). *Investment in learning: The individual and social value of American higher education*. San Francisco: Jossey-Bass.

Bringle, R., & Hatcher, J. (1999, Summer). Reflection in service-learning: Making meaning of experience. *Educational Horizons*, 179–185.

Buechner, F. (1993). *Wishful thinking: A seeker's ABC*. New York: HarperOne.

Burns, J. M. (1978). *Leadership*. New York: Harper & Row.

Carlyle, T. (1891). *Sartor resartus: On heroes, hero-worship and the heroic in history*. London, UK: Chapman & Hall.

Chase, C. (2012). *Creating your personal mission statement*. Unpublished, Portland State University, Portland, OR.

Collier, P. J., & Driscoll, A. (1999). Multiple methods of student reflection in service-learning classes. *Journal of General Education*, 48(4), 280–292.

Collier, P., Fellows, C., & Holland, B. (2008). *Students first: Improving first-generation student retention and performance in higher education*. U.S. Department of Education, FIPSE Comprehensive Grant Program. Retrieved from http://fipsedatabase.ed.gov/fipse/grantshow.cfm?grantNumber=P116B041080

Collier, P. J., & Morgan, D. L. (2002). Community service through facilitating focus groups: The case for a methods-based service-learning course. *Teaching Sociology*, 30, 185–199.

Collier, P. J., & Morgan, D. L. (2003). Is that paper really due today?: Differences in first-generation and traditional college students' understandings of faculty members' class-related expectations. *Proceedings of 2003 Hawaii International Conference on Education*. University of Hawaii-West, Oahu.

Collins, P. H. (1993). Toward a new vision: Race, class, and gender as categories of analysis and connection. In A. Ferber, C. M. Jiménez, A. O. Herrera, & D. R. Samuels (Eds.), *The matrix reader: Examining the dynamics of oppression and privilege* (pp. 97–108). New York: McGraw-Hill Higher Education.

Colvin, J. W., & Ashman M. (2010). Roles, risks, and benefits of peer mentoring relationships in higher education. *Mentoring & Tutoring: Partnership in Learning*, 18(2), 121–134.

Community-Campus Partnerships for Health. (2001). *Principles of good community-university partnerships*. http://futurehealth.ucsf.edu/ccph/principles.html

Cress, C. M. (2004). Critical thinking and development in service-learning activities: Pedagogical implications for critical being and action. *Inquiry: Critical Thinking across the Disciplines*, 23, 87–93.

Cress, C. M. (2012). Civic engagement and student success: Leveraging multiple degrees of achievement. *Diversity and Democracy*, 15(3), 2–4. Retrieved from http://www.diversityweb.org/DiversityDemocracy/vol15no3/vol15no3.pdf

Cress, C. M., Astin, H. S., Zimmerman-Oster, K., & Burkhardt, J. (2001, January/February). Developmental outcomes of college students' involvement in leadership activities. *Journal of College Student Development*, 42 (1), 15–27.

Cress, C., Burack, C., Giles, D., Elkins, J., & Stevens, M. (2010). *A promising connection: Increasing college access and success through civic engagement*. Boston: Campus Compact.

Cress, C. M., Stokamer, S., & Drummond Hays, S. (2010). *Youth-to-college: Three-year outcomes*. San Francisco: California Campus Compact.

Dewey, J. ([1916] 1966). *Democracy and education*. New York: Collier Books.

Dewey, J. (1933). *How we think*. New York: D.C. Heath.

Donelson, F. (1999). *Group dynamics*. Belmont, CA: Wadsworth.

Dreyfus, H. L., & Dreyfus, S. E. (1996). *The relationship of theory and practice in the acquisition of skill*. New York: Springer.

Duda, J. L. (1986). A cross-cultural analysis of achievement motivation in sport and the classroom. In L. Vander Velden & J. Humphreys (Eds.), Current selected research in the psychology and sociology of sport (pp. 115–132), New York: AMS Press.

Eby, L. T., & Dobbins, G. H. (1997). Collectivistic orientation in teams: An individual and group level analysis. *Journal of Organizational Behavior*, 18, 275–295.

Edelman, J., & Crain, M. (1993). *The tao of negotiation: How you can prevent, resolve and transcend conflict in work and everyday life*. New York: HarperCollins.

Ehrlich, T. (2000). *Civic responsibility and higher education*. Phoenix, AZ: The American Council on Higher Education and The Oryx Press.

Eliot, G. (1986). *Middlemarch*. Oxford University Press.

Engelken, L. C., & Washington, J. (2001, September). Who am I and what do I bring? In L. C. Engelken (Ed.), *Capstone retreat materials*. Symposium conducted at Portland State University Capstone Program, Portland, OR.

Eyler, J., & Giles, D. (1999). *Where's the learning in service-learning?* San Francisco: Jossey-Bass.

Eyler, J., Giles, D., & Schmiede, A. (1996). *A practitioner's guide to reflection in service-learning: Student voices and reflections*. Nashville, TN: Vanderbilt University.

Fisher, B. A. (1970). Decision emergences: Phases in group decision-making. *Speech Monographs*, 37, 53–66.

Folger, J., Poole, M., & Stutman, R. (1995). Conflict and interaction. In J. Stewart (Ed.), *Bridges not walls* (6th ed.). New York: McGraw-Hill.

Gabrielli, C. A. (2003). *Reflecting in thirds*. Unpublished classroom exercise, Portland State University, Portland, OR.

Geertz, C. 1973. *The interpretation of culture: Selected essays.* New York: Basic Books.

Gelmon, S. B., & Agre-Kippenhan, S. (2002). A developmental framework for supporting faculty roles for community engagement. *The Journal of Public Affairs, 6*(Supplement 1), 161–182.

Gelmon, S. B., & Connell, A. (2001). *Program evaluation: Principles and practices.* Portland, OR: Northwest Health Foundation.

Gelmon, S. B., Foucek, A., & Waterbury, A. (2005). *Program Evaluation: Principles and Practices* (2nd ed.). Portland, OR: Northwest Health Foundation.

Gelmon, S. B., Holland B. A., Driscoll, A., Spring, A., & Kerrigan, S. (2001). *Assessing service-learning and civic engagement: Principles and techniques.* Providence, RI: Campus Compact.

Gibb, J. (1961). Defensive communication. *Journal of Communication, 11*(3), 141–148.

Gibbs, G. (1994). *Learning in teams: A student guide.* Oxford Brookes University, Oxford Center for Staff Development.

Giroux, H. A. (1983). Theories of reproduction and resistance in the new sociology of education: A critical analysis. *Harvard Educational Review, 53*(3), 257–296.

Goleman, D. (1995). *Emotional intelligence.* New York: Bantam.

Greenleaf, R. K. (1977). *Servant leadership: A journey into the nature of legitimate power and greatness.* Mahwah, NJ: Paulist Press.

Guskin, A. E. (1991). Cultural humility: A way of being in the world. *Antioch Notes, 59*(61), 1–11. Yellow Spring, OH: Antioch College Publications Office.

Hamner, D. (2001). *Building bridges: The Allyn and Bacon student guide to service learning.* Boston, MA: Pearson Allyn and Bacon.

Harkins, S. G., & Jackson, J. M. (1986). The role of evaluation in eliminating social loafing. *Personality and Social Psychology Bulletin, 11,* 457–465.

Harris, T. H., & Sherblum, J. C. (1999). *Small groups and team communication.* Needham Heights, MA: Allyn & Bacon.

Heider, F. (1958). *The psychology of interpersonal relations.* New York, NY: Psychology Press.

Heldman, C. (2011). Solidarity, not charity: Issues of Privilege in Service-Learning. In C. Cress & D. Donahue (Eds.), *Democratic dilemmas of teaching service-learning: Curricular strategies for success* (pp. 33–39). Sterling, VA: Stylus.

Hoffman, J., & Wallach, J., (2005). Effects of mentoring on community college students in transition to university. *Community College Enterprise, 11*(1), 67–78.

Hovland, C., Janis, I., & Kelley, H. 1953. *Communication and persuasion.* New Haven, CT: Yale University Press.

Iyer, P. (1998). The unknown rebel. *Time Magazine.* Retrieved from http://www.time.com/time/magazine/article/0,9171,988169,00.html#ixzz2IwA1q78t

Janis, I. (1983). *Groupthink: Psychological studies of policy decisions and fiascos.* Boston, MA: Houghton Mifflin.

Johnson, D. W., Maruyama, G., Johnson, R., Nelson, D., & Skon, L. (1981). Effects of cooperative, competitive, and individualistic goal structures on achievement: A meta-analysis. *Psychological Bulletin, 89*(1), 47–62.

Kelly, K. (2011, 5 August). *Kathy Kelly in Afghanistan, Pakistan, & Iraq: The costs of war, the price of peace* [Speech]. Portland Community College, Portland, OR.

Kivel, Paul. (2000). *Social service, or social change?* Retrieved from http://www.paulkivel.com/index.php?option=com_flexicontent&view=items&cid=23:article&id=97:social-service-or-social-change&Itemid=15.

Kolb, D. (1984). *Experiential learning: Experience as the source of learning and development.* Englewood Cliffs, NJ: Prentice-Hall.

Korzybski, A. (1921). *Science and sanity.* San Francisco: International Society for General Semantics.

Kram, K. E. (1985). *Mentoring at work: Developmental relationships in organizational life.* Glenview, IL: Scott Foresman.

Kuh, G. D. (1995). The other curriculum: Out-of-class experiences associated with student learning and personal development. *Journal of Higher Education, 66*(2), 123–155.

Leavitt, H. J. (1951). Some effects of certain communication patterns on group performance. *Journal of Abnormal and Social Psychology, 46*(1), 38–50.

Lee, J. J. (2004), Home away from home or foreign territory?: How social class mediates service-learning experiences. *NASPA Journal, 24*(3), 310–325.

Liang, D. W., Moreland, R., & Argote, L. (1995). Group versus individual training and group performance: The mediating role of transactive memory. *Personality and Social Psychology Bulletin, 21,* 384–393.

Lieberman, D. (1996). *Public speaking in the multicultural environment.* Needham Heights, MA: Allyn and Bacon.

Lipman-Blumen, J. (2000). *Connective leadership: Managing in a changing world.* Oxford, UK: Oxford University Press.

Luft, J. (1984). *Group processes: An introduction to group dynamics.* New York: Mayfield.

Luft, J., & Ingham, H. (1955). The Johari Window: A graphic model of interpersonal awareness. In *Proceedings of the Western Training Laboratory in Group Development.* Los Angeles: University of California, Los Angeles.

Mabry, J. B. (1998). Pedagogical variations in service-learning and student outcomes: How time, contact and reflection matter. *Michigan Journal of Community Service-Learning, 5*, 34.

Markus, H. G., & Kitayama, S. (1991). Culture and the self: Implications for cognition, emotion, and motivation. *Psychological Review, 98*(2), 224–253.

Maslow, A. H. (1948). Some theoretical consequences of basic need-gratification. *Journal of Personality, 16*(4), 402–416.

Maslow, A. H. (1954). *Motivation and personality.* New York: Harper.

McClure, M. (2006). Solidarity not charity: Racism in Katrina Relief Work. *A Katrina Reader.* Retrieved from http://www.cwsworkshop.org/katrinareader/node/461

McIntosh, P. (1988). White privilege: Unpacking the invisible knapsack. http://www.utoronto.ca/acc/events/peggy1.htm. Excerpted from Working Paper 189, *White privilege and male privilege: A personal account of coming to see correspondences through work in women's studies.* Wellesley, MA: Wellesley College Center for Research on Women.

McMinn, T. F. (2001). *The conceptualization and perception of biblical servant leadership in the southern Baptist convention* (Digital dissertations, 3007038).

Mead, M. (1971). *Coming of age in Samoa: A psychological study of primitive youth for Western civilization.* New York: HarperCollins.

Mezirow, J. (2002). *Transformational learning.* San Francisco: Jossey Bass.

Miller, J. G., Bersoff, D. M., & Harwood, R. L. (1990). Perceptions of social responsibilities in India and in the United States: Moral Imperatives or personal decisions? Journal of Personality and Social Psychology, 58, 33–47.

Morgan, K. P. (1996). Describing the emperor's new clothes: Three myths of educational (in)equality. In S. M. Shaw & J. Lee, *Women's voices, feminist visions* (p. 47). New York: McGraw-Hill Higher Education.

Morris, M., & Peng, K. 1994. Culture and Cause: American and Chinese Attributions for Social and Physical Events. *Journal of Personality and Social Psychology, 67*(6), 949–971.

Morrison, M. C. (1983). In praise of paradox. The Episcopalian. (As quotes in K. K. Smith, & D. N. Berg, 1987). *Paradoxes of group life: Understanding conflict, paralysis, and movement in group dynamics.* San Francisco: Jossey-Bass.

National Academy of Sciences. (2008). *Adviser, teacher, role model, friend* (8th ed.). Washington, DC: National Academy of Sciences, National Academy of Engineering, Institute of Medicine, National Academy Press.

Oshyn, K., & Wang, T. A. (2007). *Youth vote 2008.* Retrieved from http://www.whatkidscando.org

Pagan, R., & Edwards-Wilson, R. (2002). A mentoring program for remedial students. *Journal of College Student Retention, 4*, 207–226.

Pascarella, E. T., & Terenzini, P. T. (2005). *How college affects students: A third decade of research. Volume 2.* Indianapolis, IN: Jossey-Bass.

Peet, M. R., Walsh, K., Sober, R., & Rawak, C. S. (2010). Generative knowledge interviewing: A method for knowledge transfer and talent management at the University of Michigan. *International Journal of Educational Advancement, 10*, 71–85.

Pennebaker, J. (1990). *Opening up: The healing power of expressing emotions.* New York: Guilford Press.

Pennebaker, J., Kiecolt-Glaser, J., & Glaser, R. (1988). Disclosure of trauma and immune function: Health implications for psychotherapy. *Journal of Consulting and Clinical Psychology, 56*(2), 239–245.

Piercy, M. (1980). *The moon is always female.* New York: Random House.

Portland State University, Center for Academic Excellence. (2011). *2010–2011 annual report.* Portland, OR: Author.

Remen, R. N. (1999, September). Helping, fixing or serving? *Shambhala Sun,* Retrieved from http://www.shambhalasun.com/index.php?option=com_content&task=view&id=2328

Renner, T., Axlund, R., Topete, L., & Fleming, M. K. (2011). Service-learning is like learning to walk: Baby steps to cultural competence. In C. Cress & D. Donahue (Eds.), *Democratic dilemmas of teaching service-learning: Curricular strategies for success* (pp. 92–97). Sterling, VA: Stylus.

Russell, C. (1999). *Culture, language and behavior.* San Francisco: International Society for General Semantics.

Schon, D. (1987). *Developing critical thinkers: Challenging adults to explore alternative ways of thinking and acting.* San Francisco: Jossey-Bass.

Smith, R. (1995). Competence is what you do when you make a mistake. *Focus on Faculty, 3*(2), 1. Provo, UT: BYU Faculty Center.

Solorzano, D. G. (1997). Images and words that wound: Critical race theory, racial stereotyping and teacher education. *Teacher Education Quarterly, 24*(3), 5–19.

Stasser, G. (1992). Pooling of unshared information during group discussion. In S. Worchel, W. Wood, & J. H. Simpson (Eds.), *Process and production* (pp. 48–67). Newberry Park, CA: Sage.

Sue, D. W. (2010). *Microaggressions in everyday life: Race, gender, and sexual orientation.* Hoboken, NJ: Wiley.

Timmons, T. (1991). *Communicating with skill.* Dubuque, IA: Kendal/Hunt.

Toole, J., & Toole, P. (2001). *The service-learning cycle.* Minneapolis: The Compass Institute.

Tuckman, B. W. (1965). Developmental sequences in small groups. *Psychological Bulletin, 63,* 384–399.

Vygotsky, L. (1978). *Mind in society: The development of higher psychological processes.* Cambridge, MA: Harvard University Press.

Washington, B. (1901). *Up from slavery: An autobiography.* New York: Doubleday.

Weiner, B. (1985). An attributional theory of achievement motivation and emotion. *Psychological Review, 92*(4), 548–557.

Wheatley, M. J. (1994). *Leadership and the new science: Learning about organization from an orderly universe.* San Francisco: Berrett-Koehler.

Wheatley, M., & Frieze, D. (2011). *Walk out walk on.* San Francisco: Berrett-Koehler.

Whelan, S. A., & McKeage, R. L. (1993). Developmental patterns in large and small groups. *Small Groups Research, 24*(1), 60–85.

Witty P. (2009). Behind the scenes: Tank man of Tiananmen. *New York Times.* http://lens.blogs.nytimes.com/2009/06/03/behind-the-scenes-tank-man-of-tiananmen

About the Authors

Susan Agre-Kippenhan is vice president for academic affairs and dean of faculty at Linfield College, McMinnville, Oregon.

Janet Bennett is executive director of the Intercultural Communication Institute. She designs and conducts intercultural training for academic institutions, corporations, and social service agencies around the world. In addition, she directs a master's degree program in intercultural relations with the University of the Pacific.

Peter J. Collier is professor of sociology and an affiliated scholar with the Center for Interdisciplinary Mentoring Research at Portland State University.

Christine M. Cress is professor of Postsecondary, Adult, and Continuing Education (PACE) in the Department of Educational Leadership and Policy at Portland State University. She coordinates the Master's Specialization and Graduate Certificate in Community-Based Learning at Portland State University and is the lead author of *Democratic Dilemmas of Teaching Service-Learning: Curricular Strategies for Success* (Sterling, VA: Stylus, 2011).

Chithra Edwin is professor of mathematics and coordinator of the International Service-Learning Programme at Lady Doak College, Madurai, South India.

Sherril B. Gelmon is professor of public health and chair of the Division of Public Administration in the Mark O. Hatfield School of Government at Portland State University. One of her research areas focuses on assessing the impact of service-learning and community engagement in higher education.

Kevin Kecskes is associate professor of public administration in the Mark O. Hatfield School of Government at Portland State University. One of his research areas focuses on developing service-learning partnerships and curricula that builds students' public leadership skills and abilities.

Seanna M. Kerrigan is the Capstone program director of University Studies at Portland State University.

Devorah Lieberman is president of the University of La Verne in Southern California. Her research background focuses on intercultural communication, diversity in higher education, institutional transformation, community engagement, assessment, and current issues affecting higher education.

Judy Patton is professor of dance in the School of Theater and Film in the College of Arts at Portland State University.

Vicki L. Reitenauer is an instructor in the women, gender, and sexuality studies department and the University Studies (general education) program at Portland State University. She provides faculty development support for service-learning curriculum development and instruction across the disciplines, and she was a recipient of the John Eliot Allen Outstanding Teaching Award from the College of Liberal Arts and Sciences in 2012.

Amy Spring is assistant director for University-Community Partnerships for Learning in the Center for Academic Excellence at Portland State University.

Stephanie T. Stokamer is the director of the Center for Civic Engagement and an assistant professor in the Peace and Social Justice Studies program at Pacific University.

Thomas J. Van Cleave is an instructor in the Postsecondary, Adult, and Continuing Education (PACE) Program in the Graduate School of Education at Portland State University. His research focuses on short-term global service-learning and effective pedagogical strategies.

Janelle DeCarrico Voegele is interim director of Teaching, Learning, and Assessment in the Center for Academic Excellence/Center for Online Learning at Portland State University.

Dilafruz R. Williams is professor of education in the educational leadership and policy department at Portland State University. In 2001 she was the recipient of the prestigious Ehrlich Faculty Service-Learning Award.

Index